THE JOY OF LESS

the joy of less

a minimalist living guide

*how to declutter, organize,
and simplify your life*

FRANCINE JAY

ANJA PRESS
MEDFORD NJ

The Joy of Less, A Minimalist Living Guide: How to Declutter, Organize, and Simplify Your Life

Cover photo: iStockphoto.com

ISBN 10: 0-9840873-1-1
ISBN 13: 978-0-9840873-1-0
Library of Congress Control Number: 2010908579

Printed in the United States of America

Contents

PART THREE • ROOM BY ROOM

PART FOUR • LIFESTYLE

The small butterfly
moves as though unburdened by
the world of desire

Poem from *The Spring of My Life: And Selected Haiku*
by Kobayashi Issa (Author) and Sam Hamill (Translator)

Introduction

What if I told you that having less stuff could make you a happier person? It sounds a bit crazy, doesn't it? That's because every day, and everywhere we turn, we receive thousands of messages to the contrary: buy this, and you'll be prettier; own this, and you'll be more successful; acquire this, and your happiness will know no bounds.

Well, we've bought this, that, and the other thing. So we must be in seventh heaven, right? For most of us, the answer is "no." In fact, quite often, the opposite is true: many of these items, and their empty promises, are slowly sucking the money out of our pockets, the magic out of our relationships, and the joy out of our lives.

Do you ever look around your house, at all the things you've bought and inherited and been given, and feel overwhelmed instead of overjoyed? Are you struggling with credit card debt, and can barely recall the purchases on which you're making payments? Do you secretly wish a gale force wind would blow the clutter out of your home, leaving you an opportunity for a fresh start? If so, then a minimalist lifestyle may well be your salvation.

First, let's pull this term "minimalism" down to earth. It seems to have acquired a somewhat intimidating, elitist air, as it's often associated with chic, multimillion-dollar lofts with three pieces of furniture. The word conjures up images of spare, cool interiors, concrete floors, and gleaming white surfaces. It all sounds very sober, serious, and sterile. What role could it possibly play in lives filled with kids, pets, hobbies, junk mail, and laundry?

Most people hear the word "minimalism" and think "empty." Unfortunately, "empty" isn't altogether appealing; it's usually associated with loss, deprivation, and scarcity. But look at "empty" from another angle—think about what it *is* instead of what it isn't—and now you have "space." Space! That's something we could all use more of! Space in our closets, space in our garages, space in our schedules, space to think, play, create, and have fun with our families...now *that's* the beauty of minimalism.

Think of it this way: a container is most valuable when it's empty. We can't enjoy fresh coffee when old grounds are in our cup; and we can't showcase our garden's blooms when wilted flowers fill the vase. Similarly, when our homes—the containers of our daily lives—are overflowing with clutter, our souls take a backseat to our stuff. We no longer have the time, energy, and space for new experiences. We feel cramped and inhibited, like we can't fully stretch out and express ourselves.

Becoming minimalists puts us in control of our stuff. We reclaim our space, and restore function and potential to our homes. We remake our houses into open, airy, receptive containers for the substance of our lives. We declare independence from the tyranny of clutter. It's positively liberating!

Sounds great—but how do we get there? Where do we start? How is this book different from all those other books on organizing your life?

Well, unlike other organizational books, this one isn't about buying fancy containers or storage systems to shuffle around your stuff; it's about *decreasing* the amount of stuff you have to deal with. Furthermore, you won't have to answer quizzes, make checklists, or fill out charts—who has time for that? And there won't be dozens of case studies about other people's junk; the focus here is on *you*.

We'll start by cultivating a minimalist mindset. Don't worry; it's not hard! We're just going to think about the rewards and benefits of a decluttered life; it'll provide the motivation we need later when dealing with grandma's old china. We'll learn to see our stuff for what it is, and weaken any power it may hold over us; and discover the freedom of living with just "enough" to meet our needs. We'll even get a little philosophical, and ponder how our new minimalism will enrich our lives and effect positive change in the world.

Why all the talk? Because decluttering is like dieting. We can jump right in, count our possessions like we count calories, and "starve" ourselves to get fast results. All too often, however, we'll end up feeling deprived, go on a binge, and wind up right back where we started. First, we have to change our attitudes and our habits—kind of like switching from a meat-and-potatoes to a Mediterranean diet. Developing a minimalist mindset will transform the way we make decisions about the stuff we have, and the stuff we bring into our lives. Instead of being a short-term fix, it'll be a long-term commitment to a new, wonderful way of life.

After our mental warm-up, we'll learn the STREAMLINE method—the top ten most effective techniques for achieving, and maintaining, a decluttered home. This is where the fun starts! We're going to have a fresh start for every drawer, every closet, and every room, and make sure that each thing we own makes a positive contribution to our households. We'll give every item a proper place, and establish limits to keep things under control. We'll steadily reduce the amount of stuff in our homes, and set up systems to ensure it doesn't pile up again in the future. Armed with these techniques, we will conquer clutter for good!

Each area of the house presents unique challenges. Therefore, we'll proceed room by room, exploring more specific ways to tackle each one. We'll start in the family room, creating a flexible, dynamic space in which to pursue our leisure activities. We'll debate the merits of each piece of furniture, and figure out what to do with all those books, DVDs, video games, and craft supplies. Then we'll move into the bedroom, where we'll purge the excess to produce a peaceful oasis for our weary souls. Our goal: a clear, calm, uncluttered space that relaxes and rejuvenates us.

Since so many of us suffer from overstuffed closets, we'll spend a whole chapter dealing with wardrobe issues. (Heed the advice therein, and you'll look fabulous with a fraction of your current clothes.) Then once we're in the groove, we'll attack the stacks of paperwork in our home offices, and reduce the flow into our inboxes from a flood to a trickle. Our minimalist makeover will tame even the messiest of workspaces!

Next, we'll turn a keen eye on our kitchens. We'll pare down our pots, pans, and place settings, and see how clean countertops and simple cookware can enhance our culinary prowess. After that, we'll take a bathroom break; and while we're in there, we'll cull its contents to create a chic, spa-like ambience. We'll even simplify our grooming routines, so we can make ourselves gorgeous with a minimum amount of fuss.

Of course, we can't forget about our basements, attics, and garages. The stuff here may be out of sight, but it's certainly not out of mind. After we get down and dirty in these storage spaces, the clutter will have nowhere left to hide! We'll also spend a little time talking about gifts, heirlooms, and souvenirs. We'll see how these critters sneak into our lives, and devise some creative ways to handle them.

Why stop at our four walls? Once we've decluttered our homes (and wondered why we didn't do this sooner!), we'll use our new minimalist attitude to streamline our schedules. We'll learn to say "no," set priorities, and get things done with ease and efficiency. We'll trim our to-do lists, and reclaim our time like we did our space—being sure to leave enough of it open, empty, and free.

Finally, we'll explore how being minimalists makes us better citizens of the planet, and helps us conserve its bounty for future generations. We'll look at the true impact of our consumer choices, examining both the human and environmental toll of the things we buy; and learn the far-reaching benefits of living lightly and gracefully on the Earth. The best part: we'll discover how saving space in our closets, and saving the world, go hand in hand.

Ready to sweep away the clutter once and for all? Just turn the page for your first dose of minimalist philosophy; in a few minutes, you'll be on the road to a simpler, more streamlined, and more serene life.

PART ONE

Philosophy

Imagine that we're generals going into battle, or athletes before a big game: to perform at our best, we must mentally prepare ourselves for the challenges ahead. In the following pages, we'll develop our secret to success: a minimalist mindset.

This section is all about attitude. Before we can take control of our stuff, we need to change our relationship with it. We'll define it, see it for what it is and what it isn't, and examine its effects on our lives. The principles we learn will make it easier for us to let stuff go, and help us keep more stuff from coming in the door. Most importantly, we'll realize that our stuff exists to serve us, not the other way around.

1

See your stuff for what it is

Take a look around you; chances are, at least twenty or thirty items are in your direct line of vision. What is this stuff? How did it get there? What is its purpose?

It's time to see our stuff for what it is. We want to name it, define it, and take the mystery out of it. What exactly are these things we spend so much time and energy acquiring, maintaining, and storing? And how did there get to be so many of them? (Were they multiplying while we slept?)

Generally speaking, our stuff can be divided into three categories: useful stuff, beautiful stuff, and emotional stuff.

Let's start with the easiest category: useful stuff. These are the items that are practical, functional, and help us get things done. Some of them are essential to survival; others make our lives a little easier. It's tempting to think that *all* our stuff is useful—but have you ever read a book on survival techniques? It's quite illuminating how little we actually need to keep ourselves alive: a simple shelter, clothing to regulate our body temperature, water, food, a few containers, and some cooking implements. (If this is all you own, you can stop reading now; if not, join the rest of us, and press on!)

Beyond the bare essentials are items not necessary to survival, but still very useful: beds, sheets, laptops, tea kettles, combs, pens, staplers, lamps, books, plates, forks, sofas, extension cords, hammers, screwdrivers, whisks—you get the picture. Anything you use often, and which truly adds value to your life, is a welcome part of a minimalist household.

Ah, but remember: to be useful, an item must be *used*. That's the catch: most of us have a lot of *potentially useful* things that we simply don't use. Duplicates are a prime example: how many of those plastic food containers make it out of your pantry and into your lunch bag or freezer? Does your cordless drill really need an understudy? Other things languish because they're too complicated, or a hassle to clean: food processors, fondue sets, and humidifiers come to mind. Then there are the "just in cases" and the "might need its," biding their time in the backs of our drawers, waiting to make their debuts. Those are the items whose days are numbered.

Intermixed with our useful things are those that have no practical function, but satisfy a different kind of need: to put it simply, we like to look at them. Throughout history, we human beings have felt compelled to beautify our surroundings—as evidenced from Paleolithic cave paintings to the pictures hanging over our sofas.

Aesthetic appreciation is an important part of our identities, and should not be denied. The brilliant glaze on a beautiful vase, or sleek lines of a modernist chair, may bring a deep and joyful satisfaction to our souls; therefore, such items have every right to be part of our lives. The caveat: they must be respected and honored with a prominent place in our homes. If your collection of Murano glass is collecting dust on a shelf—or worse yet, is packed away in the attic—it's nothing more than colorful clutter.

As you're taking stock of your possessions, don't give an automatic pass to anything artsy. Just because it appealed to you one summer's day at a craft fair, doesn't mean it deserves a lifelong lease on your living room mantel. On the other hand, if it always brings a smile to your face—or if its visual harmony stirs your soul with a deeper appreciation for the beauty of life—its place in your home is well-deserved.

Now if all the stuff in our houses were either beautiful or useful, this would be easy. But as sure as the day is long, you will come across plenty of items that are neither. So where did they come from, and why are they there? Nine times out of ten, they represent some kind of memory or emotional attachment: your grandmother's old china, your dad's pipe collection, that sarong you bought on your honeymoon. They remind us of people, places, and events that are of particular importance to us. Most often, they enter our homes in the form of gifts, heirlooms, and souvenirs.

Again, if the item in question fills your heart with joy, display it with pride and enjoy its presence. If, on the other hand, you're holding on to it out of a sense of obligation (like Aunt Edna would turn over in her grave if you gave away her porcelain teacups) or proof of an experience (like nobody would believe you visited the Grand Canyon if you ditched the kitschy snow globe), then some soul-searching is in order.

As you walk around your house, have a conversation with your stuff. Ask each item, "What are you and what do you do?" "How did you come into my life?" "Did I buy you, or were you given to me?" "How often do I use you?" "Would I replace you if you were lost or broken, or would I be relieved to be rid of you?" "Did I ever want you in the first place?" Be honest with your answers—you won't hurt your stuff's feelings.

In the course of asking these questions, you'll likely come across two sub-categories of stuff, one of which is "other stuff's stuff." You know what I mean—some stuff just naturally accumulates other stuff: like accessories, manuals, cleaners, stuff to go with the stuff, display the stuff, contain the stuff, and fix the stuff. There's some great decluttering potential here: ditching one thing could lead to a cascade of castoffs!

The second sub-category is "other people's stuff." This is a tricky one. With the possible exception of your (young) children, your authority over other people's stuff is pretty limited. If it's the kayak your brother asked you to store in your basement—and hasn't reclaimed in fifteen years—you have the right to take matters into your hands (after a phone call requesting prompt removal, of course). However, if it's your spouse's overflowing hobby supplies, or your teenager's outgrown pop star memorabilia, a more diplomatic attitude is required. With any luck, your decluttering will become contagious, and result in those other people taking care of their own stuff.

For now, simply stroll around and get to know your stuff: that thing is useful, that one is beautiful, that belongs to someone else (easy as pie!). Don't be concerned about decluttering just yet; we'll get to that soon enough. Of course, if you happen to stumble across something useless, ugly, or unidentifiable—go ahead, get a head start, and give it the heave-ho!

2

You are not what you own

Contrary to what marketers would have you believe, *you are not what you own*. You are you, and things are things; no physical or mathematical alchemy can alter these boundaries, despite what that full-page magazine ad or clever commercial tries to tell you.

Nevertheless, we occasionally fall prey to the advertiser's pitch. Therefore, we must account for another sub-category of items we own: "aspirational stuff." These are the things we buy to impress others, or to indulge our "fantasy selves"—you know, the one that's twenty pounds thinner, travels the world, attends cocktail parties, or plays in a rock band.

We may be reluctant to admit it, but we likely acquired many of our possessions to project a certain image. Take automobiles, for example. We can satisfy our need for transportation with a simple car that gets us from Point A to Point B. Why then, would we pay double (or even triple) the price for a "luxury" car? Because automakers pay advertising firms big bucks to convince us that our cars are projections of ourselves, our personalities, and our positions in the corporate world or social hierarchy.

It doesn't stop there, of course. The compulsion to identify with consumer products reaches deep into our lives—from our choice of homes to what we put into them. Most people would agree that a small, basic house more than satisfies our need for shelter (especially compared to Third World accommodations). However, aspirational marketing decrees that we "need" a master suite, bedrooms for each child, his-and-her bathrooms, and kitchens with professional grade appliances; otherwise, we haven't quite "made it." Square footage becomes a status symbol; and naturally, it takes many more sofas, chairs, tables, knickknacks, and other stuff to outfit a larger house.

We're told that the contents of our homes are reflections of ourselves—and we should take care to display the "right" things to convey the desired impression. Bear rugs and deer antler chandeliers proclaim our outdoorsy, pioneer spirit; Old World antiques speak to our refined European tastes; Moroccan lanterns and floor pillows reveal our exotic, bohemian side. Yet none of these things are really necessary to communicate our interests or personalities; it's what we do—not what we have—that's far more illuminating.

Ads also encourage us to define ourselves through our clothing—and ideally, with brand name apparel. These designer labels don't make our clothes any warmer, our handbags any sturdier, or our lives any more glamorous. Furthermore, such trend-setting items seem to go out of style mere minutes after their purchase—leaving our closets packed with outdated duds which we hope someday will return to fashion. In reality, the majority of us have no need for celebrity-sized wardrobes, as our clothes and accessories will never garner widespread comment or attention. Nevertheless, marketers try to convince us that we live in the spotlight, and would do well to dress accordingly.

It's not easy to be a minimalist in a mass media world. Advertisers constantly bombard us with the message that material accumulation is the measure of success. They exploit the fact that it's a lot easier to *buy* status than to earn it. How many times have you heard that "more is better," "fake it 'til you make it," or "clothes make the man?" They tell us that more stuff means more happiness, when in fact, more stuff often means more headaches and more debt. The purchase of all this stuff is certainly benefiting someone...but it's not us.

Truth be told, products will never make us into something we're not. Designer handbags won't make us rich, premium lipsticks won't make us supermodels, and expensive pens won't make us successful executives. Pricey garden tools won't give us green thumbs, and high-end cameras won't turn us into award-winning photographers. Yet we feel compelled to buy, and keep, stuff that holds a promise—to make us happier, prettier, smarter, a better parent or spouse, more loved, more organized or more capable.

But consider this: if these things haven't delivered on their promises yet, it may be time to let them go.

Similarly, consumer products are not surrogates for experience. We don't need to own a garage full of camping gear, sports equipment, and pool toys when what we're really seeking is quality time with our family. Inflatable reindeer and piles of presents do not make a joyous holiday; gathering with our loved ones does. Accumulating mountains of yarn, stacks of cookbooks, and boxes of art supplies will not automatically make us accomplished knitters, master chefs, or creative geniuses. The activities themselves—not the materials—are what's essential to our enjoyment and personal development.

We also identify with stuff from our past, and hold on to certain things to prove who we were, or what we accomplished.

How many of us still have cheerleading uniforms, letter sweaters, swimming trophies, or notebooks from long-forgotten college classes? We rationalize keeping them as evidence of our achievements (as if we might need to dig out our old Calculus tests to prove we passed the course). However, these items are usually stuffed in a box somewhere, not proving anything to anybody. If that's the case, it may be time to release these relics of yesterday's you.

As we examine our things with a critical eye, we may be surprised how much of it commemorates our past, represents our hopes for the future, or belongs to our imaginary selves. Unfortunately, devoting too much of our space, time, and energy to these things keeps us from living in the present.

Sometimes we fear that getting rid of certain items is equivalent to getting rid of part of ourselves. No matter that we rarely play that violin, and have never worn that evening gown—the moment we let them go, we'll eliminate our chance to become virtuosos or socialites. And heaven forbid we throw away that high school mortarboard—it'll be like we never graduated.

We have to remember that our memories, dreams, and ambitions aren't contained in these objects; they're contained in ourselves. We are not what we own; we are what we do, what we think, and who we love. By eliminating the remnants of unloved pastimes, uncompleted endeavors, and unrealized fantasies, we make room for new (and *real*) possibilities. Aspirational items are the props for a pretend version of our lives; we need to clear out this clutter, so that we have the time, energy, and space to realize our true selves, and our full potential.

3

Less stuff = less stress

Think of the life energy expended in the ownership of a single possession: planning for it, reading reviews about it, looking for the best deal on it, earning (or borrowing) the money to buy it, going to the store to purchase it, transporting it home, finding a place to put it, learning how to use it, cleaning it (or cleaning around it), maintaining it, buying extra parts for it, insuring it, protecting it, trying not to break it, fixing it when you do, and sometimes making payments on it even after you've disposed of it. Now multiply this by the number of items in your home. Whoa! That's positively exhausting!

Being the caretaker of all our things can be a full-time job. In fact, entire industries have sprung up to help us service our stuff. Companies make fortunes selling us specialty cleaning products for every item—detergents for our clothes, polishes for our silver, waxes for our furniture, spray dusters for our electronics, and conditioners for our leather. The insurance business flourishes on the chance that our cars, jewelry, or art might be damaged or stolen. Locksmiths, alarm companies, and safe manufacturers promise to protect our things from theft.

Repairmen are standing by to fix our stuff when it breaks, and movers are ready to gather it all up and schlep it someplace else.

With all the time, money, and energy it demands, we may start to feel like our stuff owns us—instead of the other way around.

Let's take a closer look at how much of our stress can be attributed to stuff. First of all, we stress about *not having* stuff. Maybe we saw something in the store, or in an ad, and suddenly we can't imagine how we've lived until now without it. Our neighbor has one, our sister received one as a gift, and our coworker bought one last week; oh my goodness, are we the only ones in the world without one? A sense of deprivation starts to kick in…

So next we stress about how to acquire this thing. Unfortunately, we don't know anyone who will give us one, so we're going to have to buy it for ourselves. We drive from store to store (or surf from website to website) to check out prices, and wish that it would go on sale. We know we really can't afford it at the moment, but we want it *now*. So we scrape up some cash, put in extra hours at work, or charge it to a credit card and hope we can make the payments later.

The glorious day comes that we finally buy it. At long last, it is ours! The sun is shining, birds are singing, and all the stress melts away. Right? Think again. Now that we've spent good money on it, we're going to have to take good care of it. We've acquired not only a new possession, but also a load of responsibility.

We have to make sure we clean it regularly, as dust and dirt may inhibit its function and its lifespan. We have to keep it out of reach of the kids and pets. We have to use extra caution when we use it ourselves, so that we don't break or ruin or stain it. Sound crazy? How many times have you parked a new car at the far end of a parking lot, or had your day ruined when you discovered a scratch or dent? How did you feel when you splashed tomato sauce on that expensive silk blouse?

Then when something goes wrong with it—as it inevitably will—we stress over how to fix it. We pore over manuals or search the Web for advice. We go out and buy the appropriate tools, or replacement parts, for the repair. When we fail, we drag it into a repair shop. Or maybe we procrastinate because we can't figure out how (or don't particularly want) to deal with it. It sits there in the corner, or in a closet, or in the basement, weighing on our minds. Maybe we didn't break it, but simply got bored of it. Whatever the case, we feel a little guilty and uneasy for spending so much time and money on it.

Then we see another ad, and are captivated by an entirely different thing; this one's even more exciting than the last. Oh no, here we go again…

We never seem to have enough time in our days—perhaps our stuff is what's to blame. How many precious hours have we wasted running to the dry cleaners, how many Saturdays have been sacrificed to oil changes or car repairs, how many days off have been spent fixing or maintaining our things (or waiting for a technician to make a service call)? How often have we agonized (or scolded our children) over a broken vase, chipped plate, or mud stains on our area rugs? How much time have we spent shopping for cleaners, parts, and accessories for the stuff we already have?

Let's take a breather, and reminisce about how carefree and happy we were in college. Not coincidentally, that period was likely when we had the least amount of stuff. Life was so much simpler then: no mortgage, no car payments, no motorboat to insure. Learning, living, and having fun were far more important than the things we owned. The world was our oyster, and anything was possible! Now *that's* the joy we can recapture as minimalists. We simply need to put our stuff in its place, so it doesn't command the lion's share of our attention.

That doesn't mean we have to rent studio apartments, or furnish them with milk crates and secondhand couches. Instead, for now, let's imagine that we have only *half* of our current amount of stuff. Wow—that's a huge relief in itself! That's fifty percent less work and worry! Fifty percent less cleaning, maintenance, and repair! Fifty percent less credit card debt! What are we going to do with all this extra time and money? Ah, the light bulb's gone on... We're beginning to see the beauty of becoming minimalists.

4

Less stuff = more freedom

What if you were presented with a fabulous, once-in-a-lifetime opportunity—but you had to move across the country in three days in order to take it? Would you be filled with excitement and start making plans? Or would you look around your house and worry about how to get everything packed up in time? Would you despair at the thought of transporting your stuff across thousands of miles (or worse yet, find it completely ridiculous)? How likely would you be to decide it's just not worth the hassle, you're "settled" here, and maybe something else will come along some other time?

It seems crazy to consider—but would your stuff have the power to hold you in place? For many of us, the answer may very well be "yes."

Things can be anchors. They can tie us down, and keep us from exploring new interests and developing new talents. They can get in the way of relationships, career success, and family time. They can drain our energy and sense of adventure. Have you ever sidestepped a social visit because your house was too cluttered for company? Have you missed a child's soccer game because you were working overtime to keep up with credit card payments? Have you passed up an exotic vacation because there was nobody to "watch the house?"

Look around at all the things in the room where you're sitting. Imagine that each of these objects—every individual possession—is tied to you with a length of rope. Some are tied to your arms, some to your waist, some to your legs. (For extra drama, visualize chains instead.) Now try to get up and move around, with all this stuff dragging and clinging and clanging behind you. Not too easy, huh? You probably won't be able to get very far, or do very much. It won't be long before you give up, sit back down, and realize it takes much less effort to stay where you are.

In a similar way, too much clutter can weigh on our spirits. It's like all those items have their own gravitational field, and are constantly pulling us down and holding us back. We can literally feel heavy and lethargic in a cluttered room, too tired and lazy to get up and accomplish anything. Contrast this with a clean, bright, sparsely furnished room—in such a space, we feel light and liberated and full of possibility. Without the burden of all those belongings, we feel energetic and ready for anything.

With this in mind, we may be tempted to enact a quick fix and create the *illusion* of uncluttered space. We'll just nip on down to the superstore, nab some pretty containers, and make a minimalist room *tout de suite*. Unfortunately, simply stuffing everything into drawers, baskets, and bins won't do the trick: out of sight, out of mind doesn't work here. Even stuff that's hidden away (be it in the hall closet, down the basement, or across town in a storage unit) stays in the back of our minds. In order to free ourselves mentally, we must shake off the stuff entirely.

Here's something else to consider: in addition to crowding us physically, and stifling us psychologically, things also enslave us financially, via the debt used to pay for them. The more money we owe, the more sleepless our nights, and the more limited our opportunities. It's no picnic to get up every morning and drag ourselves to jobs we don't like, to pay for stuff we may no longer have, use, or even want. We can think of so many other things we'd rather be doing! Furthermore, if we've exhausted our paychecks (and then some) on consumer products, we've dried up our resources for other, more fulfilling pursuits: like taking an art class or investing in an up-and-coming business.

Travel is a wonderful analogy to the freedom of minimalist living. Think about what a pain it is to drag around two or three heavy suitcases when you're on vacation. You've anticipated the trip for ages, and when you disembark from your plane you can't wait to explore the sights. Not so fast—first you have to wait (and wait and wait) for your bags to appear on the luggage carousel. Next, you need to haul them through the airport. You might as well head to the taxi stand, as maneuvering them on the subway would be nearly impossible. And forget about getting a jump on sightseeing—you *must* head directly to your hotel, to rid yourself of this enormous burden. When you finally reach it, you collapse in exhaustion.

Minimalism, on the other hand, makes you nimble. Imagine traveling with only a light backpack instead—the experience is positively exhilarating. You arrive at your destination, leap off the plane, and zip by the crowds awaiting their luggage. You then jump on the subway, catch a bus, or start walking in the direction of your hotel. Along the way, you experience all the sights, sounds, and smells of a foreign city, with the time and energy to savor it all. You're mobile, flexible, and free as a bird—able to tote your bag to museums and tourist sites, and stash it in a locker when need be.

In contrast to the first scenario, you hit the ground running, and spent the afternoon seeing the sights instead of lugging around your stuff. You arrive at your hotel energized by your experience, and ready for more.

It's much the same with life. When we surround ourselves with things, we're like a tourist in a taxi—cut off from other people and all the interesting things that are happening *out there*. Our stuff builds up to form a prison around us. In becoming minimalists, we dismantle these dungeons, item by item, and regain our freedom.

When we're no longer chained to our stuff, we can savor life, connect with others, and participate in our communities. We're more open to experiences, and better able to recognize and take advantage of opportunities. The less baggage we're dragging around (both physically and mentally), the more living we can do!

5

Become detached from your stuff

Bashō, the famous haiku poet, wrote:

> "Since my house burnt down,
> I now own a better view
> Of the rising moon."

Now that's someone who's detached from his stuff!

While we don't have to go to such extremes, we'd do well to cultivate a similar sense of non-attachment. Developing such an attitude will make it significantly easier to declutter our homes—not to mention ease the pain when things are taken from us by other means (such as theft, flood, fire, or a collection agency).

Therefore, we'll spend this chapter doing mental exercises to loosen the grip our stuff has on us. To achieve our goals, we'll need to stretch, limber up, and get into shape for the task ahead. In the next few pages, we'll build up our minimalist muscles—and gain the psychological strength and flexibility we'll need for a showdown with our stuff.

We'll start out with something easy to get ourselves warmed up: let's imagine life without our stuff. This is a cinch—we don't even really have to imagine it, we can *remember* it.

Many of us look back on our young adult days as one of the happiest, most carefree times of our lives. No matter that we were living in a shoebox (sometimes with two or three other people), and had little disposable income. No matter that we couldn't afford designer clothes, fancy watches, or electronic gadgets. All of our possessions fit in a few crates, and we didn't have to worry about car repairs, home maintenance, or even going to the dry cleaners. What little stuff we had took a backseat to our social lives. We were footloose and fancy-free!

Think such liberty is a thing of the past? Not necessarily. Many of us get the chance to relive our "stuff-free" lives once or twice a year—when we go on vacation. The word vacation, in fact, comes from the Latin *vacare*, meaning "to be empty." No wonder we love to get away from it all!

Think about the last time you went camping, for instance. You carried everything you needed, for both comfort and survival, in your pack. You fussed little over appearance, and functioned perfectly well with the clothes on your back. You cooked your supper in a portable pan, over an open fire, and dined with nothing fancier than a plate, cup, and fork. Your tent, the simplest of shelters, kept you warm and dry. Your minimal possessions were in synch with your needs, leaving you plenty of time to relax and commune with nature.

So why do we need so much *more* when we get back to our "real" lives? Well, we don't, actually—and that's the point of these exercises. We'll come to recognize that much of the stuff that surrounds us is hardly necessary to our health and happiness.

Now that you're loosened up, let's kick things up a notch: pretend you're moving overseas. But don't start dialing your local self-storage company—this is a permanent move. You can't just stash your stuff away in anticipation of returning. Furthermore, transporting items across the globe is complex and costly; so you'll have to pare down to what you can't live without.

Survey the contents of your house and decide exactly what you'll take. Would your old, beat-up guitar make the cut? How about your ceramic animal collection? Would you devote precious cargo space to that ugly sweater you received three Christmases ago, the shoes that pinch your feet after fifteen minutes of wear, or the oil painting you inherited, but never liked? Of course not! Doesn't it feel great? It's amazing what you're able to ditch when you suddenly have the "permission!"

Okay, you're on your game now, so let's tackle a tough one: it's the middle of the night, and you're awakened by the piercing sound of the fire alarm. Holy smokes! You have only minutes— maybe seconds—to decide what you'll save as you head out of the house.

Admittedly, you'll have little opportunity for decisions here, and will have to rely mainly on instinct. If you have the time, you might grab some important files, the family photo album, and maybe your laptop. In all likelihood, however, you'll have to sacrifice all your stuff in order to get yourself, your family, and your pets out alive. In that moment, you won't care a whit about all those *things* that so thoroughly consumed your attention in the past.

Whew! Let's take a moment after that one to slow down our heartbeats. Actually, we're going to slow them way, way down…until they stop. What!

As much as we hate to think about it, our time here on earth will someday end; and unfortunately, it could occur sooner than we expect. And what's going to happen after that? People are going to look through our stuff. Yikes! It's a good thing we won't be able to blush, because that could be downright embarrassing.

Like it or not, the things we leave behind become part of our legacy—and I can't imagine any of us want to be memorialized as junk collectors or packrats. Wouldn't you rather be remembered as someone who lived lightly and gracefully, with only the basic necessities and a few special items?

Take some time and mentally catalog your "estate." What story does your stuff tell about you? Hopefully, it's not, "Boy, she had quite an affinity for takeout containers" or "That's odd, I didn't know he collected old calendars." Do your heirs a favor, and don't make them slog through a houseful of clutter after your demise. Otherwise, when you peer down from your afterlife, you'll likely see strangers pawing through your "treasures" at a giant yard sale.

All right, I promise, no more doom and gloom—this is a happy book! The point is, a jolt from our everyday routines (be it from a vacation or disaster) helps put our stuff in perspective; and in the latter case, it's a lot better to imagine it than actually experience it. Such scenarios help us see that in the grand scheme of things, our stuff isn't all that important; and with that realization, we can weaken the power it has over us, and be ready (and willing) to let it go.

6

Be a good gatekeeper

British writer and designer William Morris penned one of my favorite minimalist quotes: "Have nothing in your houses that you do not know to be useful or believe to be beautiful." It's a wonderful sentiment, but how exactly do we put it into practice? After all, we don't intentionally bring useless or ugly things into our homes; yet somehow, some less-than-desirables seem to find their way in. The solution: we have to become good gatekeepers.

It's pretty straightforward, actually. Things come into our houses by one of two ways: we buy them, or they're given to us (in other words, we get them for free). No matter what we'd like to think, they don't slip in when we're not looking, seeking shelter from the great outdoors. They don't materialize out of thin air, nor are they reproducing behind our backs (except perhaps the paperclips and Tupperware). Unfortunately, the responsibility lies squarely on our shoulders: we let them in.

As you evaluate your possessions, ask how each item came into your life. Did you seek it out, pay for it, and excitedly bring it back to your house or apartment? Did it follow you home from that conference in Chicago, or from that trip to Hawaii? Or did it sneak in disguised in colorful paper and a pretty bow?

Our homes are our castles, and we devote plenty of resources to defending them. We spray them with pest control to keep the bugs out; we use air filters to keep pollutants out; and we have security systems to keep intruders out. What are we missing? A stuff blocker to keep the clutter out! Since I have yet to see such a product on the market (and if one appears in the future, you heard it here first), we must take matters into our own hands.

Of course, we have the power to exercise complete control over what we buy; we just need to use it. Don't let down your defenses when something slips into your cart—in fact, don't escort any item to the checkout counter without extensive questioning. Ask the following (in your head!) of each potential purchase: "Do you deserve a place in my home?" "What value will you add to my household?" "Will you make my life easier?" "Or are you going to be more trouble than you're worth?" "Do I have a place to put you?" "Do I already have something that could accomplish the same task?" "Will I want to keep you forever (or at least a very long time)?" "If not, how hard will it be to get rid of you?" The last question alone saved me from lugging home a suitcase full of souvenirs from Japan—because once something has memories, it's a bugger to get rid of.

See, that's not too difficult. All we need to do is stop and think "Why?" before we buy. But what about those things we don't *choose* to acquire—and oftentimes don't even want? (Gifts, freebies, promotional items, I'm looking at you!) It can be hard (or rude) to refuse them; yet once they take up residence in our homes, they can be even harder to evict.

The best defense is a good offense, especially when it comes to freebies. Learning to decline them politely is a valuable technique, which comes in handy more often than you think. Pass up the magnets, pens, and paperweights with corporate logos and accept a business card instead. Turn down the perfume and cosmetic samples at the mall (hey, wait—what are you doing at the mall?), and the miniature detergents and dishwashing liquids from the supermarket. Decline the toaster when you open a bank account, and ask for an equivalent deposit in cash (it's worth a try!).

If you're attending a professional meeting or conference, review the booklets, pamphlets, and other materials while you're there; if they somehow hitch a ride in your luggage, distribute them at the office. And by all means, leave those little lotions, shampoos, and conditioners in the hotels where they belong. Unless you honestly plan to *use* them, don't let these miniatures (cute as they may be) clutter up your cabinets and drawers.

Gifts, on the other hand, require a different game plan. I've found it best to accept them graciously, without going overboard on the gratitude (because if you make a big fuss, you're sure to receive something similar next year). Yet that leaves a dilemma: what should you do with gifts you don't want? We certainly don't want to shove them in drawers, or the backs of our closets—we're trying to declutter, after all!

The solution is simple: never let them settle in. Keep a donation box outside of your living space (like in the basement), and stash unwanted stuff in there immediately. When it's full, cart it to your favorite local charity. The time delay between receiving the item and donating it (while waiting to fill the box), can actually work in your favor. For example: if Aunt Maude visits in the intervening months, you can quickly retrieve those bookends she gave you and set them out for display. Photographing the gift also works wonders: if it's a tchotchke, snap a shot of it on your mantelpiece; if it's a sweater or scarf, put it on and pose for a picture. Send the photo to the gift giver, and the item to charity, and happiness will reign all around.

In order to be a good gatekeeper, you have to think of your house as sacred space, not storage space. You're under no obligation to provide a home to every stray object that crosses your path. When one tries to sneak or charm its way in, remember that you have the power to deny entrance. If the item won't add value to your life in terms of function or beauty, hang out the "Sorry, No Vacancy" sign. A simple refusal up front will save you tons of decluttering down the road!

7

Embrace space

I hope you like quotes, because I'm starting this chapter with another one of my favorites: "Music is the space between the notes." My interpretation of composer Claude Debussy's words: beauty requires a certain amount of emptiness to be appreciated—otherwise, you have only chaos and cacophony.

For our purposes, we'll put a minimalist twist on this idea and say, "Life is the space between our things." Too much clutter can stifle our creativity, and make our lives discordant. Conversely, the more space we have, the more beautifully and harmoniously we can live.

Space: it's not anything, really, but we never seem to have enough of it. The lack of it distresses us to no end; in fact, we'd do almost anything to have more space in our houses, more space in our closets, and more space in our garages. We remember having larger amounts of it sometime in the past, and its disappearance is cause for concern. We look around with puzzled expressions and wonder, "Where did all our space go?"

We have fond memories of how it looked the first day we moved into our homes; oh, all that glorious space! But what happened? It's not nearly as impressive as we remember it. Well, our space didn't go anywhere. It's still right there where we left it. The space didn't change; our priorities did. We focused so much of our attention on stuff that we completely forgot about the space. We lost sight of the fact that the two are mutually exclusive: that for each new thing we bring into our homes, a little bit of space disappears. The problem: we put more value on our stuff than on our space.

Here's the good news: space may be easy to lose, but it's just as easy to reclaim. Get rid of an item, and voilà! Space! Get rid of another item, and voilà! More space! This is fun! Soon, all those little spaces add up to a big space, and we can actually move around again. Take advantage of all that newfound space and do a little happy dance!

What we need to keep in mind (and which is way too easy to forget) is that the amount of stuff we're able to own is limited by the amount of space we have to contain it. It's simple physics. No amount of stuffing, scrunching, pushing, or pulling will change that. Seal it up in "magic" vacuum bags if you want, but even they have to go somewhere. So if you live in a small apartment, or you don't have a lot of closets, you can't bring home a lot of stuff. Period. Otherwise, you're going to have a problem.

By the same token, we don't need to fill all the space we have. Remember, space is of equal value to things (or greater, depending on your perspective). If you live in a four-thousand-square-foot house, you don't *need* to acquire four thousand square feet of stuff. If you're lucky enough to have a walk-in closet, you don't *need* to pack every inch of it. Really! In fact, you'll live and breathe a lot easier if you don't.

We talked a little bit about the value of containers in the introduction, and how they hold the greatest potential when they're empty. When we want to enjoy a pot of tea, we need an empty cup to pour it in. When we want to make a meal, we need an empty pot to cook it in. When we want to do the tango, we need an empty room to dance it in.

Likewise, our houses are the containers of our domestic lives. When we want to relax, create, and play with our families, we need some empty space in which to do it. Alternatively, we can think of our homes as the stages on which the dramas of our lives play out. For the best performance, we must be able to move about and express ourselves freely; it's certainly no fun (nor particularly graceful) if we're tripping over the props.

We also need space for our ideas and thoughts—a cluttered room usually leads to a cluttered mind. Say you're sitting on your sofa, maybe reading a book or listening to music, and a truly profound thought captures your imagination: perhaps you've had an insight into human nature, or are on the brink of uncovering the meaning of life. You're deep in thought, solving the mysteries of mankind, when your gaze falls on the stack of magazines on the coffee table, or the broken sewing machine in the corner. "Hmm, I really must attend to that," you think; "I wonder if there's time before dinner..." Your mind immediately takes a detour and your train of thought is lost—and with it, your legacy as a great philosopher.

Of course, you don't have to be channeling Aristotle to appreciate an uncluttered environment. Even activities of a more mundane variety benefit greatly from space and clarity; for instance, it's much easier to give your full attention to your partner or toddler when there aren't a million doodads around to confuse and distract you.

In fact, that's the greatest thing about space: it puts the things (and people) that are truly special to us in the spotlight. If you owned a beautiful painting, you wouldn't crowd it with other décor—you'd hang it on its own, with enough space around it to show it off. If you had an exquisite vase, you wouldn't bury it in a pile of junk—you'd put it on its own pedestal. We need to treat what's important to us with similar respect; which, in effect, means removing all the other stuff that's not so important.

By creating space in our homes, we put the focus back where it should be: on what we do, rather than what we own. Life is too short to waste fussing over stuff. For when we're old and gray, we won't wax poetic on the things we had—but rather on what we did in the spaces between them.

8

Enjoy without owning

What if someone offered you the Mona Lisa—with the stipulation that you couldn't sell it? Sure, you'd have the opportunity to gaze on a breathtaking painting twenty-four hours a day; but suddenly the responsibility of one of humanity's greatest treasures would rest squarely on your shoulders. It'd be no small task to keep her secure from theft, clean from dust and debris, protected from sunlight, and stored at the optimum temperature and humidity. You'd no doubt also have to deal with a steady stream of art lovers wanting to view her. In all likelihood, any pleasure you'd derive from her ownership would be usurped by the burden of her care and upkeep. Before long, that mysterious smile may no longer seem so charming.

On second thought, thanks but no thanks—we'll leave her in the Louvre instead!

We're incredibly lucky, in our modern society, to have access to so many of mankind's masterpieces—without having to acquire and maintain them ourselves. Our cities are such amazing resources of art, culture, and entertainment, we have no need to create artificial approximations of them within our own four walls.

I learned this lesson years ago, when I was fresh out of college. I had studied art history in school, and worked part-time in a contemporary art gallery. I attended scores of exhibitions, read dozens of monographs, and fancied myself quite the connoisseur. So when I had the opportunity to acquire a print by a well-known artist, I couldn't hand over my money fast enough. It was a big step in my young adult life—I was on my way to becoming an art collector.

The joy of acquisition waned a bit when I faced the responsibility (and expense) of having the print archivally matted and properly framed. Next, I had to tackle the issue of where to display it. Naturally, I hadn't stopped to think how a modern work of art would look in my prewar apartment. Nor had I considered such things as lighting, glare, and sight lines. In the end, I settled on the place of honor above the fireplace. Although it clashed a little with the vintage tile work, I wanted it to be the centerpiece of my décor (I'd paid good money for it, after all!).

Once I worked through these issues, I was finally able to sit back and admire my treasure. Imagine my surprise when one day I spotted a big black bug, smack dab in the middle of my precious print! I couldn't fathom how it had gotten under the glass of the professional frame; but there was nothing I could do but let it be. I'm not sure what it did in there, but it added its own artistic smudge and went on its way.

Nevertheless, I displayed it proudly—and carefully wrapped it up and carted it with me when I moved. My new apartment lease prohibited wall hangings, so the print acquired a less glamorous position on the floor. After several more relocations, I became decidedly less enthusiastic about hauling it around and finding places to put it. It spent five years covered in bubble wrap and stuffed in a closet before I finally sold it. From then on, I decided to let the museums handle the art, and I'd go and enjoy it at my leisure!

In fact, finding ways to "enjoy without owning" is one of the keys to having a minimalist home. Case in point: those cappuccino makers gathering dust in our kitchen cupboards. In theory, it seems convenient (and somewhat decadent) to be able to make a steaming cup of frothy java in the comfort of our own homes. In reality, the contraption is a pain to drag out, set up, and clean up when we're finished; and to top it off, the brew never seems to taste quite as good. It's somehow less *special* when we can have it anytime. After playing barista a few times, we realize it's more fun to visit the local coffee shop, and soak in the ambience while sipping our drink.

In pursuing a minimalist lifestyle, we need to resist the temptation to recreate the outside world within our abodes. Unfortunately, however, trends in home design have been moving in the opposite direction: media rooms, fitness centers, and bathroom "spas" are all the rage in the luxury home market. It's almost as if we're going to hunker down and never leave our houses. But instead of purchasing, maintaining, and repairing all that equipment, why not have a fun night out at the movies, go to the gym (or take a walk), or treat yourself to a day at the local spa? That way, you can enjoy such activities when it strikes your fancy—without having to store and care for all the stuff.

For even less work and worry, apply the same principle to your backyard. Keep it neat and maintained, but don't feel compelled to create a botanical extravaganza behind your house. Instead, do as city dwellers do, and take advantage of public parks and gardens. There, professional landscapers do all the hard work, leaving you free to enjoy an ever-changing panorama of flowers and foliage. It's a great way to get your greenery fix, without having to own a garage full of lawn and garden equipment. Likewise, there's no need to turn your yard into a five-star resort, complete with pool, tennis courts, fire pit, and outdoor living rooms when you can enjoy similar amenities (and much less upkeep) at the local community center or swim club.

If you're particularly susceptible to buying "pretty" things, repeat "enjoy without owning" as a mantra when you're out shopping. Admire the delicacy of a glass figurine, the metalwork on an antique bracelet, or the vibrant colors of an artisan vase—but instead of bringing them home, leave them in the showcase. Think of it like a museum trip: an opportunity to admire the beauty and design of well-crafted objects, without the possibility (or pressure) of ownership. I do the same while surfing the Internet; and to be honest, I get just as much satisfaction from looking at the pictures as I would from owning the pieces.

In our quest to become minimalists, we want to reduce the amount of things in our homes that require our care and attention. Fortunately, we have ample opportunity to do so—simply by shifting some of our pleasures and activities into the public realm. In fact, such action produces a pretty wonderful side effect. For when we hang out in parks, museums, movie houses, and coffee shops—instead of trying to create similar experiences in our own homes—we become significantly more socially active and civically engaged. By breaking down the walls of stuff around us, we're able to get out into the world and enjoy fresher, more direct, and more rewarding experiences.

9

The joy of enough

Chinese philosopher Lao Tzu, author of the *Tao Te Ching*, wrote, "He who knows he has enough is rich."

Enough—it's a slippery concept. What's enough for one is too little for the next guy and too much for another. Most of us would agree we have enough food, enough water, enough clothing, and enough shelter to meet our basic needs. And anyone reading this book probably feels that they have enough things. So why do we still feel the urge to buy, and own, *more?*

Let's investigate this word "enough" a little more closely. Dictionary.com defines it as "adequate for the want or need; sufficient for the purpose or to satisfy desire." Ah, there's the problem: even though we've satisfied our needs, there's still the matter of our wants and desires. In order to experience the joy of "enough," that's where we'll need to focus. It's quite simple, actually: happiness is wanting what you have. When your wants are satisfied by the things you already have, there's no need to acquire any more. But wants can be pesky little things; and in order to get them under control, we have to understand what drives them.

Let's imagine we live out in the middle of nowhere, with no access to television or the Internet, and no magazine or newspaper subscriptions. We may live simply, but we're perfectly satisfied with what we have. We're warm, well-fed, and safe from the elements. To put it simply, we have enough. Then one day a family builds a house next door to us; it's bigger than ours, and filled with more things. Our enough doesn't look like so much anymore. Then more families move in, with all different kinds of houses, cars, and things; holy cow, we never realized how much stuff we *didn't* have! A satellite connection brings us TV and Internet, and we get a glimpse into the lavish lives of the rich and famous. We still have the same possessions as before—which with, up until this point, we'd felt perfectly satisfied—but now we can hardly help but feel deprived.

What happened? We fell victim to the classic dilemma of "keeping up with the Joneses." Suddenly, we're not measuring our "enough" in objective terms (is our house sufficient for our family?), but rather in relative terms (is our house as nice, as big, or as new as the one next door?). Worse yet, the problem is compounded because the bar keeps moving; once we've made it to the level of one Jones, we focus on the next Jones up. Let's face it, though: there's *always* going to be someone else who has more than us. So unless we truly believe we're going to become the richest people in the world, it's an exercise in futility to define our "wealth" relative to others. The funny thing is, even billionaires aren't immune to this phenomenon; they've been known to try to outdo each other in the sizes of their yachts. If contentment with stuff is out of reach even at the loftiest levels, then *what's the point?*

The fact of the matter is, once we've covered our basic needs, our happiness has very little to do with the amount of stuff we own. Beyond this point, the marginal utility (or satisfaction) derived from consuming additional goods diminishes rapidly; and, at what economists call the "satiation point," it actually turns negative. (Perhaps the reason you're reading this book!) That's why "more" often fails to satisfy us— and in some cases, can even make us less happy. Consumer one-upmanship, therefore, is a shell game; the only winners are the companies selling the goods. We'd actually be happier, more relaxed, and more satisfied people if we disengaged from it entirely.

Cultivating an attitude of gratitude is far more conducive to a minimalist lifestyle. If we recognize the abundance in our lives, and appreciate what we have, we will not want for more. We simply need to focus on what we have, rather than what we don't have. If we're going to make comparisons, we have to look globally, as well as locally; we have to look down the ladder, as well as up. Even the poorest of First World families are rich by Third World standards. So while we may feel deprived relative to the more affluent in our own country, we're living like royalty compared to many others around the world.

I used to feel discontent because my house had just one bathroom. How inconvenient when nature is calling, and someone else is taking a shower! How awkward to have to share with overnight guests! Then one day a wonderful book came into my hands: *Material World: A Global Family Portrait* by Peter Menzel. It featured "average" families from around the world, photographed in front of their houses with all of their possessions spread around them. If you ever feel the slightest bit deprived, just open this book—most middle-class Americans will find they own more material goods than other First World families; and the humblest of our abodes would be palaces to the poorest ones. It's truly eye-opening how little some people possess; I learned that even indoor plumbing is a rarity in some parts of the world. It gave me a new perspective on my relative "affluence," and made me realize how lucky I am to have any bathroom at all!

Now that we have a better understanding of where we stand in the world (and not just compared to celebrities or our neighbors), let's wrap up our discussion of "enough" with a little exercise. It's very straightforward; all you'll need is paper and pencil (or a computer, if you prefer). Ready? Go through your house, and make a list of everything you own. I know some of you are looking at this page incredulously; but no, I'm not kidding. Make a list of every book, every plate, every fork, every shirt, every shoe, every sheet, every pen, every knickknack—in short, every single object—that resides inside your home. Too difficult? Try just one room. Still can't do it? How about just one *drawer*. It's pretty overwhelming, isn't it? *Do you still feel like you don't have enough?*

10

Live simply, so that others may simply live

Mahatma Gandhi said, "Live simply, so that others may simply live." As it turns out, this may be the greatest incentive of all for becoming a minimalist.

Now that we're thinking globally, let's consider this: we share the world with over six billion other people. Our space, and our resources, are finite. How can we guarantee that there's enough food, water, land, and energy to go around? *By not using any more of it than we need.* Because for every "extra" we take, someone else (now, or in the future) will have to do without. That "extra" may not add significantly to *our* well-being; but to someone else, it may be a matter of life or death.

We must realize that we don't live in a vacuum; the consequences of our actions ripple throughout the world. Would you still run the water while you brush your teeth, if it meant someone else would suffer from thirst? Would you still drive a gas guzzler, if you knew a world oil shortage would bring poverty and chaos? Would you still build an oversized house, if you witnessed first-hand the effects of deforestation? If we understood how our lifestyles impact other people, perhaps we would live a little more lightly.

Our choices as consumers have an environmental toll. Every item we buy, from food to books to televisions to cars, uses up some of the earth's bounty. Not only does its production and distribution require energy and natural resources; its disposal is also cause for concern. Do we really want our grandchildren to live among giant landfills? The less we need to get by, the better off everyone (and our planet) will be. Therefore, we should reduce our consumption as much as possible, and favor products and packaging made from minimal, biodegradable, or recyclable materials.

Our purchases have a human toll as well. Unfortunately, global outsourcing has fostered an out-of-sight, out-of-mind mentality with regards to this issue. Manufacturing has moved out of our own communities, where we could see first-hand the conditions under which our neighbors worked—and where we could count on laws, unions, and other regulations to protect them and ensure their safety. Now the things we buy are made on the other side of the world, where labor is cheap and regulations scarce. Whenever we purchase something, we need to consider the people who made it. Under what kind of conditions did they labor? What effect did the production of this item have on their lives, their communities, and their environment? If it's negative, is our need (or desire) for this thing worth their suffering?

Of course, it's practically impossible to calculate the human and environmental impact of every item we buy. We should educate ourselves the best we can, but our research will never be comprehensive; manufacturers are rarely transparent about their overseas operations, and often change locations in their quest to cut costs. It could conceivably take us months to gather the appropriate information for a single purchase. However, we can do an end run around this issue, and still minimize our personal consumer footprints: by buying local, buying used, and buying less.

Buying local has significant ethical, environmental, and economic benefits. First, locally-made goods are much more likely to have been produced under fair and humane working conditions. Second, eliminating long-distance transportation saves massive amounts of energy. Purchasing vegetables from your local farmer's market, for example, is considerably kinder to the planet than having them shipped halfway around the globe. And third, supporting our local economies keeps our hard-earned dollars in our communities, where they can be used to provide infrastructure and services to enrich our lives and those of our neighbors.

Buying used enables us to obtain the things we need, without putting further pressure on the earth's resources. Why waste materials and energy on a new item when an existing one will do? Instead of going to the mall, shop the secondhand market for furniture, appliances, electronics, clothing, books, toys, and more. Thrift shops, classifieds, and websites such as eBay (www.ebay.com), Craigslist (www.craigslist.org), and Freecycle (www.freecycle.org) are treasure troves of perfectly good, previously used items. Take pride in becoming the second (or third, or fourth) owner of something; it's a financially-savvy, as well as eco-friendly, way to meet your needs.

Finally, buying less is the cornerstone of our minimalist lifestyles. Limiting our purchases to essentials is the best way to curb the impact of our consumption. By doing so, we can ensure that we, as individuals, are responsible for less resource depletion, human hardship, and waste. If we truly don't need another sweater or pair of shoes, let's not buy them simply for the sake of fashion. Let's think about the resources used to make them, the factories in which they were made, the cost of transporting them around the globe, and the eventual impact of their disposal. Let's base our purchasing decisions on our needs, and the entire life cycle of a product—rather than the fact that we like the color or saw it in an advertisement.

Let's reject being "consumers," and become "minsumers" instead. We'll strive to minimize our consumption to what meets our needs; minimize the impact of our consumption on the environment; and minimize the effect of our consumption on other people's lives.

As an added bonus, such a philosophy helps us accomplish our other minimalist goals: for as we reduce our consumption to save the world, our living rooms will stay clean, serene, and clutter-free!

PART TWO

STREAMLINE

Now that we've established our minimalist mindset, we're ready to put our new attitude into practice. The following chapters outline the STREAMLINE method: ten sure-fire techniques to rid our houses of clutter, and keep them that way. They're easy to use, and easy to remember; each letter of the word represents a particular step in our decluttering process. Once we get these under our belts, there'll be no stopping us!

S Start over
T Trash, Treasure, or Transfer
R Reason for each item
E Everything in its place
A All surfaces clear
M Modules
L Limits
I If one comes in, one goes out
N Narrow it down
E Everyday maintenance

11

Start over

The most difficult aspect of any task is knowing where to start. As we look around our houses, we see piles of stuff everywhere—in corners, in closets, in drawers, in dressers, in pantries, on counters, and on shelves. We may also have stuff hidden in basements, in attics, in garages, and in storage units; although out of sight, it's certainly not out of mind. If you feel overwhelmed, don't despair—you're not alone.

Sometimes it seems that nothing short of a force of nature, or extreme circumstance, will clear the clutter from our homes. We almost wish we had to move cross-country on a moment's notice, or that a great wind would sweep away everything but our most precious and needed items. Unfortunately, however, decluttering doesn't happen instantaneously; it's something we have to work at, slowly and deliberately. Here's the good news, though: as we get into the groove, we get better at it; and believe it or not, it actually becomes fun!

In fact, nothing prepared me for the rush I got when that first bag of discards hit the curb. What I expected to be a tedious, and rather onerous, task turned out to be exhilarating. I was instantly addicted. I decluttered in the morning; I decluttered in the evening; I decluttered on the weekends; I decluttered in my dreams (really!). When I wasn't actually decluttering, I was planning what I could declutter next. The high I experienced while decluttering was like no other; it's as if I could feel the physical weight being lifted from my shoulders. After I'd been particularly productive, I'd twirl around in my (newly) empty space with a huge grin on my face. (I told you this would be fun!)

Before we begin, let's think back to the first day we moved into our house or apartment. We walked around the bare rooms, imagining what life would be like within its walls. How wonderful it felt to savor the space before a single box was unpacked! It was a beautiful blank canvas, empty and full of potential, ready to be personalized with our own special touch. We relished the thought of a clean slate—what a fabulous opportunity to start fresh and do things right!

We vowed to unpack slowly and methodically, finding each item its own special place and getting rid of anything that didn't belong. We looked forward to putting everything into perfect order. But then life got in the way: we had to start a new job, prepare the kids for school, accommodate guests, or spruce up the place for a housewarming party. We had to put things away fast, with minimal disruption to daily life, and had no time to judge the worthiness of each individual item. We did the best we could to stash our stuff, and throw the emptied boxes into the attic or basement.

Well, now's our chance to Start Over. We're not going to vacate the premises, or empty the contents of our houses onto our front lawns. We're just going to redo moving day—but now we're going to take our time, breaking up the gargantuan task into little pieces. We're going to orchestrate a fresh start for each area of our homes. We'll simply pick a single section at a time—as big as a room or as small as a drawer—and start over again, as if it's the first day we moved in.

The key to Starting Over is to *take everything out* of the designated section. If it's a drawer, turn it upside down and dump out its contents. If it's a closet, strip it down to bare hooks, rods, and shelving. If it's a box of hobby materials, spill them all out. Tackling an entire room at once is a little more challenging, as you'll need somewhere to put all the stuff you remove; a nearby room is most convenient, and will cut down on walking, or climbing steps, as you put things back. If that's not possible, consider using your front porch, backyard, or basement as a temporary holding area; the effort it takes to schlep things back to the room in question may be all the deterrent you need.

I can't emphasize enough the importance of *completely* emptying the section on which you're working. We become so accustomed to seeing certain things in certain places, it's like they've earned the right to be there (whether they belong there or not). It's tempting to say, "Oh, I know that'll stay, so I'll just leave it there for now and work around it—what's the point of taking it out if I'm going to put it right back?"

No—take it *all* out—every single item. Sometimes just seeing something out of its usual spot—and how great that spot looks without it—will completely change your perspective on it. The broken chair that's been in the corner of your living room for as long as you can remember seems to have staked its claim to the space; it's like a member of the family, and it feels disloyal (or even sacrilegious) to move it. But once it's out in the backyard, with the light of day shining on it, it's suddenly nothing more than an old, forlorn broken chair. Who would want to bring *that* into their house? Especially when the corner it used to sit in now looks so clean and spacious...

Decluttering is infinitely easier when you think of it as deciding what to keep, rather than deciding what to throw away. That's why Starting Over—emptying everything out, then bringing things back one by one—is so effective. You're selecting what you truly love and need; and it's much more fun to single out things to treasure, than to single out things to toss. A curator at an art museum starts with an empty gallery, and chooses the best works with which to beautify the space. Well, Starting Over makes us the curators of our homes. We'll decide which objects enhance our lives, and put only those things back into our space.

Remember, the things with which we choose to surround ourselves tell our story. Let's hope it's not "I choose to live in the past," or "I can't finish the projects I start." Instead, let's aim for something like, "I live lightly and gracefully, with only the objects I find functional or beautiful."

12

Trash, Treasure, or Transfer

Now that we've dumped out our stuff, we need to sort through it and decide what to do with it. We're going to separate our things into three categories: Trash, Treasure, and Transfer. For the first, grab a large, heavy-duty garbage bag (a smaller one will do if you're working on a single drawer). For the latter two, use boxes, tarps, or whatever's convenient for the area you're tackling. Boxes work well if you're dealing with smaller items; but if the stuff you're sorting is bigger than a breadbox, designate sections of the floor (with or without tarps), and make separate piles for each category.

Keep an extra box on hand as well; we'll call it Temporarily Undecided. As you sort through your stuff, you'll come across things that you're not sure you want to keep, but you're not quite ready to part with. Perhaps you just need a little more time to think it over. You don't want a few tricky objects to throw you off track, or slow your momentum; so if you can't make a quick decision on something, put it here for now. You can revisit it later and assign it to a pile.

Truth be told, you may very well end up with a full box of Undecideds, even after further consideration. In that case, seal it up and write the date on it with permanent marker. You're going to put it into "temporary" storage: in the basement, attic, garage, or back of a closet. If, after six months (or a year), you haven't opened it to retrieve anything, take it to your favorite charity. This box should only be used as a last resort—not as an excuse to avoid hard decisions. The point isn't to save these items, but rather to save your *space* from items you're not sure you need.

So let's start with the Trash: this stuff is a no-brainer. Throw away everything that's clearly garbage, like food packaging, stained or ripped clothing, expired cosmetics and medicines, spoiled food, nonworking pens, old calendars, newspapers, flyers and pamphlets, junk mail, bottles and containers that can't be reused, and any broken items that can't be fixed or aren't worth fixing. If it's not good enough for Goodwill, it belongs in this pile.

And I know you know that when I say "throw away," I mean "recycle if possible." While tossing things in the trash is easy, we must keep the environment in mind. I don't think any of us want to be responsible for something sitting in a landfill for the next hundred years. So err on the side of good karma, and recycle what you can: most communities will accept cardboard, paper, glass, metal, and some plastics. Of course, before you pitch anything, consider if someone else can use it; if so, put it in the Transfer pile instead. It's always better to send something to a good home than to a landfill or recycling plant—even if it takes a little more time and effort. We have to take responsibility for the entire life cycle of the things we buy, including their proper disposal. Be mindful of these issues when you're shopping—it's actually a pretty effective way to curb impulse purchases.

The Treasure pile is for the items you'll keep, and should contain just what the name implies: the things you truly cherish, for either their beauty or their functionality. If you haven't used something in over a year, it probably doesn't belong here. Consider giving it to someone with more use for it; or if you have that much difficulty parting with it, put it in the Temporarily Undecided box. We don't want to devote valuable space to unused stuff; we want to save it for the good stuff! Ditto for knickknacks, collectibles, and other decorations: if you're not displaying them proudly and prominently, and if you don't derive true pleasure from their presence, send them off to a new home where they'll get the attention they deserve.

Finally, let's discuss the Transfer pile. In here belong all those perfectly good items that are no longer good for *you*. Don't feel guilty about letting them go; set them free, and give them a new lease on life. Above all, resist the urge to hold on to something because you "might need it" someday—if you haven't needed it yet, you likely never will. If by some chance you did, would you even be able to find it? Would it be in usable condition? Or would you probably run out and buy a shiny new one anyway? If it's easily obtainable, or replaceable, better to let someone else use it now, than keep it waiting in the wings for a day that may never come.

As you're sorting, divide the Transfer pile into Give Away and Sell sections. Be generous! Something that's been sitting in your house, unused and unloved, may bring a great deal of joy to, or fill the genuine need of, someone else. Make their day, and give yourself a pat on the back. Knowing that you're doing good can make it much easier to part with your stuff. If you don't have a specific recipient in mind for an item, offer it up on Freecycle. Simply list the things you're giving away, and interested parties will contact you to retrieve them. Alternatively, give seldom-used items to someone who'll use them more—like your power saw to a woodworking neighbor, or your sewing machine to a seamstress cousin—with the understanding that you can borrow them if the need arises.

Don't worry, you don't have to spend weeks putting your possessions up for adoption. If you don't have the time or inclination to find them specific homes, charitable organizations accept a wide range of goods. Goodwill, the Salvation Army, the Red Cross, religious organizations, homeless shelters, domestic violence shelters, thrift stores, and senior centers are well-equipped to distribute your donations to those who need them most. Your castoffs can do a world of good in your own community: consider giving books to your local library, office supplies to your children's school, pet items to an animal shelter, and professional clothing to Dress for Success (www.dressforsuccess.org). You may be able to take a tax deduction for your generosity, so keep a list of donated items and their values, and obtain a receipt from the organization.

Selling your stuff is another effective way to ease separation anxiety. Sometimes, it's much easier to let something go when you can get some (or all) of your money back. In fact, the cash may bring you more happiness than the item itself! You have a choice of outlets through which to peddle your unwanted wares, from the traditional to the high-tech. If your castoffs are large in quantity and low in value, hold a garage or yard sale, or send them to a consignment shop. To unload more unique, collectible or expensive items, turn to the Internet: try online classifieds like Craigslist or auction sites like eBay. You can even sell used books, CDs, DVDs, video games, and other goods through retail giant Amazon (www.amazon.com).

Great! Now that you've set up your sorting system, and you know what goes where, you can get to the business of clearing out some stuff. Focus like a laser beam, and declutter the drawer, closet, or room you chose to Start Over. Have fun with it—put on some upbeat music, dance around your piles, and kiss those castoffs goodbye! Once you've assigned every item to a category, those Trash and Transfer piles get a one-way ticket out of the house—and you're that much closer to living only with your Treasures.

13

Reason for each item

As you sort through your items, stop and question each one headed for your Treasure pile. Nothing gets a free pass! Put on your gatekeeper cap and conduct an entry interview with each item; make sure it has a good *reason* for being part of your household. Just because it's a stray (the tote bag that followed you home from a business conference), or seeking asylum from another home (the mismatched china your sister unloaded on you), doesn't grant it clearance. It must be able to make a positive contribution to be considered for residency. Careful screening, after all, is the only way to keep out the riffraff.

You may run into situations where items have strong credentials for staying in your home—but they're identical (or nearly so) to something else you own. Being a minimalist is about getting rid of the excess, so cull these duplicates from your Treasure pile. How did multiple versions enter your household in the first place? In some cases, they may have been gifts. In others, however, you may have purchased something new, then decided to hang on to the old one. You bought a new TV, and put the old one in the bedroom; you bought a new dining table, and stored its predecessor in the basement; you bought new shoes, and saved the grungy pair for a rainy day.

Other things are only sold in excessive quantities: paperclips, rubber bands, and bobby pins come to mind. When you purchase such things, you usually end up with a lifetime supply of them. Still others—like pens, buttons, and safety pins—seem to multiply of their own accord. The extras end up in the back of a drawer until the end of time, no questions asked. But let's shake things up: if you can't envision yourself ever using a thousand paperclips, or a hundred safety pins, retain a reasonable amount and pass along the rest. If you only need a handful, why hang on to a bucketful?

Once you've dealt with the duplicates, it's time to scrutinize the remaining candidates. As you consider each one, ask what it's used for and how often you use it (if you can't answer those two questions, it shouldn't be anywhere near your Treasure pile!). Have you used it in the past year? Do you expect to use it in the near future? Does it make your life easier, more beautiful, or more pleasurable? How? Do you have something similar? Is it hard to maintain or clean, and if so, is it worth the effort? Would it be difficult or expensive to replace? Would you take it with you if you were moving? How would your life change if you didn't own it?

Finally, no matter what the other answers, always be sure to ask this question: what is more valuable to you—the item, or the space it occupies?

If you're having difficulty making decisions, recruit an objective friend to provide assistance. Explaining to someone else the reason why you're keeping something can be difficult, illuminating...and sometimes a little embarrassing! What seems perfectly legitimate in your head can sound ridiculous when spoken aloud. ("I might need this feather boa if I moonlight as a cabaret singer.") Furthermore, when there's a third party present, your pride will kick in—and you'll be much less likely to squirrel away something old and ratty. Don't enlist the help of a packrat or sentimental type, though; unless, of course, you can get them to cart away some of your rejects.

During this process, you'll find plenty of good reasons for keeping something: you use it often, it makes your life easier, you find it beautiful, it would be difficult to replace, it's multifunctional, it saves you time, it's a cherished part of your heritage or family. A not-so-good reason, on the other hand, is that it "might be worth something." This excuse can bring your decluttering to a screeching halt, and compel you to continue providing refuge to useless items. If this happens, get thee on the Internet and do some research. Almost everything imaginable has been auctioned on eBay, from antique jewelry to kitschy cookie jars—making it a wonderful reference with which to value your items. (It's probably where you'd end up selling them anyway.)

Chances are, most of your clutter is *not* fetching a fortune. But don't despair—celebrate! You're no longer obligated to provide it with long-term, climate-controlled storage in the (false) hope that it may fund your retirement. You're free to let it go; and if the need ever arises for it, look how inexpensively you can acquire it. Once in awhile, however, one of your Treasures may live up to its title—giving you the opportunity to pocket some serious cash. If you don't need it, and don't love it, why not go for it? Take some snaps and put it up for auction. You'll have the photographs for memories, some extra dough in your wallet, and some extra space in your house.

As we determine what belongs in our Treasure piles, we should keep the Pareto principle (also known as the 80/20 rule) in mind. In this context, it means we use 20 percent of our stuff

80 percent of the time. Read that again, closely: *we use 20 percent of our stuff 80 percent of the time.* That means we could get by with just a fifth of our current possessions, and hardly notice a difference. Woo-hoo! This is going to be easier than we thought! If we rarely use most of our stuff, we should have no problem paring down to the essentials. All we have to do is identify our "20 percent," and we'll be well on our way to becoming minimalists.

14

Everything in its place

A place for everything, and everything in its place. Memorize this mantra, repeat it often, sing it out loud, say it in your sleep—it's one of the most important minimalist principles. When each thing you own has a designated spot (ideally in a drawer, cupboard, or container), stray items won't wander your household and congregate as clutter. With this system in place, you can easily spy something that doesn't belong—and immediately escort it out of your home.

When assigning a place to each item, consider where, and how often, you use it. Think of your house in terms of zones. On the broadest level, your house is divided into rooms, including the kitchen zone, bathroom zone, bedroom zone, and family room zone. Each of these can then be broken up into smaller zones: within the kitchen, you have cleaning, preparation, and eating zones; within the bathroom, grooming and bathing zones; within the family room, television, hobby, and computer zones. An item's ideal place depends on the zone in which you use it, and how accessible it needs to be.

Is the item in question used daily, weekly, monthly, once a year, or less? The answer determines whether it belongs in your Inner Circle, Outer Circle, or Deep Storage.

Stand in one of your zones and stretch your arms out around you. This area defines your Inner Circle, the space to keep frequently used items—like your toothpaste, dishwashing liquid, checkbook, and underwear—within easy reach. You want to be able to access such things without bending, stretching, struggling, or moving other things out of the way to retrieve them. This not only makes them easy to find and access, it makes them easy to put away. Remember the Pareto principle? Well, your Inner Circle should hold the 20 percent of things you use 80 percent of the time.

Your Outer Circle is a little more difficult to reach, and should be reserved for things that are used less often. It includes higher and lower shelves, out-of-the-way closets, upper cabinets, and under the bed. Use these places to store backups of toiletries and cleaning supplies, infrequently worn clothing, wrapping paper and ribbons, specialty pots and cooking supplies, and the myriad other things that aren't part of your regular routine. A good rule of thumb: if it's used less than once a week, but more than once a year, your Outer Circle is where it belongs.

Deep Storage is typically outside of your living space, and includes attics, basements, and garages. This is where to stash your spare parts, seasonal decorations, old paperwork and tax returns, and other things you use once a year or less. However, don't make Deep Storage a catch-all for everything that doesn't fit in your house; try to keep it lean. If you never use or look at the item in question, and it's not a financial or legal document that must be kept indefinitely, out it goes. Sometimes the best place for something is somebody else's house!

Keep in mind that "a place for everything" applies to decorative items as well. If an item is truly special to you, establish a proper and prominent place to display it. It doesn't deserve to be pushed aside, around, and out of the way, or to fight for position in a crowd of clutter. And it certainly shouldn't be stuffed in a box in the basement! The whole point of a decorative item is to be able to *see* it; so if you're storing any such things (other than seasonal items) out of sight, it's time to question why you're keeping them at all.

Once you've designated a place for everything, don't forget about the second part: always return everything to its place. What's the use of having assigned seats, when everything's lounging all over the house? To this end, it helps to label shelves, drawers, and boxes with their appropriate contents. Then everyone will know exactly where to put something after they've finished using it—and you'll be less likely to find the corkscrew holed up in the sock drawer, or the stapler getting cozy with the baking supplies.

Get yourself, and your family members, into the habit of putting things away. A neat household gives clutter fewer places to hide. Hang up your clothes (or put them in the hamper) after you undress, rather than piling them on the floor or chair. Put spices, condiments, and utensils back where they belong, instead of leaving them out on the counter. Keep shoes in a designated spot, rather than scattered throughout the house. Return books to their shelves, and magazines to their rack. Encourage children to pick up their toys, and put them away, when playtime is over.

In fact, whenever you leave a room, collect any stray items and return them to their rightful place. This simple habit takes only a few minutes out of your day, but makes a huge difference in your household. Clutter is a social creature; it's never alone for long. Let a few pieces hang out in your living room, one thing leads to another, and before long they're hosting a full-fledged party! If things are regularly returned to their spots, however, stray items never get settled. It's like a game of musical chairs: when the melody stops (or the day's activities are over), anything stranded without a spot doesn't get to stay.

Now I know that some of you with less-than-adequate storage space are probably crying foul. How can you be expected to put everything in its place, when you don't have enough places to put them? Don't despair—*you're the lucky ones!* The more space we have to put things, the more things we tend to keep—things we don't always need. Those with walk-in closets and extra cupboards must summon up extra motivation to declutter; while you, on the other hand, get the benefit of a little tough love. Having less space is an asset, not a liability, and puts you on the fast track to becoming a minimalist.

15

All surfaces clear

Horizontal surfaces are a magnet for clutter. Walk in your front door with your hands full, and I guarantee the contents will land on the first available surface. Their large, flat expanses are an irresistible invitation to stray items; you can almost feel the gravitational pull.

Take a look around at the surfaces in your house. Is there anything on your dining table besides plates, flatware, and perhaps a centerpiece? Is your coffee table free of objects, save any drinks or snacks currently being consumed? Do your end tables hold anything other than lamps, or maybe the remote control? How about your bed? Are its contents limited to the sheets, blankets, and pillows you'll use tonight? Are your kitchen counters completely clear, ready for the preparation and serving of your next meal? How much of your desk can you still see?

Unless you're already a full-fledged, dyed-in-the-wool minimalist (or an exceptionally good housekeeper), you're likely struggling with some sort of surface problem. It may be confined to one area, like your desk or workspace; or perhaps it's affecting all the tables and counters in the house. It may be a recent phenomenon, caused by something like an upsurge in your children's craft activities, or a pile of work you brought home from the office. On the other hand, the problem may have been building for weeks, months, or even years—to the extent that you're no longer quite sure what the top of your dining room table looks like.

What's the big deal, you ask? Well, if we don't have clear surfaces, we don't have space to *do* anything. Clear surfaces are full of potential and possibility; they're where the magic happens! Think of all the things we can't do when our surfaces are cluttered: we don't have room to prepare a delicious dinner, we don't have a place to sit down with our families and enjoy it, and we don't have the space to play a board game afterwards. We don't have a spot to pay our bills, do our homework, or enjoy our hobbies. In some cases, we may not even have a place to lie down at the end of the day.

Never fear! All we need to conquer our surface clutter is a new attitude, and enthusiastic adherence to the following principle: *surfaces are not for storage*. Rather, surfaces are for activity, and should be kept clear at all other times. Put this minimalist principle into practice, and you'll be thrilled with the results: not only will your home look neater, more organized, and more serene, it'll be infinitely more useful and easier to clean.

To achieve this, we have to change the way we think about surfaces—in particular, how we imagine their physical properties. By nature, surfaces are "sticky;" they're big, flat, and extremely adept at providing a resting place for items. Once an object lands on one, it's liable to stay there for days, weeks, or even months. Sometimes it stays there so long, we don't even notice it anymore. We grow accustomed to its presence, and it becomes part of the landscape. Another one joins it, and so on, and so on. Before we know it, our surfaces are no longer smooth, but a bumpy terrain consisting of items that got "stuck" to them.

Instead, we need to imagine our surfaces as slippery. If they were slick as ice, or tilted just a few degrees, nothing would be able to stay on them for very long. We'd be able to do our business, but then anything left over would slide right off. Until someone invents such a "magic" minimalist countertop (and pays me royalties for such a superb idea), we'll just have to *pretend* that that's how our surfaces function. To wit: everything we place on our "slippery" surfaces leaves with us when we leave the room. If we put a cup on the coffee table, a book on an end table, or a craft project on the dining table, we pick it up and take it with us when we make our exit—and encourage family members to do the same.

The only exceptions: those items whose "place" is on that particular surface—such as the centerpiece and candlesticks on your dining table, or the reading lamps on your end tables. This special dispensation also covers the remote control on your coffee table, the cookie jar on your kitchen counter, and the alarm clock on your nightstand. If you choose to keep such functional or decorative items on your tables, however, limit their numbers—to three "permanent" items per surface, for example. That'll keep clutter from gathering in these spots, reducing their functionality, and crowding the things that deserve to be there.

Finally, don't forget about the biggest surface of all: the floor! It presents a particular challenge, simply because there's *so much* of it. When our tables, closets, and drawers are full—or when we just don't feel like putting things away—our next inclination is to pile them on the floor. Don't give in to the temptation! The floor has no strict boundaries (nothing's going to fall off of it), so once stuff lands on it, it tends to spread...and spread...and spread. I've been in houses where the floors are completely buried, save a narrow path to walk through the room. You can hardly move—let alone accomplish anything productive—in such an environment. Reserve your floors for feet and furniture, and keep them free of anything else.

After we've made the effort to declutter our surfaces, we have great incentive to keep them that way. Who wants to repeat all that hard work? The most effective way to maintain them is to develop the habit of scanning them. Before you leave a room or turn out the lights, survey the tables, the countertops, and the floor. If they're not as "smooth" as they should be, spend a few minutes clearing them of their contents. This quick and easy act goes a long way toward keeping your home clutter-free. Heed this rule: if the room is empty, the surfaces should be, too.

16

Modules

In this section, we're going to learn a valuable organizational technique that combats clutter, keeps our stuff under control, and helps us in no small part to achieve our minimalist goals.

We talked about zones in an earlier chapter, defining them according to rooms (such as kitchen, bathroom, and bedroom) and sections of rooms (such as the television, hobby, and computer zones in our family room). The idea was that all objects pertaining to the activities of a certain zone should reside in that zone, instead of wandering aimlessly about the house. We then went further, and broke each zone down into our Inner Circle, Outer Circle, and Deep Storage—containing those things that we use (respectively) often, sometimes, or hardly ever.

Now we'll organize things even more, by sorting our stuff into "modules." The concept of modules comes from systems design; basically, it means dividing a complex system into smaller, task-specific components. A computer program, for example, might consist of millions of commands. To keep track of them, programmers arrange them into modules—sets of related instructions that perform particular tasks. That way, the commands can be "stored" more efficiently, and moved around easily in the program.

Well, our households are also pretty complex systems, with lots of things to store and keep track of. They could certainly benefit from a more efficient arrangement of stuff—so let's take this module concept and run with it! For our purposes, a module is a set of related items that perform a particular task (like paying the bills, or decorating a cake). To create them, we'll need to gather things of similar functions together, eliminate the excess, and make sure they're easy to access and move around when needed. In short, we'll need to consolidate, cull, and contain our stuff.

The first step is to consolidate like items. Store all similar (or related) things together: DVDs, extension cords, paperclips, first aid supplies, craft materials, hardware, photos, spices, and more; you get the idea. Consolidating your stuff makes it much easier to find things. When you're in need of a bandage, you won't have to tear the bathroom cabinets apart; just go straight to the first aid module. When you want to watch your favorite DVD, you won't have to scour the shelves, rummage through the bedrooms, or crawl under the couch to find it; it'll be waiting for you in the DVD module. When you're looking for a certain size screw to make a home repair, you won't have to launch a search expedition in the basement; simply go to the appropriate hardware module, and pluck it from the pile.

Even more importantly, consolidating your stuff lets you see *how much you have.* When you've gathered all sixty-three ballpoint pens into one place, you know you don't need to buy another. Nor will you splurge on another pair of earrings, when faced with a pile of fifteen others. This technique is particularly suited to curbing the accumulation of craft materials, which seem to grow unchecked if scattered throughout the house; in fact, the effect of seeing them all together can be quite sobering. ("How on earth did I get all this yarn!") It'll also keep you from inadvertently bringing home duplicates of things you already own. How many times have you run out to buy something, only to find later you already had one? Being able to quickly check the appropriate module for it can eliminate lots of unnecessary clutter and expense.

Now for the task all you budding minimalists have been waiting for: once you've gathered like items together, it's time to cull them. As you consolidate, you'll undoubtedly come across excess supplies of certain items; cut them down to what you actually use now, and can realistically use in the future. Few of us will ever need all the twist-ties, chopsticks, and matchbooks lurking in our junk drawers; set some of them free, and reclaim the space! Likewise, why keep all sixty-three pens when ten is more than enough? How many can you write with at one time, anyway? Consider how long it takes to use up a pen: if each one lasts six months, you have a thirty-year supply—most of which will have dried up by the time you touch them to paper. Go through your collection, and save only your favorites. Apply the same principle to socks, t-shirts, coffee cups, plastic containers, hand towels, and anything else you have in abundance.

Finally, once we've consolidated and culled our items, we need to contain them; this step keeps them from spreading out through the house again. The "container" can be a drawer, shelf, box, plastic storage bin, ziplock bag—whatever's appropriate for the size and quantity of the contents. I prefer transparent containers, since you can see what's inside without opening them. If you're using opaque ones, label or color code them for easy identification.

The advantage of using physical containers is their portability. Suppose that while watching a DVD with your family, you'd like to work on your knitting. Simply retrieve the knitting module, and you're ready to go. When you're finished, you'll have little temptation to leave your supplies on the coffee table; just pop them back into the container for instant cleanup. If you lack a dedicated office space, keep your checkbook, calculator, pens, and other implements in an office module—and tote it into the dining room, kitchen, or other space when it's time to pay bills. Teach your children to do the same with their toys, books, and games, and you'll have much less "picking up" to do at the end of the day.

I'd like to emphasize the importance of consolidating and culling your stuff, *before* containing it. All too often, when we get the urge to "simplify," we run out to our nearest organizational superstore and bring home a trunkful of pretty containers. We think that by arranging our stuff into neat little bins, we can automatically create a sense of order and serenity. But if we haven't first weeded out the Treasures from the Trash, we're spinning our wheels. The containers may make our houses look tidy, but they serve no higher purpose than to hide our junk. Instead of simplifying our homes (and our lives), we're merely arranging our clutter.

Instead, declutter as much as you possibly can before putting anything into a box. Pare down to the essentials first, and *then* find a convenient way to house them. Being a minimalist means going one step beyond simply straightening up and organizing our homes. In creating our modules, we're establishing a system that eliminates and discourages excess—making our possessions equivalent to our needs, and then literally putting a lid on them.

17

Limits

Minimalist living means keeping our possessions in check, and the most effective way to do this is by establishing limits. Okay, I can hear you thinking, "Whoa, wait a second! Limits? I didn't sign up for that. I don't want to feel deprived of anything…" No need to worry—the limits are for your stuff, not you! They help you gain the upper hand over your things, so you have more power, more control, and more space. Limits work *for you*, not against you.

Let's use books as an example: we're all familiar with how quickly they can accumulate. We buy one, we read it, and somehow it earns a permanent spot in our collection—no matter whether or not we liked it, or ever intend to crack it open again. We reason that we paid good money for it, and devoted time and effort to it, so we may as well have something to show for it. Sometimes we'll keep a tome just to prove we read it. (Time to 'fess up: who has *War and Peace* on their shelf? Are you *really* going to read it again?) Perhaps the bigger our library, the more intellectual we *feel*.

Remember: you are not what you own. Storing all those books doesn't make you any smarter; it just makes your life more cluttered. Instead of keeping every one you've ever read, apply a limit: for example, restrict the number of volumes to what easily fits on your bookshelf. Don't let them spill onto the floor or end tables, or grow into miniature towers on the side of the room. Limit your collection to the allotted space, and cull it as you add new ones. Your library will be much more special, consisting of only your freshest and favorite titles—it'll be a pleasure to peruse! Put the excess books back in circulation: donate them to your local library, or pass them on to friends and family.

Limits also help tame those ever-multiplying craft and hobby supplies. Whether you're a beader, knitter, scrapbooker, model builder, woodworker, or soapmaker, limit your materials to *one* storage bin. When it starts to overflow, use up some of your old stash before acquiring anything new—it's great motivation to finish the projects you've started. Not only does it reduce your clutter, it's a good reality check: do you enjoy doing the craft as much as collecting the materials for it? If not, perhaps you should rethink your hobby; and if so, you should have no problem using up those supplies.

Limits can, and should, be applied to just about everything. Have fun setting boundaries for your stuff: require that all your DVDs fit on their assigned shelf, all your sweaters in their designated drawer, all your makeup in one cosmetic case. Limit the number of shoes, socks, candles, chairs, sheets, pots, cutting boards, and collectibles you own. Limit your magazine subscriptions, and the number of items on your coffee table. Limit your holiday decorations to one box, and your sports equipment to one corner of the garage. Limit your plates, cups, and utensils to the size of your family, and your garden supplies to the needs of your yard.

Back in the old days, limits were applied by external factors: most significantly, the price and availability of material goods. Items were generally handmade and distributed locally—making them scarcer and more costly (relative to income) than in modern times. It was easy to be a minimalist a hundred years ago, as it was difficult enough to acquire the necessities—let alone anything extra. Nowadays, we can zip over to our local superstore and purchase whatever our heart desires; mass production and global distribution have made consumer items cheap, widely available, and easy to obtain. Sure, it's convenient; but as many of us have learned, it can be too much of a good thing. If we don't voluntarily limit our consumption, we can end up drowning in stuff!

Setting limits not only helps *you*; it also eases other members of your household into a more minimalist lifestyle. Explain to your family that stuff must fit into the space allotted—and that when things overflow, they must be pared down. Limit your children's toys to one or two storage bins, and your teenager's clothing to the size of her closet. They'll benefit enormously from this guidance, and develop valuable habits for later in life. At the very least, limit each person's possessions to what fits into his or her room—be it a child's bedroom or playroom, or a spouse's office, craft room, or workshop. That way, you'll prevent personal stuff from spilling over into family space.

Of course, the ultimate limit on your possessions is set by the size of your house—which, as a minimalist, you may someday decide to reduce. Stuff expands to fill the space available (I'm pretty sure there's a physics equation for that!). Limiting that space means less stuff, less clutter, less worries, and less stress. If you don't have a big house, you can't have a big houseful of stuff. Imagine moving from a studio apartment into a house with an attic, basement, and two-car garage—those storage spaces will undoubtedly fill up just because they're *there*. If you stopped using an exercise bike in your small apartment, you'd likely dispose of it; but in your bigger house, it would surely end up in the basement. Smaller digs put a natural limit on the number of things you can own—making it that much easier to live a minimalist lifestyle.

You may initially think that limits will be stifling; but you'll soon discover that they're absolutely liberating! In a culture where we're conditioned to want more, buy more, and do more, they're a wonderful breath of relief. In fact, once you've discovered the joy of limits, you'll be inspired to apply them to other parts of your life. Limiting commitments and activities can lead to a less harried lifestyle and free up valuable time. Limiting your spending slashes your credit card bills and boosts the balance in your bank account. Limiting processed, fatty, and sugary food can reduce your waistline and improve your health. The possibilities are, well...unlimited!

18

If one comes in, one goes out

Sometimes we declutter, and declutter, and declutter some more—but when we look at our homes, we don't see any progress. We can't understand it—we've filled up trash bags to put on the curb; we've filled up our trunks with stuff for charity; and we've filled up boxes to give to our brother-in-law. Yet it seems like we have just as much stuff in our closets, drawers, and basements. We're working hard, and we want to see results. What's the problem?

Think of your house, and all the stuff in it, as a bucket of water. Decluttering is like drilling a hole in the bottom—causing the bucket to empty slowly, drip by drip, as you rid your household of unwanted things. Great, that sounds like progress! As long as you keep up the good work, your stuff level should steadily decrease.

Here's the catch: the stuff level only goes down if you stop pouring more in the top. Every item that enters your home is inflow into the bucket. So if you're still shopping, and buying things, and bringing home freebies from business conferences, those drips out the bottom won't do much good. The bucket will never empty, and may in fact overflow!

You can solve this problem by following a simple rule: if one comes in, one goes out. Every time a new item comes into your home, a similar item must leave. For every drip into the bucket, there must be one drip out. This strategy ensures that your household won't flood, and threaten the progress you're making.

The One In-One Out rule is most effective when applied to like items. For every new shirt that goes in the closet, an old shirt comes out. For every new book that joins your collection, an old one leaves the shelf. For every new pair of shoes that waltzes in, an old pair takes a hike. It's very straightforward. If a new set of plates moves in, the old set moves out. If a new duvet says hello, an old duvet says goodbye. If a gorgeous new vase makes its household debut, a less gorgeous one takes its final bow. You can mix it up a little if you feel the need to rebalance your possessions. For instance, if you have too many pants and too few shirts, ditch a pair of trousers when you buy a new top. Keep it equitable, though: tossing socks to offset a coat—or trading a paperclip for an office chair—doesn't fit the bill!

Too often, when we buy something new, we keep the item it's supposed to replace. Here's how it usually goes down: we spy something in our house that's no longer up to snuff— perhaps it's out of style, falling apart, or just doesn't meet our needs. So we set out on a shopping mission, eager to ditch the old version in favor of a better, brighter, shinier, more technologically up-to-date one. We do our research, compare prices, read reviews, and finally make our purchase. Then something strange happens: when we bring home our new model, the old one doesn't look so forlorn. Although we'd deemed it "not good enough" to use, it still seems "too good" to throw away. We begin to imagine all the scenarios (however unlikely) in which we "might need it." (As if we're expecting its brand-new, state-of-the-art replacement to up and stop working the following day.) Before we know it, the tired old thing is comfortably ensconced in our basement or attic, "just in case" it'll come in handy.

The One In-One Out strategy helps you show your rejects the door—rather than house them in their retirement. As soon as that new model enters your home, bid your final farewell to the old. There's no magic to the system, but it does require discipline. I can tell you from experience that it's tempting to cheat, and promise yourself you'll purge something "later." You're so excited to wear that new sweater, or play that new video game, that you don't feel like finding an appropriate swap. Nevertheless, summon up your minimalist powers, and commit to "one out" before you open, hang up, or use the "one in"— because unless you do it immediately, it'll likely never happen. I've gone so far as to keep new items, still packaged, in the trunk of my car until I was able to oust something old.

When you're starting to declutter, the One In-One Out rule is a wonderful stopgap measure. It caps your number of possessions, and keeps you moving in the right direction. There's nothing more disheartening than working to purge ten items—agonizing over the decisions, summoning the strength to let them go—only to discover you accumulated twelve new ones in the meantime. Following this principle prevents such a scenario. From the second you commit to it, your household enters a steady state of stuff: as long as you stick with the program, you'll never own more than you do at that moment.

Better yet, as you continue to purge your possessions, you'll see a marked decrease in your stuff level. Since you've "shut off the tap," those drips out the bottom have a noticeable (and satisfying) effect. Of course, the more stuff you get rid of, the more rewarding the result; so in the next chapter, we'll turn the decluttering trickle into a steady flow.

19

Narrow it down

In the previous chapter, we learned how to achieve a steady state of possessions, by offsetting each item entering our home with a similar one leaving it. Fantastic! Now we no longer have to worry about taking one step forward, and two steps back. With this system in place, each additional item we purge gets us that much closer to our minimalist goals.

To really make progress, though, we need to kick our decluttering efforts into high gear. Streamlining isn't about getting rid of a few things, and then going on with business as usual. Quite the contrary! It's designed to help us reach the holy grail of minimalist living: owning just enough to meet our needs, and nothing more. Therefore, when it comes to the stuff in our closets and drawers, and in our modules and zones, we have one mission: to narrow it down.

Ideally, we want to reduce our possessions to the bare necessities. Now, before you get worried about having to live in a tent or sleep on the floor, let me explain. The "bare necessities" means different things to different people. The minimalist residing on his sailboat may be able to meet his culinary needs with a single hotplate. Those of us with full kitchens, on the other hand, may consider our microwaves, pizza stones, and rice cookers indispensable. At the same time, the scuba gear he deems a necessity would likely be superfluous in our households.

Our personal essentials depend on a wide range of factors—like age, gender, occupation, hobbies, climate, culture, families, and peers. Minimalists in professional jobs may find business suits and dress shoes *de rigueur*, while those working from home can get by with smaller wardrobes. Parents with young children will have a different list of essentials than a bachelor living alone. Bookworms will have different necessities than sports enthusiasts, students will have different necessities than retirees, men will have different necessities than women.

Therefore, there's no master list of what's in a minimalist home. No decree outlines the items we should have in our kitchens, living rooms, bathrooms, or bedrooms. (That would be too easy, wouldn't it?) In fact, contrary to popular belief, there's not even a magic number. It doesn't matter if you own fifty, five hundred, or five thousand things—what matters is whether it's just enough (and not too much) for *you*. You must determine your own list of must-haves, then narrow your stuff down to match it.

This step, then, is about reducing our possessions to our personal "optimum" levels. Whenever we pick up an item, we should stop and think if we really need it—or can just as well get by without it. When we discover we have multiples, we should immediately cull the excess. When we unearth a box of unused stuff, we should seriously consider just dumping the lot. The good news: as we progress on our minimalist journeys, our number of "necessities" will slowly but surely decrease.

In addition to simply decluttering our stuff, we can also "narrow it down" by more creative means—like choosing multi-functional items over single-use ones. A sleeper sofa eliminates the need for a separate guest bed. A printer with a scanner function means one less piece of office equipment. A smartphone can do the work of a calendar, wristwatch, calculator, appointment book, and more. Our goal is to accomplish the greatest number of tasks with the least amount of items.

By the same token, we should favor versatile items over specialty ones. A large sauté pan can do the same job as a drawer full of specialty cookware. A classic black pump coordinates with both work and dress clothes, doing double duty in our wardrobe—as opposed to those fuchsia heels that hardly go with anything. An all-purpose cleaner can keep our homes sparkling, replacing separate sprays for the sink, tub, mirror, and countertops.

As we're happily narrowing down our items, however, some things will stop us in our tracks—and more often than not, they'll be sentimental or commemorative in nature. Things with memories are just difficult to part with. But don't worry—we minimalists have ways of dealing with them, too! "Miniaturizing" them, for example, is a tried-and-true strategy. No, I don't mean turning a shrink ray gun on them (although that would be fun!). Rather, we simply save a *piece* of the item instead of the whole thing. The logic: if an item's purpose is to evoke memories, the same memories can be evoked by a smaller piece.

Consider "miniaturizing" items like old wedding gowns, christening outfits, baby quilts, graduation memorabilia, sports uniforms, and letter sweaters. For instance, rather than keep the entire wedding dress, snip off a swatch; display it with a photo, invitation, or dried flower from the bouquet. Instead of squirreling away your college mortarboard, keep only the tassel. Do the same with collections you inherit: rather than stash all twelve place settings of your grandmother's china in the attic, keep just a single plate and display it in a place of honor. Alternatively, take snapshots of the items, and then declutter them; the photos preserve the memories, without taking up the space. They're also more accessible—and easier to enjoy—than an item tucked away in storage.

Finally, we can narrow down our possessions by digitizing them. Again, we don't need a magician's wand or a sci-fi laser beam—we have the power of technology. Entire collections of stuff—music, movies, video games, books—can now be reduced to intangible bits and bytes. No longer must we devote shelf space to CDs and their jewel cases; we can simply store our music on our computers and iPods. Digital movies eliminate the need for physical DVDs. Electronic readers can replace entire bookshelves by holding hundreds of tomes on one device (and giving us online access to thousands of others). It's a wonderful time to be a minimalist!

If you embrace minimalism wholeheartedly, you'll find yourself continually on the lookout for new ways to narrow down your stuff. Be creative. Regard it as a personal challenge to do more with less, and have *fun* exploring all the possibilities. You may be surprised at what you can do without!

STREAMLINE

20

Everyday maintenance

Once we've worked through all the STREAMLINE steps—starting over; separating our stuff into Trash, Treasure, and Transfer piles; making sure we have a good reason for each item we own; finding a place for everything, and putting everything in its place; keeping all our surfaces clear; arranging our things into modules; imposing limits on our possessions; heeding the "if one comes in, one goes out" rule; and narrowing down our stuff—we can't simply call it a day and return to our old ways. Goodness no! We need to keep things up with some everyday maintenance.

Becoming a minimalist isn't like going on a crash diet. We can't simply purge all our possessions in a no-holds-barred decluttering session, and then check it off as "done." If so, we're likely to suffer a rebound effect—stuff will accumulate again as sure as rapidly lost weight. Instead, we need to change our underlying attitudes (that's why we did all those mental exercises) and develop new habits (that's why we learned the STREAMLINE method). We must approach minimalist living in the same way as a new, healthier diet—not as a one-off activity, but as a wholesale lifestyle change.

Most importantly, we must continue to be vigilant about what enters our homes. Remember how we discussed being good gatekeepers? To maintain our minimalist lifestyles, we can never really let our guard down; things can get out of control quickly if we let them. Fortunately, the task is easier than it sounds, and soon becomes second nature. We simply have to establish routines to handle incoming stuff—like mail, catalogs, gifts, and freebies—and stick to them. Placing recycling and donation boxes near the front door, for example, works wonders—preventing tons of potential clutter with hardly any effort.

Yet sometimes it can feel like you're always on the defense—trying single-handedly to stop the tsunami of stuff threatening your home. But you can play offense, too: by getting off mailing lists, canceling magazine subscriptions, opting out of gift exchanges, and generally making it known that you're pursuing a minimalist lifestyle. The last point is more important than you might think: because when they see your "empty" rooms, well-meaning friends and relatives may misinterpret your lack of stuff as a *need* for stuff. At best, you may be showered with unwanted gifts; and at worst, you may receive *their* cast-off clutter.

In addition to monitoring the front door, keep a sharp eye on clutter hotspots. As you know, clutter begets clutter. Once you let one item hang out for awhile, it makes itself comfortable and invites over some friends. Don't let the party get started! It's a lot easier to kick out one unwelcome guest than a whole pack. In fact, if you don't act at the first signs of clutter, your radar becomes somewhat dulled. Think about it: there's a big difference between a perfectly clear surface, and a surface with an item that doesn't belong. The wayward object sticks out like a sore thumb. However, the contrast between a surface with one wayward item, and one with two, isn't quite so jarring; and even less so between one with two, and one with three (and so on). Best to clear off clutter as soon as you see it, than risk a new accumulation.

In the process, you'll often have to deal with OPC—other people's clutter. As you're generally not at liberty to dispose of it yourself, the best option is to return it post-haste to its rightful owner. If the items belong to a non-resident—like the stuff your sister stashed in your basement while moving (and still hasn't retrieved), or the craft project your friend abandoned on your dining room table—a quick phone call or email explaining your decluttering efforts should motivate them to collect their belongings.

More often, however, the wayward items belong to other household members. In that case, simply return them to the owner's personal space (like just inside their bedroom or office door). The idea is not to become everyone's maid, but to establish a boomerang effect—reinforcing the concept that anything that ventures into family space will be promptly returned. With any luck, they'll eventually get the picture and think twice before leaving things behind. Pointing out the offending clutter to its owner, and giving them the choice of removal or disposal, also does the trick quite nicely.

Finally, keep decluttering! The initial sweep through your house isn't the be-all and end-all of your purging; in fact, it's just the beginning. You'll find that your minimalist powers will grow stronger with time—and those must-haves that survived your first decluttering won't look as essential in the second round. For that reason, I recommend purging in cycles; after your initial decluttering, take another look around after a few weeks or months. You'll see your possessions with fresh eyes and a more seasoned perspective. In the meantime, you'll have started to experience the joy and freedom of a minimalist lifestyle—which will make you motivated (and excited) to dispose of more stuff. You'll be amazed how much easier it becomes to part with things in the second, third, fourth (or tenth or twentieth!) round.

Practice, of course, makes perfect. Therefore, instead of purging in spurts, you may prefer a slow and steady approach like the One-A-Day Declutter. Simply commit to disposing of one item each and every day. It can be anything: a worn-out pair of socks, a book you'll never read, a gift you could live without, a shirt that doesn't fit, or an outdated magazine article. It takes little time or effort (just a few minutes per day), and at the end of the year, your home will be 365 items lighter. To avoid putting useful items in a landfill, keep a donation box tucked away in your basement or hall closet. Add your discards one by one, and when it's full, donate it to Goodwill, the Salvation Army, or other charitable organization.

Alternatively, set decluttering goals for certain time periods: like ten items a week, or one hundred items a month. Keep a running tab of your castoffs, to track your progress and maintain your motivation. Most importantly, have *fun* with it! The best part about minimalist living is that the rewards are immediate: every item you jettison instantly lightens your load. Do it daily, and you'll feel fantastic. You'll only regret that you didn't start sooner!

PART THREE

Room By Room

How exciting—it's time to put our decluttering skills to work! In the following chapters, we'll apply the STREAMLINE method to specific rooms, addressing the issues and challenges unique to each. Feel free to skip around, and start anywhere you like. Just because we discuss the rooms in a certain order doesn't mean you have to tackle them that way. Start with the easiest, the hardest, the smallest, the largest—whatever strikes your fancy. Okay, then—let the minimalist makeover begin!

21

Living or family room

In this chapter, we'll focus on the living room (or what you may call your family room). It doesn't matter how your walls are arranged—for our purposes, it's the area where family members congregate, and guests hang out when they visit. In most homes, it's the largest space, and the one that sees the most action; so our decluttering efforts here will set a wonderful tone for the whole household.

Start over

Before we begin, however, I'd like you to leave your house. (Yes, you read that correctly.) Get up, walk out the door, and close it behind you. Once you're outside, clear your mind and enjoy the fresh air for a bit. By the time you return, I'll have decluttered your entire home with my magical minimalist superpowers! Just kidding, of course—but there is a point to this exercise.

Okay, you can go back inside now—but when you walk through the front door, *pretend you don't live there*. Enter as if you were a guest, with fresh eyes and an objective perspective. Act as if you were seeing your living space for the very first time, from a stranger's point of view. (It's an easier way to Start Over than emptying your living room onto the front lawn.) So what's your first impression? Do you like what you see? Is your living room serene and inviting, welcoming you to stay? Or is it chaotic and cluttered, making you want to run away? More pointedly: if all this stuff wasn't yours, would you have any desire to sit down and hang out in the middle of it?

We're taking a fresh look at our living rooms because clutter "disappears" when we grow accustomed to it. If the coffee table has been covered in magazines, knickknacks, craft supplies, and children's toys for weeks, months, or even years, we get used to it. We get used to the laundry basket in the corner, the books stacked next to the couch, and the DVDs piled around the TV. Somehow, the clutter becomes invisible to us; our perspective shifts, and instead of looking *at* it, we look *around* it.

After you've assessed the big picture, look closely at the room's contents. Scrutinize each piece of furniture, each throw pillow, and each tchotchke. Is every one of these items either useful or beautiful? Do they look harmonious with each other, and appropriate in their places? Or does the scene resemble a flea market—or worse yet, the inside of a storage unit? If you *did* empty the contents onto your front lawn, would you bring it all back in—or would you be happy to evict a good portion?

Now close your eyes, and visualize your ideal living room. Picture which pieces of furniture you'd keep and how you'd arrange them; imagine what would be on your tables and shelves, and in your drawers and cabinets. How does your fantasy room differ from your real one? Which items remained, and which ones disappeared? Chances are, you can transform your current space into your dream space with just a little decluttering.

Trash, Treasure, or Transfer

First things first: let's ditch those items that didn't make it into your dream room. Life is short—so why live with things that don't make you happy?

Common advice says to start small, and build up to larger tasks. Not a bad idea, but let's do something different here— let's do something BIG. Your living room houses some substantial items, and offers a great opportunity to start with a bang. Purging just one piece of unnecessary (or unloved) furniture can make a dramatic impact—and provide wonderful incentive to slog through smaller items. It's like that ratty old chair or orphan end table is a giant plug in your stopped-up sink of stuff; and once you yank it out, it clears the way for a gush of clutter.

So focus first on your big stuff. Is every piece of furniture used regularly, or are some items there for no better reason than "they always have been"? Consider how you and your family use the room. Do you congregate on the couch or the floor? Does anyone ever sit in the corner chair? Does the console serve a useful purpose, or is it little more than a repository for junk? Would you have more room for activities (lounging, playing games, gathering for a movie) if you had fewer pieces of furniture?

By all means, don't feel obligated to own certain items simply because they're expected (as in, "My goodness, what would the neighbors think if we didn't have a recliner?"). When my husband and I lived overseas, we decided we didn't need a couch. Although we'd never seen a home without one, it simply didn't suit our lifestyle (we had neither a TV, nor frequent visitors, and spent our evenings and weekends out on the town). Therefore, we furnished our living room with just two lounge chairs and a coffee table. Those three pieces were enough to meet our needs; anything more would have been too much.

If you target a major item you'd like to toss—but still feel a little hesitant—move it out of the room for a few days. Temporarily stow it in the basement or attic, and note if anyone misses it. Does its absence hinder your enjoyment of the room—or enhance it? Sometimes, simply moving a piece out of the way gives you a better perspective on it; and once it's left its spot, it's easier to sever ties with it.

After you've dealt with the large items, it's time to move on to the smaller ones—and depending on your living room, there may be quite a few. Don't panic; this is where we'll break things up into smaller, more manageable tasks. The best way to tackle it: go shelf by shelf, drawer by drawer, pile by pile. (One shelf doesn't sound so bad, does it?)

Simply clear off the contents (or dump them out), and sort them into your Trash, Treasure, and Transfer piles. Clean up any garbage that's accumulated (like packaging, junk mail, and food wrappers), and send plates, glasses, and coffee cups to the sink. Comb through your collections of CDs, DVDs, and video games, and donate those that have fallen out of favor. Clear the magazine rack of outdated issues. Go through hobby supplies, board games, and books to make sure they're in "active" use. Size up your knickknacks and decorative items, and pinpoint those that are truly Treasures (you know what to do with the rest!).

Most importantly, don't rush through it. Take the time to do a thorough job—even if it takes weeks, or months, to sort through every last drawer. Such attentiveness will bring far greater rewards in the long run.

Reason for each item

Because of its public nature (and proximity to the front door), the living room can be a dumping ground for clutter. Therefore, you'll need to be particularly vigilant that every object in the room actually belongs there. Remember, it's a *living* room, not a storage room: only those things that are used by you (or your family) on a regular basis should reside in this space. If you think of the room as a stage, is there enough space for everyone to interact (in other words, is there enough space for actual *living*)? Or is the action stifled by the presence of too many props?

Walk around the room, and name the reason for each item's existence. For example: the couch is here because we sit on it to talk, play games, and watch TV. The coffee table holds our drinks and food, and provides a surface on which we can pursue our hobbies. The DVD player allows us to enjoy movies together. The clock on the mantle is a cherished family heirloom. The end table holds a pile of magazines that no one ever looks at. (Hmm…we might have to do something about that one.) As you evaluate your living room's contents, don't just gloss over the DVD collection or bookshelves. Consider each item individually, and question whether anyone still reads a certain book, watches a certain movie, or plays a certain game.

Be similarly thorough with your décor, considering each knickknack in turn. Do the decorative items in the room really bring you joy to look at? Or did they just accumulate over the years, and do nothing more than take up space? Try clearing the room entirely of non-functional pieces—sweep them from the shelves, the mantle, the console, and the side tables. Store them away in a box, and live without them for a week. Sometimes extraneous items can stifle our enjoyment of a space without us even realizing it. When they're gone, we feel a wave of relief—

like we finally have the room to stretch out and move around (without hitting or breaking anything). Notice how family members and guests react to the decluttered space—are they more relaxed? Do they move around more freely? Are they more enthusiastic to engage in activities?

Of course, if you truly miss an item—like a souvenir from a special trip, or a beautiful artisan bowl—feel free to retrieve it from the box and restore it to its rightful place. If its presence makes you genuinely happy, it has just as much reason to be part of the room as the practical stuff. The key: selecting and highlighting just one or two of these treasures, rather than turning your living room into a gallery of them.

Everything in its place

Since the living room sees so much action, it's particularly important that everything has a place. Otherwise, things can become truly chaotic!

Therefore, establishing zones or activity areas is especially useful. Define the regions where you watch TV, store movies, read magazines, play games, and use the computer. Make sure that the objects involved with said activities are housed in their appropriate zone, and do everything you can to prevent them from straying into another. DVDs shouldn't be piled on the coffee table; they should be on their own designated shelf or in an assigned drawer. Likewise, magazines shouldn't be stacked on top of the television, and playthings shouldn't reside on the couch. Involve all household members in the process of defining the zones—then everyone will understand the system, and share responsibility for maintaining it.

If the living room also functions as someone's office or craft space, restrict the activity (and its accessories) to a well-defined area. Set up a desk or worktable in a corner, against the wall, or in another space as far removed as possible from the main action of the room. If it helps, use a standing screen or floor plant to evoke a visual (and psychological) boundary. The reason is two-fold: first, you want to keep the office supplies from spilling over into the main living space. Second, you want to keep the office area free of clutter and distraction—you'll be much more productive when you don't have to clear toys from your desk before using it.

After dividing the space into zones, assign your stuff to your Inner Circle, Outer Circle, and Deep Storage. As you recall, your Inner Circle items are those you use on a regular (daily, or almost daily) basis. They should be kept in easy-to-access locations, such as mid-level shelves and drawers close to your activity zones. Candidates for your living room's Inner Circle include the remote control, current magazines, frequently used electronics and computer peripherals, and favorite books, CDs, DVDs, and games. Your Outer Circle should house items used less than once a week, like certain hobby and craft supplies, reference books, and items for entertaining guests. Store these on upper and lower shelves, and in less accessible drawers and cabinets. Seasonal decorations, and pieces you treasure but can't currently display (in an effort, perhaps, to toddler-proof the room) belong in Deep Storage—preferably in the basement, attic, or other out-of-the-way place.

All surfaces clear

If a neighbor dropped by at this very moment, could you set refreshments on the coffee table? If your kids wanted to play a game or work on an art project, is there any place to do so? Or would either scenario be delayed (or forsaken) because you have to clear off too much stuff? If you felt inspired to do a little yoga, is there ample room on the floor—or would you get more of a workout moving around furniture and other contents to make some space?

Our living rooms are for living. If we treat them as makeshift storage units, and fill them to the brim with stuff, we're destroying the functionality of the room—and cheating ourselves (and our families) out of very valuable space. The surfaces in particular—like the coffee table, side tables, worktable, or desk—are of supreme importance. If they're haphazardly piled with magazines, junk mail, toys, books, and unfinished craft projects, they're useless for our current activities. Likewise, if they're used as display space for innumerable tchotchkes, knickknacks, and other decorative objects, they bring the "living" in the room to a halt. Family room surfaces shouldn't be reserved for a lifeless parade of ceramic figurines—quite the opposite. They're meant for four-year-olds to color, teenagers to play games with their friends, and adults to enjoy a cup of coffee.

We should keep the floor (our largest surface) as clear as possible, too. Children in particular need space to roam, frolic, and explore; they shouldn't be cramped into a tiny play area, barely visible among wall-to-wall furniture and mountains of clutter. Adults also benefit from a serene, uncluttered space. When we come home after a long workday, we need room to unwind, both mentally and physically. If we're tripping over objects on the way to the couch, or looking around at a jumble of stuff, we feel stressed, stifled, and irritated. By contrast, when the room is spare and tidy, we have plenty of space—and peace of mind—to kick back, relax, and breathe. Therefore, make an effort to corral loose items and keep them from underfoot.

To borrow a term from the corporate world, we should think of our living rooms as "flex space." In an office, flex space is a work area open for anyone's use. When an employee arrives in the morning, he sets up at an available (empty) desk for the day. When he leaves in the evening, he takes all his belongings with him, leaving the desk free and clear for someone else to use the following day. Our living rooms should function similarly: the floor and surfaces should stand empty, ready to accommodate the day's activities; and when those activities cease, they should be cleared of all items, leaving them open and available for the next person to use.

Modules

In the largest sense, each room is a container that holds all the stuff related to its function. However, our living room (like many of our other rooms) serves *multiple* functions—so without some organization, things can fall into disarray. For this reason, we divided it into zones, defining specific areas for specific activities. Now we'll go a step further and set up modules, consolidating specific items for specific tasks.

In your living room, create modules for your various collections—like CDs, DVDs, and video games. Instead of storing them in a jumbled mess, separate them from each other and designate a specific shelf, drawer, or container for each category. Consolidating like items helps us easily spot duplicates, weed out undesirables, and grasp the size of our collections. It also helps us, and other family members, return things to their dedicated spots—preventing them from drifting throughout the room, or straying into other parts of the house. Do the same for books (on assigned shelves), magazines (on a shelf or rack), and electronic and computer equipment (in a special drawer, cabinet, or container).

Modules are particularly useful for organizing craft and hobby supplies. Instead of housing them in a common drawer or cabinet, separate the materials by activity: knitting, scrapbooking, painting, model building, jewelry making, et cetera. Assign each activity its own container; clear plastic storage bins work well, as do the heavy cardboard boxes in which reams of paper are sold (cover them with fabric or contact paper to make them more attractive). Deep, rectangular baskets will also do the trick. When you're ready to engage in a particular hobby, simply retrieve its module and unpack its supplies onto a convenient (clear!) surface. When you're finished, cleanup is a cinch: put everything back into the container, and return it to its proper storage space. By making it easy to cart things away, modules effectively preserve the living room's flex space.

Imagine this scenario: your family finishes dinner and retires to the living room. The kids, opting to watch a favorite movie, simply pluck it from the DVD module and pop it in the player; there's no mad search for it under the couch, behind the bookshelves, or among the CDs and video games (and no one accused of "having it last"). Your spouse settles in with a magazine, pulling the current issue from the rack without having to dig through piles of clutter to find it. And you decide to do some scrapbooking, retrieving your container of supplies from a nearby cabinet and spreading your work on the empty coffee table. At the end of the evening, the DVD is returned to its bin, the magazine to its rack, and your craft supplies to their container. With everything tucked away in its modules, the living room is already clear for the next day's activities!

Limits

As minimalists, we want to limit our collections to our favorite items; otherwise, they tend to grow unchecked, and before we know it, we're inundated with stuff. The limits can be defined as either a certain number, or a certain amount of space. When dealing with books, for example, you may decide to cap your collection at one hundred, or the available space on your bookshelf. Either way, you're putting a lid on the total amount, and ensuring that your library contains only your most loved, and most frequently read, volumes.

In your living room, put limits on every type of possession that resides there, including books, CDs, DVDs, and games. Once you've reached them, purge the old before adding something new. Our tastes change over the years; we grow tired of the movies, music, and pastimes we once loved. Yet for some reason we often hold on to these out-of-favor items—whether from guilt for the money spent, or with hope that we'll regain interest in them. Instead of retaining them indefinitely, periodically cull through them and donate the ones you no longer enjoy. A fresh, pared-down collection is much more pleasant to browse than an indiscriminate hodgepodge of titles. If you crave novelty, borrow from the library instead of buying; that way, you can enjoy a wide variety of entertainment, without the headache (or expense) of ownership.

In the case of hobby and craft supplies, your modules provide a natural limit on the amount of materials you keep on hand. If they're reaching full capacity, refrain from further accumulation until you've winnowed down your current supply—either by tackling planned projects, completing unfinished ones, or simply clearing out what you don't intend to use. Imposing limits gives you the perfect excuse to purge unwanted materials (like the chartreuse yarn, chintzy beads, or cheap fabric)—the mere sight of which can dampen your enthusiasm for the activity in question. Pick your favorites, and pitch the rest!

Limit your collectibles as well. I don't know if the drive to collect is inherent in human nature, but at some point in our lives, most of us have accumulated certain things simply for the sake of it: be it baseball cards, Beanie Babies, vintage teacups, first edition books, movie memorabilia, commemorative coins, foreign stamps, or antique nutcrackers. We enjoy the thrill of the hunt, and the excitement of finding a new item (the rarer, the better) to add to our collection.

Unfortunately, however, the Internet (and eBay in particular) has made tracking down such "treasures" far too easy. In the past, our collections were curbed by limited availability and access; we actually had to scour antique stores and flea markets for new finds. Now a world of "stuff" is at our fingertips; in a few hours online, we can acquire a collection that formerly took years to build! Therefore, we must impose our *own* limits on collectibles—restricting our acquisitions to a fixed number, instead of purchasing everything we can find.

Finally, impose limits on your decorative items. Take inspiration from traditional Japanese homes, in which only one or two carefully chosen pieces are displayed at a time. In this way, you can honor and appreciate those items that are most meaningful to you—instead of making them compete for attention with a dozen others. That doesn't mean you have to toss the rest of your décor (unless, of course, you want to). Simply create a "décor module" to store your favorite pieces; bring them out for display a few at a time, and rotate them throughout the year. It'll give a fresh look to your room, and put your treasures in the spotlight.

If one comes in, one goes out

While we slowly declutter our living rooms, we need to make sure that nothing *more* comes in. By following the One In-One Out rule—offsetting each incoming item with an outgoing one—we can ensure a zero net gain of stuff.

In contrast to occasionally culling through our collections, this method requires immediate decision and action. If we bring home a new book, game, or DVD, an old one must leave at once. Thus, instead of growing in quantity, our collection grows in quality. Why hang on to that movie you only watched (or book you only read) once—and didn't even particularly like? Don't let it hog your precious space; swap it for something new and exciting. Make this a habit, and it'll transform your living room: instead of being a stale memorial to old interests and pastimes, it'll be a dynamic space reflecting your family's current tastes.

Likewise, when the latest issue of a magazine arrives, toss the old one in the recycling bin (or pass it on to friends or relatives). If you haven't found time to crack it open, you're probably not that interested in the content. At the very least, quickly flip through it and pull out intriguing articles; a few sheets of paper in your reading pile are less daunting than an entire issue. Furthermore, if you sign up for a new subscription, drop an old one. We may have lots of interests, but we only have so much time in our days; select just one or two periodicals, so you can give them the attention they deserve. You can always swap them for new ones next year.

Apply the same logic to crafts and hobbies. Again, our leisure hours are limited; instead of indulging every passing fancy, choose one or two pursuits about which you're truly passionate. If you start a new hobby, give up an old one that no longer excites you—it'll free up your time as well as your space. Perhaps you've lost enthusiasm for jewelry making, but would love to learn to play the guitar; make a clean break with the former, in order to pursue the latter. Sell any leftover supplies on Craigslist or eBay, or donate them to a local school.

The One In-One Out rule pertains to décor as well. Suppose you're out shopping, and something striking catches your eye. You think it's perfect for your home, and imagine you'd derive great happiness from looking at it every day. As a minimalist, however, you hesitate (and rightly so)—do you *really* want to bring another object into your house? If the piece is that special, you don't have to deny yourself its aesthetic pleasure—as long as you give up something in return. What you want to avoid is accumulating *more*; but it's not off-limits to *replace* something you have with something *better*. If you decide the new object doesn't merit such a sacrifice, better to skip it and wait for something more worthy to come along.

Narrow it down

Achieving a steady state of stuff is good, but narrowing it down is even better (and essential to developing a minimalist lifestyle). Ideally, we want to own nothing more than that which meets our needs.

At the bare minimum, a living room needs some sort of seating for household members. Extreme minimalists (and those of non-Western cultures) may be perfectly content with a few floor cushions. A bachelor may get by with a lounge chair. A family, on the other hand, may deem a sofa a necessity. Do the math—if you only have three people in your household, do you really need furniture that seats eight? You can always rustle up some folding chairs if you have guests (or create a fun, bohemian atmosphere by lounging on the floor). Consider the footprint of the furniture, too; I've seen overstuffed, oversized sectionals that nearly filled the entire room. Is the "comfort" of such a behemoth really worth the floor space it devours? Could you meet your seating needs with something smaller and slimmer?

Next, let's talk tables. Again, most living rooms will require at least one table to accommodate the family's activities. A small coffee table may be perfectly adequate. If the room also serves as an office or craft space, an additional desk or worktable may be needed. Anything beyond that, however, is often merely decorative. Think long and hard about whether you really need the end tables, side tables, console tables, and other tables that currently dwell in the room. If the end table's only function is to hold a magazine and remote control, consider reassigning that role to the coffee table and saving the space. Do the same for the console table that does nothing more than display your knickknacks; ditch the tchotchkes, and you no longer need the table. Wow! Major decluttering in one swoop!

Another way to "narrow it down" is to invest in multi-functional furniture. As mentioned earlier, a sleeper sofa can serve as both your family's couch and guest bed. A coffee table with built-in drawers or cabinets can eliminate the need for other storage pieces, and free up significant floor space. The same goes for ottomans: if you're going to have one, make it do double-duty and stash some of your stuff. Such pieces provide maximum functionality with a minimum footprint, leaving us much more room to move around.

Your living room might also contain an entertainment center for the television and electronics. But ask yourself this: do you really need the TV? Shocking as it may seem, plenty of people (my husband and I included) live perfectly fulfilling, entertaining, and informed lives without one. News is readily available on the Internet, and with a broadband connection, you can watch plenty of shows online. I'm not asking you to ditch the TV today, but simply presenting the idea as a *possibility*. Ruminate on it (or turn it off for a week and see if you miss it). Once you consider the option, you may decide it's not such a bad idea—and when your current set kicks the bucket, perhaps you'll choose not to replace it. The bonus: when you don't have a TV, you don't need a cabinet, stand, or any other piece of furniture to hold it. (Alternatively, you can bypass the stand— and still keep the TV—by mounting it on the wall.)

Most of our living rooms also have some sort of shelving, where we store our books, magazines, games, CDs, DVDs, hobby supplies, knickknacks, and so on. All I can say is that the less stuff you have, the less shelving you need—so get to work culling those collections! Cultivate hobbies that require little in terms of supplies, like singing, origami, or learning a new language; and play games that involve a small deck of cards, instead of large boards and hundreds of plastic pieces. Use creative strategies to meet your entertainment needs—like borrowing items from friends or the library instead of owning them. (There's certainly no point in owning something you plan to read, watch, or listen to just once.)

For those titles you *do* wish to own, consider going digital. Download movies from the Internet instead of buying DVDs. Convert your music into MP3 files, and purchase it in that format from now on; not only will it reduce your clutter, you'll have access to your library (on an iPod or MP3 player) wherever you go. Invest in an electronic reader, and buy digital books instead of physical ones. A single, paperback-size device can hold hundreds of titles (and give you access to thousands of others), eliminating the need for entire bookshelves.

Use the power of technology to downsize your photo albums as well. Instead of storing those bulky books, scan the contents into digital format. You can print the ones you'd like to display, one by one, when it strikes your fancy. The benefits of digital photographs are numerous. First, they're much easier to access. If you want to view pictures from your trip to Paris or the office Christmas party, they're right at your fingertips on your computer. (If you had to dig through a closet or shoebox to find them, you might not even bother.) Second, they're much easier to share. It's quicker, more convenient, and less costly to email your friends recent snaps of your baby or vacation, than to send paper copies through the mail (or wait for them to visit and look through your albums). Third, paper photos can deteriorate with age, or be destroyed in a flood, fire, or other disaster. Digital photos can be stored in multiple ways (on a hard drive, online, and on DVDs in multiple locations), so you're less likely to lose those irreplaceable images.

Everyday maintenance

Since so much activity occurs in the living room, we must always be aware of its contents. Devoting some time to everyday maintenance is well worth the effort; you and your family will have a much more pleasant space to relax, and enjoy each other's company.

Of course, we must always keep our defense shields at the ready. This room is only steps from the front door, and is often the first place incoming objects tend to rest. (In fact, some of them seem to get stuck here forever!) Patrol the area for intruders. (What's in that box by the door? Whose jacket is draped over the couch? Is that junk mail on the coffee table?) When you spot stuff that doesn't belong, don't throw up your hands in exasperation and slump on the sofa—fight back. Flush out those invaders at first sight, and make sure that anything entering, or traveling through the room, doesn't get a chance to stop. Hang up coats, put away shoes, handle the mail, and take new purchases directly to their appropriate spots.

Keep a close eye on where clutter tends to gather—such as the coffee table, end table, or any other surfaces in the room.

After you've enjoyed a snack, take plates, cups, and leftover food *immediately* to the kitchen. After you've played a game, or worked on a craft project, stash all materials in their modules and tuck them away. After your kids have played with their toys, encourage them to return all items to their appropriate places. If you straighten up after each and every activity, the clutter has no chance to accumulate. Furthermore, if you discover wayward items while vacuuming or dusting, don't clean around them—clean them up!

To complicate matters, the living room is where you'll most often encounter other people's clutter. Ideally, this problem will wane with time, as household members learn to respect the flex space and take personal items with them when they leave the room. In the meantime, however, you may have to roll up your sleeves, dive in there, and boomerang that stuff right back to its owners. Get in the habit of doing a clean sweep of the space each evening before bed, and clearing it of stuff that doesn't belong. It takes just a few minutes, but makes a huge difference. You can nag, and preach, and talk about keeping things tidy until you're blue in the face—but the best way to inspire others is to lead by example.

Finally, continue decluttering on a regular basis—unless you're already a minimalist extraordinaire, there's usually something more you can get rid of. Constantly scan your books, CDs, and DVDs for titles you no longer want; what you liked last month (or even last week) may no longer appeal to you. If you spot an outdated magazine, toss it out; if you've grown bored of certain hobbies, ditch the supplies; and if any item has a layer of dust on it, seriously consider showing it the door. When it comes to your living room, keep it simple, keep it fresh, and keep it serene!

22

Bedroom

In this chapter, we'll work our minimalist magic in the bedroom. This room, more than anywhere else in the house, should be a place of peace and serenity, a haven from our hectic lives. Therefore, we have some important work ahead—but after we're through, we'll have the perfect environment for a well-deserved rest.

Start over

Your bedroom should be the most uncluttered room in your house. It serves an incredibly important function: providing solace for your weary soul after a hard day of work, school, childcare, housecleaning, and every other activity you manage to fit into your day. It should be a place of rest and relaxation—not only for your body, but also for your mind.

Take a few moments, close your eyes, and envision your ideal bedroom. Picture every detail, as if it were a magazine layout: the style of bed; the color of the sheets, duvet, and blanket; the pillows, the lighting, the flooring, the décor, and the other furnishings in the room. What kind of mood does it have?

(I'm guessing probably not chaotic.) Is it a calm oasis? A romantic retreat? A luxurious suite? Although I don't know your personal tastes, I'm pretty sure of one thing: there's not a stitch of clutter in your dream room. And rightly so: it's hard to feel pampered when you're buried in stuff, and there's nothing romantic about a storage facility.

To Start Over, then, move everything out of the room except the bed. Since the room by definition is for sleeping (and we don't want to throw our backs out), this piece of furniture can stay. Likewise, leave in place any large, wardrobe-related items that you'll definitely keep, like an armoire or dresser. But for now, everything else goes: desks, tables, chairs, storage boxes, laundry bins, potted plants, treadmills, ab crunchers, televisions, computers, lamps, books, magazines, vases, knickknacks, and so forth. Empty it down to its bare bones, and put everything in an adjacent room for the time being.

Now lie down on the bed, and look around. Quite a change, isn't it? You probably never realized how much space you actually have. Does it feel more open, peaceful, and relaxing? Is it easier to stretch out, clear your mind, and breathe? That's how a bedroom *should* feel! It should refresh and rejuvenate you, not make you stressed out and tired. The best part: creating this idyllic atmosphere doesn't require an interior decorator or expensive renovation. All you have to do is declutter!

Trash, Treasure, or Transfer

Make your Trash, Treasure, and Transfer piles, and start sorting through your bedroom's contents. Don't bother with clothing or accessories just yet; that's a job unto itself, and we'll tackle it in a later chapter. For now, concentrate on everything else— particularly those items that have nothing to do with sleeping or dressing.

You'll likely encounter an interesting dilemma here: you'll find items that aren't appropriate for *any* of those piles. You don't want to dispose of them in the Trash pile, or put them in the Transfer pile to sell or give away; in fact, you'd really like to keep them. However, they can't go in your bedroom's Treasure pile, because they aren't related to sleep or clothing. The problem: the items may belong in your life, but they don't belong in the bedroom.

Unfortunately, our bedrooms tend to function as overflow drains for our stuff. When a sink gets too full, the excess water sloshes into the hole at the back of the basin; similarly, when our living areas get too full, the spillover stuff leaks through our bedroom doors. Imagine you're expecting guests in an hour, and are frantically picking up the living and dining rooms. You've shoved what you can in the closets and drawers, but inevitably run out of space. So what do you do? Stash the excess in the bedroom. At least you can shut the door, and hide it from sight while entertaining. All too often, though, that refugee stuff gains asylum there—and before long, you're using your bedroom as an ad hoc solution to your clutter problem.

Feel free, then, to redefine your Transfer pile to "Transfer Out of the Room," and include in it any object that belongs elsewhere in the house. This pile might contain anything from magazines, to your children's toys, to your rowing machine. You may even decide to add some keepsakes and sentimental items to the mix. Make sure, however, that the items contained herein have a rightful place *somewhere*. The last thing you want to do is shuffle a pile of homeless junk from room to room. If an item's function is so vague that you don't know where to put it, the best place for it may be in your donation box.

Reason for everything

The main function of our bedrooms is to provide space for sleeping and clothes storage. Therefore, when we ask the resident items their *raison d'être*, the answer better have something to do with rest, relaxation, or wardrobe—otherwise, they may face deportation.

Your bed's probably feeling pretty smug right now, knowing it'll pass this test with flying colors. The objects on your nightstand, vanity, or dresser may be a little more nervous—but some of them actually have every right to be there. The alarm clock is safe, as are your glasses, tissues, and the book you're currently reading. You might keep that vase of flowers, and a few candles—they're certainly conducive to a romantic, and relaxing, atmosphere. A handful of other objects may also gain access to this coveted, cozy space—but to be honest, I can't think of too many. "Because there's nowhere else to put them" is *not* a good reason to keep them here!

Now let's discuss those things that don't belong here, but often try to muscle their way in. That pesky laundry basket, for example; sure, the bed provides an excellent surface for folding clothes—but do it and be done with it already! Or if it's collecting your next load, find another place to keep it. When you're enjoying a spontaneous, romantic evening with your partner, nothing kills the mood faster than a pile of dirty socks. The same goes for your toddler's toys; it's hard to heat things up when you're under the gaze of a herd of stuffed animals.

Craft supplies are another issue. They often migrate to this room when they can't find shelter elsewhere. Unless you're knitting in your sleep, however, yarn and needles should be banished from the bedroom. If it's a pre-bedtime activity, we'll make an exception; in that case, stash the stuff in a box or bag, slip it under the bed, and I won't make a fuss. Just don't turn your boudoir into a fully stocked craft shop—if only out of consideration for your partner. By the same token, find somewhere else to store exercise equipment and computer supplies; hand weights and hard drives are *not* a turn-on!

Perhaps I don't give a fair shake to knickknacks, but I think they have little place in the bedroom. A few special pieces are acceptable; but do question whether you need fifteen of them lined up across your dresser. A room full of tchotchkes can feel stale and museum-like; and if you make a wrong move, you might damage something fragile. Plus, the more stuff on your surfaces, the harder they are to clean—and who wants to spend *any* extra time on housework?

Everything in its place

For our bedrooms to be peaceful and serene, everything in them must have a place. When stuff is tucked away, a sense of calm prevails; stray items, on the other hand, disturb our restful ambience.

Defining zones in the bedroom is easy—you'll need one for sleeping, and one for dressing. You may also have a grooming zone (for putting on makeup, fixing your hair, and the like), particularly if you share a bathroom with other household members. I don't endorse having an office zone in the bedroom, unless you truly have no other place for it; in that case, do whatever you can to separate it from the main space. It's difficult to drift to sleep when a desk piled with work, bills, and anything else that causes you stress is in view. Set up a screen, or hang a curtain, to hide it when it's not in use.

The Inner Circle of your bedroom should contain those items in daily use: like the aforementioned alarm clock, reading glasses, grooming items, and in-season clothing. Of course, they should all be in their appropriate places, rather than strewn about the room. Clothes should be in the closet and dressers—*not* piled on the floor, or draped over chairs. Make it a habit to fold, hang up, or toss your clothing in the hamper immediately upon removal. Corral cosmetics in a makeup bag or container, and ensure that all accessories—like shoes, belts, handbags, and jewelry—have designated spots in your closet or drawers. The stuff of your Inner Circle should be within reach—though not necessarily within sight.

Reserve your Outer Circle for things like extra linens and out-of-season clothing. Keep them in nooks and crannies that are harder to access, such as under the bed (everyone's favorite storage spot), in lower dresser drawers, and on higher shelves in closets and armoires. Remember, though, your Outer Circle isn't a catch-all for things you don't know what to do with; to qualify for this space, stuff must be used at least a few times a year. If your extra linens include orphan pillowcases, your grown son's childhood sheets, or a duvet cover that no longer suits your décor, it's time to do some decluttering.

As for Deep Storage, I can't think of a single bedroom item that would be suitable. Garages, attics, and basements aren't optimal places for storing bedding; and furthermore, any bedding you own should be in regular rotation in your household. Even linens of a seasonal nature (like flannel sheets and heavy blankets) are inappropriate for such an out-of-the-way storage spot. Well, that makes it easy, doesn't it? Simply decide what belongs in your Inner and Outer Circles, and you're finished with this step!

All surfaces clear

Let's start with the most important surface in this room: the bed! It should always be clear—no ifs, ands, or buts about it. Your bed is essential to your health and well-being, and used at least a quarter of every day; therefore, it should always stand ready to serve its intended purpose.

Your bed is a functional surface, not a decorative one—so keep the fancy throw pillows and other nonessentials to a minimum. It's a drag to clear off the bed each night before climbing into it; and the less stuff you have to straighten, arrange, and fuss with, the better. Take a cue from luxury hotels, and keep it simple: crisp white sheets and pillowcases, topped with a fluffy duvet, make for a heavenly, minimalist retreat—no accessories needed! Just note that when I say the bed is a functional surface, I don't mean it should serve every function imaginable; it's not meant to be your laundry station, workspace, or play area for your kids. If it happens to serve one of these purposes temporarily, remove the clothes, paperwork, or children's toys immediately thereafter.

Of course, the bed isn't the only surface that requires monitoring. The more pieces of furniture you have—nightstands, vanities, dressers, tables—the more vigilant you need be (a great reason for having less furniture!). Don't let these pieces gather wayward items, like clothes, mail, spare change, cosmetics, and DVDs. Clear off their tops, and reserve them for the handful of things that truly belong there. If you've relegated certain knickknacks to the bedroom because they're not "good enough" for your living space, consider whether they're "good enough" to keep at all.

Last but not least, don't forget about the floor. Banish those stacks of books and magazines (how many can you read at a time, anyway?), and anything else that may have accumulated while you weren't paying attention. Above all, don't let any clothing get underfoot and lay the foundation for a pile. Once you start a "floordrobe," you have a much larger problem; a growing mountain of apparel isn't good for your ambience or your clothes! In fact, the only part of the floor that's fair game for stuff is under the bed. Use, but don't abuse, this valuable storage space; in other words, don't make it a hiding place for clutter.

Modules

If you don't have a linen closet elsewhere in the house, use modules in the bedroom for your extra bedding. Plastic, under-the-bed containers are perfect for storing additional sheets, pillowcases, and blankets. Keep them separated according to season, so that you won't have to dig through flannels and heavy quilts to find your cool summer linens. Do the same for each bedroom in your house; keep the kids' sheets and guest sheets stashed under their respective beds, in their own modules. Each person then has immediate and easy access to their own bedding, and you'll avoid the mess that can result when they're all piled together on a shelf.

Furthermore, consolidating your linens enables you to see just how many you have. Sheets seem to multiply when we're not looking. Every so often, we buy a new set—because we want a fresh look, our old ones are getting shabby, or guests are on the way—with little thought to those we already own. The old ones get relegated to a "just in case" pile, and our collection grows with each passing year. When you gather them all together, it can be startling to discover how many you own! Putting them into modules provides a wonderful opportunity to cull them to a reasonable amount.

If you keep grooming items in the bedroom, make modules for them as well. Store cosmetics, combs, hairbrushes, and styling products in a small bag or container that can be tucked away when not in use. Why display your entire arsenal of beauty items for your partner (or overnight guests) to see? Better to maintain a little mystery, than ruin a romantic atmosphere with a lineup of hairspray, foot powder, or deodorant on your dresser. You may also want to assign a small tray, box, or designated drawer for the stuff that comes out of your pockets each day: wallet, loose change, transit cards, keys, and the like. Consolidating them looks neater, and makes them much easier to find the next morning. Books, magazines, craft projects, and other supplies for pre-bedtime activities also benefit from a little modular organization—making them easy to stash away and slide under the bed when you start to doze off.

Limits

Use limits liberally in the bedroom, to create and maintain a serene atmosphere. The less clutter you see, the more calm you'll feel—which can very well make the difference between a restless or peaceful sleep.

First of all, limit the furniture you have in the room. Just because a bedroom set has six matching pieces, doesn't mean you have to buy (or keep) all of them. Instead of jamming the whole ensemble into the room, select only those pieces you truly need. Limit seating (such as chairs or benches) to the number of occupants sharing the room, and limit clothes storage (like armoires or dressers) to one per person. The latter makes for a more streamlined wardrobe, as well as a more spacious bedroom. Limiting the *contents* of your furnishings helps you limit the furnishings themselves.

Second, limit the stuff that's visible. For example, keep no more than three items on your nightstand or on top of your dresser. Such a strategy highlights decorative items, and leaves plenty of room for functional ones. Don't let the beautiful vase on your vanity, or framed photograph on your dresser, compete for attention with a pile of magazines or jumble of hairspray bottles. Likewise, don't create a situation where you'll knock over knickknacks when reaching for your snooze alarm.

Third, put a lid on your linens, by limiting them to a certain number. Two sets of sheets per bed are generally sufficient, and can be rotated with your laundry schedule. Set your limit according to the needs of your household; if you have frequent overnight guests, or toddlers of potty-training age, you may require a few extra. In the case of blankets and quilts, climate also plays a role; a household in Florida certainly won't need as many as one in Michigan. In general, don't keep more than your family (and guests) can reasonably use at any given time. A cozy household comes from the warmth, love, and hospitality of its occupants, not the number of duvets squirreled away in the linen closet.

If one comes in, one goes out

As you declutter your bedroom, take control over the stuff flowing into it. You don't want to purge ten items, and then find you've accumulated twice that in the meantime. From now on, make sure an old item leaves each time a new one enters.

Stashes of linens require particular vigilance. For some reason, when we buy a new sheet set, blanket, quilt, or duvet, we're often reluctant to throw away the old. The compulsion to hold on to extra bedding seems hard-wired into our genes. Perhaps we're afraid that we'll lose power in the middle of winter, and need to pile it on to stay warm; or we imagine that a dozen overnight guests will show up unexpectedly at our door; or we think they'll come in handy the next time we're moving, painting, or having a picnic. However we rationalize it, there's only so many linens we'll ever need; and holding on to them for some hypothetical situation in the future is taking up some very real space right now. Stick to the One In-One Out rule, and the next time you acquire new bedding, donate the old—and think of the warmth and comfort you're so generously providing someone else.

Apply the same principle to *anything* that enters the bedroom, and it'll make decluttering that much easier. Freshen up your décor by replacing or rotating pieces, rather than adding more. (Keep extras in a décor module, and switch them every so often.) If you bring in new bedtime reading, dispose of the old, or return it to its rightful place. If you acquire a new piece of furniture, swap it for something similar instead of squeezing it into the room. (If you feel you "need" it to hold more stuff, declutter the stuff first!) Stick with this strategy, and you'll keep clutter from creeping into your sleeping space.

Narrow it down

"Narrow it down" is one of my favorite steps, because that's where the real minimalist fun begins! I've always had somewhat of an anti-establishment streak, and breaking the rules of consumer (or decorative) propriety is my little way of "sticking it to the man." Nowhere is this more fun, or socially acceptable, than in the bedroom!

Our bedrooms are our own little worlds. Few outsiders enter this intimate space, and those that do know us pretty well already (and presumably won't judge us by our furnishings, or lack thereof). Therefore, we can feel free to explore our minimalist fantasies here, without regard for social norms. That sounds fun, doesn't it? In your living room, it may be awkward to seat guests on the floor; but in your bedroom, nobody knows (or cares) if you're sleeping on it.

As a child, I had a well-appointed little princess's room: a beautiful canopy bed, floral duvet and curtains, and entire suite of vanity, dressers, and bookcases. Almost every inch of floor space was occupied by a piece of furniture, save a few feet on each side of the bed. Though it was very pretty, I found it suffocating; I never felt like I had enough room to stretch out my young limbs and move around freely. As a teenager, however, I cajoled my parents into letting me "redecorate." Out went the dressers, vanity, and nightstands, and I traded the fancy bed for a mattress and box spring on a simple frame. My bedroom went from 80 percent furniture, 20 percent floor space to the opposite—and I loved the transformation. (Thus, a minimalist was born!)

Today, my husband and I have nothing in our bedroom save a futon mattress on the floor. That may not work for everyone, but it works for us. By eliminating the bed frame, we also eliminated the need for nightstands; we each keep travel-size alarm clocks on the floor beside us. Instead of using dressers, we store all clothing in our closets, organized with hanging fabric shelving and a handful of containers. We don't have a vanity, preferring to perform all grooming in the bathroom. Keeping things to the bare minimum gives our bedroom an open, airy, spacious feel—exactly what we need after a day in a crowded, urban environment.

The point I want to emphasize is that you don't have to own certain pieces of furniture simply because it's "expected." Not everyone needs a vanity; not everyone needs a dresser; not everyone needs a nightstand. Heck, not everyone needs a bed! Forget what all the design magazines tell you about how a master bedroom should look. Instead, stop and contemplate what *you* really need. If you find it fussy to have a vanity, get rid of it; if you're always bumping into the dresser, move it out; if you never sit in the corner chair, find it a new home. Narrow down the pieces in your bedroom to a functional minimum, and reclaim all that glorious space—the neighbors never have to know that you live without a nightstand.

Seek ways to minimize your linens as well. Question whether it's necessary to have separate winter and summer bedding; in most climates, simple cotton will suffice year round. By the same token, choose a duvet cover that'll work in every season; skip the heavy velvet, for example, in favor of something more versatile. By making wise choices, you can reduce the contents of your linen closet without sacrificing comfort. Instead of stockpiling sheets for an army, pare down your collection to the essential—be that two sets per bed, or just one. If you don't have frequent overnight visitors, your guest sheets can double as your backup set.

Everyday maintenance

The bedroom may not see the same traffic as other parts of the house; however, it still needs daily maintenance to keep it clean and clutter-free.

Number one on the agenda: make the bed every day! This simple action takes just a few minutes—but it can completely transform the room, and set the tone for your day. A made bed is one of life's little luxuries, inviting you to slip in and relax after a hard day's work. Furthermore, it exudes calm and order, and is a powerful influence in keeping the bedroom neat and tidy. When the bed is undone, a mess in the rest of the room doesn't seem out of place; everything just looks a wreck. In contrast, when your bedding is smoothed, tucked, and folded just so, the clutter has no camouflage, and is much less likely to accumulate.

Number two: scan the room for wayward clothes. Sometimes when we take off a jacket, sweater, or pair of stockings—especially if we're falling into bed after a long day—

the item fails to reach its appropriate spot. As soon as you notice such a stray article, put it away. Don't save the task for "later;" by that time, more items will have joined it, and the chore will have grown. It can be particularly hard to corral shoes and handbags; these items like to go out on the town, and you'll often find a crowd of them waiting at the door. Give them their own special space in the closet (to which they're returned each night), so they don't take up floor space in *your* part of the room. Properly storing clothes and accessories—on hangers and shelves, instead of heaps on the floor—makes for a longer-lasting wardrobe, and a more pleasant environment.

Third, monitor the bedroom for uninvited "guests." As private a space as it is, some things still manage to sneak in (usually in the arms of other family members). If you catch your toddler's stuffed toy or spouse's tennis racket lurking in the corner, don't invite it to stay the night—boomerang it right back where it belongs. Similarly, when you're finished reading that mystery novel, or watching your favorite romantic comedy on DVD, don't let it take up residence by your bedside. Unless you keep a bookshelf in your bedroom, return it to its appropriate module in the living room or office. Clear the room before you close your eyes, and you'll wake up to a wonderful, serene space each morning!

23

Wardrobe

It's time to tackle the clutter in our closets. If you have plenty of clothes but nothing to wear, this chapter's for you. We'll explore how paring down our attire can save us time, money, space, and stress—while making it *easier* for us to look well-dressed. Having a streamlined wardrobe is one of the true joys of being a minimalist!

Start over

Cleaning out your closet doesn't have to be a chore; on the contrary, it can be a blast! In fact, it's one of my favorite decluttering activities. The task is certainly easier than tackling an entire room: there's no furniture to worry about, tchotchkes to deliberate over, or other people's stuff to deal with. To be honest, I think of it more as "me time" than cleaning time. I like to put on some music, have a glass of wine, and stage my own personal fashion show as I rummage through my wardrobe. Purging dowdy old things and planning fabulous new outfits makes for a fun couple of hours; and having extra closet space in the end is a wonderful reward.

To Start Over, take everything out of your closet, your dressers, your armoire, and everywhere else you store your clothing, and lay it out on your bed. And by everything, I mean *everything*! Reach into those dark recesses and pull out the bell-bottoms, bubble skirt, and bridesmaid dress from your sister's wedding. Dive into the back corners and fish out those cowboy boots, platform sandals, and strappy stilettos you've never been able to walk in. Dump all the underwear, socks, pajamas, and pantyhose out of their respective drawers, and line up your handbags for inspection. Nothing stays behind—keep going until you're left with empty drawers, bare shelves, and naked hangers.

Before we continue, though, let's stop for a little soul-searching. In order to create a minimalist wardrobe, we need a good handle on what's *right* for us—because when we have a limited number of clothes, they all have to pull their weight. Therefore, spend some time pondering your personal style: is it classic, sporty, preppy, punk, bohemian, glamorous, vintage, romantic, or modern? Think about your favorite colors: do you prefer light pastels, dark jewel tones, or bold primaries? Do you look best in clothes that are closely tailored, or loose and flowing? Do you feel more comfortable in natural fabrics like cottons and wools, or high-tech ones like polyester blends? Keep your answers in mind as you evaluate your clothing; pieces that don't fit your style or preferences are likely to spend more time in your closet than on your body.

Next, imagine this situation: a fire, flood, or other disaster has wiped out your entire wardrobe, and you must rebuild it from scratch. (Yikes!) Your funds are limited, so you have to make smart choices. Consider the absolute essentials you would need to get through a typical week. Your list will likely include socks, underwear, one or two pairs of trousers, a couple of shirts, a jacket, a versatile pair of shoes, and perhaps a sweater, skirt, and pair of pantyhose or tights (forget the last two if you're a guy!). You'll want to choose items that are appropriate for both work and weekend, and can be layered to keep you comfortable in a range of temperatures. You'll need to be able to mix and match them, and create a variety of outfits from just a few pieces. This exercise illuminates your most functional articles of clothing, and lays a good foundation for your minimalist wardrobe.

Once you've nailed down your essential requirements, and your favorite looks, colors, fabrics, and silhouettes, you can make your ideal wardrobe a reality. This is the fun part: you get to be your own personal stylist! As you sort through your clothing, keep in mind the image you want to project—cool professional, chic bohemian, Ivy League prepster—and select (and reject) pieces accordingly. If you're aiming for a more glamorous look, keep the dresses and ditch the dowdy sweats. If you're climbing the corporate ladder, favor pencil skirts over peasant shirts. Be the curator of your clothes: pick out the items that fit your style, and make you look and feel your best.

Trash, Treasure, or Transfer

Now that everything's out of your closet, try everything on. If you haven't worn that cocktail dress or three-piece suit in five years, how do you know it still fits? Don each piece in turn, and do a three-sixty or two in front of the mirror. We all know that just because something looks good on a hanger, doesn't mean it looks good on us; and conversely, an item that's ho-hum on its own may come alive when we put it on. During your fashion show, mix and match individual pieces: experiment with different combinations, and figure out exactly what goes with what. In the process, you'll pin down your most flattering and versatile articles of clothing.

Make your Trash, Treasure, and Transfer piles, and psych yourself up for some heavy-duty decision making. It helps to use boxes or garbage bags for your castoffs—not because you're going to throw them away, but because it keeps them out of sight. Hence, once you've decided to toss an article, your decision will be "final;" your eye won't fall on it again, tempting you to retrieve it from the reject pile. If your resolve starts to waver, take a break and re-read the philosophy chapters; sometimes all you need is a little pep talk to steel your strength and keep you going!

In your Trash pile, put all those items that are beyond repair (or your ability, or desire, to do so): like the blouse with the stubborn wine stain, the shirt with the frayed collar, the pants with the worn-out knees, the skirt with the large tear, the threadbare jacket, the stockings with runs, the stretched-out undies, the socks without mates, and the sweaters with undarnable holes. If you can't reach into your closet, put it on, and wear it in public, it doesn't belong there. Of course, that doesn't mean these pieces are destined for the landfill. If you can recycle or repurpose them (perhaps as dust rags), all the better. Only keep them, however, if you have a specific use in mind.

If we only had to deal with worn out items, decluttering would be a snap! Unfortunately, however, most of our clothes wear out their welcome long before they wear out. Therefore, make good use of your Transfer pile; it's for all those perfectly good clothes that are no longer good for you. If it doesn't fit or isn't flattering, if it's outdated or unsuitable, or if you've simply grown bored of it, put it here. Include any clothes that make you feel self-conscious, uncomfortable, or unfashionable—you know, the ones you remove minutes after you put them on. Don't let these duds clutter up your closet. They get in the way of your good stuff, confuse you when you're getting dressed, and make you feel like you have nothing to wear.

While these pieces may be all wrong for you, they may be perfect for someone else. Instead of letting them languish in your closet, give them a chance at a second life. If an item's still sporting its tags, see if you can return it—most retailers will accept unworn clothing for a reasonable time period (usually thirty to ninety days) after its purchase. Otherwise, consider selling it on eBay, or in a consignment shop; name brands and designer pieces can net you a nice wad of cash. Alternatively, donate your duds to a thrift shop, or charitable organization like Dress for Success; you'll get a clean closet, some good karma, and maybe even a tax write-off, in return.

Work through the remaining steps to determine your Treasures, and you'll have a minimalist wardrobe in short order. However, if you prefer to proceed more slowly, here's an alternative technique that's almost effortless. Obtain three spools of ribbon: one each of green, yellow, and red. After you wear an item, tie the hanger with a bow: green if it made you feel fabulous; red if it made you feel frumpy; or yellow if you're on the fence about it. At the end of six months, keep the greens and yellows as your Treasures, and Trash or Transfer the reds. If something doesn't have a ribbon, it means you haven't worn it at all—and you know exactly where that belongs!

Reason for each item

The number one reason to keep an article of clothing is because *we wear it*. Well, that should be easy, right? Wouldn't that justify saving the majority of our apparel? Not so fast. According to the Pareto principle (or 80/20 rule), we wear 20 percent of our wardrobe 80 percent of the time. Uh-oh! That means we *don't wear* the majority of our clothing—at least not often. In fact, we could pare down our wardrobes to one-fifth their size, and hardly miss a thing! Therefore, our mission is to separate our "favorite 20" from our "unworn 80"—that is, identify the pieces that fit us, flatter us, and suit our lifestyles.

An article of clothing *that fits you* has good reason to stay in your closet. Conversely, if an item doesn't fit, you can't wear it; and if you can't wear it, then why keep it? Don't torture yourself by storing different clothes for different weights. If you keep "fat clothes," you keep the expectation that you might gain weight; if you keep "skinny clothes," you'll be depressed that you can't fit into them. Instead, reward yourself with a new wardrobe *after* you drop those pounds. What great incentive to skip dessert and hit the gym! Save only those clothes that fit you *now*, and shop for your new figure when it makes its appearance. (If you're pregnant, you're off the hook; but if you haven't returned to your pre-baby weight by your child's first birthday, it's time to declutter.)

Items *that flatter you* are also welcome in your wardrobe. Learn which colors and silhouettes suit you best, and you'll avoid crowding your closet with "mistakes." Do you look better in fitted or flowing clothes? Pleated or plain-front pants? Mini or maxi skirts? Crew or v-shaped necklines? Decide which sleeve length makes your arms look sexy, and which skirt length best shows off your legs. Determine which colors complement your skin tone, and which ones wash them out. Base your wardrobe on your body, not on trends: just because hip-huggers or cropped tops are in fashion, doesn't mean *you* should wear them. When considering an outfit, question whether you'd feel comfortable being photographed, or running into your ex, while wearing it. If the answer is "no," out it goes!

We also have good reason to keep clothes that *suit our lifestyles*—and to get rid of those that don't. List the activities for which you need apparel—such as work, social functions, gardening, housecleaning, and exercise—and evaluate your pieces accordingly. Resist the temptation to hold on to "fantasy" clothes; a closet full of cocktail dresses and ball gowns won't make you a socialite. Devote your space to what you'll wear "in real life" instead. Furthermore, consider if a recent life change has altered your clothing needs. For example, if you've left your corporate job to work at home, you can banish those business suits; or if you've moved from Minnesota to Florida, you can shed that sheepskin coat.

Finally, let's examine a *poor* reason to keep an article of clothing: because you paid "good money" for it. I know, you're wracked with guilt when you even *think* about tossing that cashmere sweater, or those designer heels—no matter how long it's been since you've worn them. You reason that if they're still in your closet, you haven't wasted your money (been there, done that!). There's two ways to deal with such clothing—and no, one of them is *not* keeping it. You can sell the item in question, and try to recoup some of your cash; or you can give it away, and think of it as a charitable donation. In the latter case, at least the money "spent" will go to a good cause!

Everything in its place

When you're organizing your clothing, remember that your wardrobe is a zone unto itself. Therefore, everything you wear should be contained within its furnishings—be that a closet, dresser, armoire, or shelving unit. Don't let your apparel stray into other parts of the room, or other rooms in the house: your sweaters shouldn't be draped over a chair, your socks shouldn't be piled in the corner, your shoes shouldn't be lounging in the living room, and your shirts shouldn't be holed up in your spouse's closet (at least not without permission). Keeping everything together gives you a better handle on the size, and contents, of your wardrobe—and prevents you from running around half-naked, looking for your "missing" pants!

Within your wardrobe zone, give everything a place; it makes dressing in the morning so much easier. Dedicate certain shelves to t-shirts, certain drawers to underwear, and certain sections of the closet to coats, suits, and dresses. If you've decluttered thoroughly, and still run short on storage, consider some "space-saving" solutions. Although I rarely advocate them (preferring to pare down further instead), they can be quite useful in such a tight area. It's better to store your sweaters in a hanging organizer than in a mound on your closet floor; or drape your pants on a multi-trouser hanger, instead of stuffing them side-by-side.

Assign your clothing to your Inner Circle, Outer Circle, and Deep Storage. Devote your Inner Circle to those items you wear on a daily, or weekly, basis: your socks, underwear, pajamas, work clothes, weekend clothes, exercise clothes, and around-the-house clothes. This is where your "favorite 20 percent" belongs. Keep these workhorses easily accessible, in your top drawers, middle shelves, and center section of your closet—not only to save you time getting dressed, but to make them easy to put away. If returning them to their spots is a hassle—requiring you to bend over, stand on a footstool, or move a stack of items—they'll likely end up on the floor, your bed, or a nearby chair.

Reserve your Outer Circle for those clothes you wear less frequently—from once or twice a month, to once or twice a year. This group will likely include your dressier clothes and formal attire. Why keep them if you so seldom wear them?

Because chances are, you'll be invited to a wedding, holiday party, or other social function this year; and it's less stressful to have something on hand, than to have to go shopping. Now, that doesn't mean you need three tuxedos or five fancy dresses at the ready; keep just the minimum amount that meets your needs. Because such occasions are few and far between, you can usually get away with repeating an outfit; unless you're a social diva, it's unlikely anyone will remember (or care) what you wore to the last one.

Your Outer Circle may also contain specialty and seasonal clothes, like your ski pants and bathing suits. In fact, you may find it convenient to store out-of-season clothes in your Outer Circle (such as on the top shelf of your closet, or under the bed), and switch them with your Inner Circle at the appropriate time of year. Your heavy sweaters will then be tucked away in summer, but accessible in winter; and your shorts and sundresses will be out of the way when it's cold, but within reach when it's warm. When you're making the seasonal switch, take the opportunity to do some decluttering.

Very little (if any) clothing should be in Deep Storage. Sentimental items (like wedding, christening, and communion dresses) are potential candidates, should you decide to keep them. Deep Storage may also be used for outgrown children's clothes that you're saving for a younger sibling. Just be careful where you store them; attic, basement, and garage spaces can be harsh environments for fabric, and may speed them into your Trash pile. If possible, find a remote, but climate-controlled, spot inside the house.

All surfaces clear

Don't let stuff from your closets and dressers spill out onto the surfaces around them; strive to keep these spaces clear. Hang up everything, or put it in the hamper, immediately after removal—don't dump it on the floor, plop it on the bed, or pile it on a chair. Storing your clothes properly will keep them cleaner, prevent them from wrinkling, and make them easier to find when you need them. At least do it out of consideration for your partner; no one likes to see someone else's dirty laundry strewn about! A "floordrobe" can quickly ruin the ambience of a romantic evening or relaxing weekend morning.

Likewise, make every effort to keep the floor of your closet empty; a jumble of items down below makes it easy for "intruders" to hide. Try to accommodate all the contents in vertical storage—like shelves, shoe racks, closet rods, or hanging organizers. Modular systems can be particularly efficient, and configured to fit your space. Such organization keeps the clutter from creeping in, and keeps your clothes in better condition. When you're getting dressed for that job interview or first date, the last thing you want to do is pluck your blouse or blazer off the closet floor.

Finally, if you have an armoire, don't pile stuff on top of it. I know it's tempting to use this high, out-of-sight hiding place as a storage spot of last resort. However, the surface is typically overlooked on housecleaning rounds, so anything you stash up there will soon be covered in dust. Besides, it's no fun to drag out a stepstool when you need to access something. Worst case—you may forget about the stuff up there entirely. Treat it like any other surface in the house, and keep it clear.

Modules

Consolidate your clothing into modules, just like your DVDs, office supplies, and kitchen gadgets. The results can be eye-opening! You may discover (perhaps to your great shock) that you have ten pairs of black slacks, twenty white shirts, or thirty pairs of shoes. When you see them all together, you'll quickly realize you have *more* than enough. The idea is to *keep* them consolidated, so you're never tempted to add to your collection. Hang all your skirts together, pants together, dresses together, and coats together. Keep pajamas, workout clothes, and sweaters stacked on their own shelves, and socks and underwear stashed in their own drawers. Be strict about keeping things in line; once your yoga pants cozy up to your business suits, or your tank tops take up with your tights, you never know what chaos can ensue!

If you'd like, you can further break down your "category" modules by color, season, or type. In this scenario, you'd store all your navy pants, brown blazers, or khaki shorts together. Similarly, you could break down your shirts into sleeveless, short sleeve, and long sleeve, and your skirts into mini, knee-length, and ankle-length. You can divide your dresses into casual and formal, and your suits into summer and winter weight. The more specific your modules, the easier it is to take stock of what you own. You'll see what you have too many of, what you have just enough of, and what you still might need—making it much easier to plan your wardrobe.

Do the same for accessories; just because they're small, they shouldn't be forgotten. Consolidate your scarves, and divide them into seasons. Consolidate your shoes, and divide them by activity (how many pairs of sneakers do you have?). Consolidate your jewelry, and divide it into earrings, necklaces, brooches, rings, and bracelets. Consolidate your handbags, and divide them by color, season, or function. Have a designated spot for each category, and make sure its contents stay there. Accessories tend to wander, and can end up in far-flung places—as anyone who's ever searched the house for a purse or pair of earrings knows too well.

Once you've gathered everything together, it's time to cull. If you discover you have too many items in a single category (like two dozen button-down shirts), keep only the finest and most flattering—that's probably what you'll end up wearing anyway. Having some multiples is certainly understandable; few people can get by with a single shirt, or pair of pants. Even Buddhist monks typically have two robes! The problem occurs when we have so many similar items that we barely wear most of them. Often, such excess is the result of chasing "perfection": the perfect pair of black pants, the perfect white shirt, the perfect handbag. We keep buying and buying and buying, and end up with more than we'll ever need. Choose your best and most beautiful, and declutter the rest.

After consolidating and culling your items, contain them as best you can so they stay in order. That doesn't mean you have to run out and buy twenty plastic bins. "Contain" can just as well mean "keep on a certain shelf, in a certain drawer, or in a certain section of your closet." It can mean that all your navy slacks are on a multi-trouser hanger, all your jeans are in one stack, or all your ties are on a single rack. Small items, however, are best corralled in actual containers; use trays, boxes, or baskets for things like pantyhose, scarves, watches, and jewelry. It'll keep them organized, and keep a lid on their accumulation.

Limits

In this era of mass production, clothing is inexpensive and readily available; we can nip down to our local mall and come back with a carload, if we're so inclined. Furthermore, fashion is always changing; what's "in" this season is "out" the next, only to be replaced by a new set of must-have items. While our great-grandparents could only afford (and obtain) a few new outfits each year, we have no such restrictions. No wonder our closets are bursting at the seams!

That's why limits play such an important role in our minimalist wardrobes; they keep our apparel and accessories to a manageable level. Without them, we'd surely be buried under an avalanche of clothes! In the largest sense, then, we should limit our clothing to the available storage space. If our armoires or dressers are overflowing, we must stem the tide—and prevent the contents from pouring into the room. Yet even if we can hold back the torrent, we don't want to teeter at the breaking point. The idea is not to stuff our closets as full as possible, but to remove enough items to create some breathing room. It's not good for our clothes (or stress levels) when we have to wrestle them out of the closet or squash them into drawers. With that in mind, I'll revise the above statement: we should limit our clothing to *less* than the available storage space.

I certainly can't tell you how many shirts, sweaters, or pairs of pants you should own—that number is up to you to decide. Some people have no problem wearing the same trousers all week, while others won't feel comfortable with less than a pair per day. Determine what's enough for *you*, and prune down to that level. Your limits may be well considered, or completely arbitrary. When I moved overseas, I could only fit four pairs of shoes in my luggage; hence, that's what I kept. When I bought a hanger that held five skirts, I capped my collection at that number. I've limited my coats to one per season, and my socks and underwear to a ten-day supply. Your limits will be different than mine, and depend on your personal situation and comfort level.

Additionally, set limits on your nightclothes, your exercise clothes, and your "messy work" clothes (the worn out items you save for when you're gardening or painting). Depending on your laundry and activity schedules, one to five outfits will generally suffice. Limit your accessories as well—scarves, ties, handbags, and jewelry can multiply when we're not keeping tabs on them. Calculate how many you wear in a typical week, and set a reasonable maximum number; alternatively, limit them to the container in which they're stored.

Most importantly, have fun with your limits! Personally, I love seeing how many unique outfits I can fashion from a fixed number of items. Regard it as a challenge: how well can you get by with only so many shirts, shoes, skirts, or handbags? It's a great opportunity to exercise your creativity and style.

If one comes in, one goes out

We can purge and purge and purge—taking items to consignment shops, selling them on eBay, and donating them to Goodwill—but if we don't turn off the inflow, our closets won't get any emptier. Our new purchases will sabotage our decluttering efforts, and hinder our progress. Fortunately, we can avoid this problem by following the One In-One Out rule; if we offset each incoming article with an outgoing one, we won't accumulate more than we already have.

Fashion changes faster than our clothes wear out; so if we purchase new items each season, our closets fill up quickly. Therefore, when we update our wardrobes, we must also purge them of the outdated, the outgrown, and the out-of-favor. The best way to do this is to make a like-for-like trade: if you bring home a new pair of sneakers, make an old pair take a hike; if you splurge on a new cocktail dress, waltz an old one out the door; and if you buy a new business suit, send an old one into retirement. Then, your wardrobe will be a fresh, ever-changing collection, rather than a stale archive of fashions past.

When you made your modules, you may have realized you had too much in some categories, and too little in others—perhaps you have enough trousers to last a lifetime, but hardly any skirts. This problem is common, as we tend to gravitate toward certain items, or stock up on them when we find something we like. In that case, feel free to tweak the One In-One Out rule to do some rebalancing. When you acquire a new skirt, toss a pair of pants instead; do the same for any other categories in need of adjustment. Once you've brought your wardrobe back into balance, you can return to swapping like-for-like.

Don't be tempted to cheat! On occasion, you'll be so anxious to wear a new outfit that decluttering an old one is the last thing on your mind. But you know what? If you don't do it immediately, you likely never will. Use your excitement to wear your new stuff as *incentive* to purge the old: don't cut the tags off that just-purchased jacket until you list the old one on eBay, or add it to your donation box. If you make it a habit, it'll become second nature (and a whole lot easier) with time. In fact, you'll likely find yourself shopping with a castoff already in mind.

Finally, if your old clothes are "too good" to get rid of, question if you really need anything new. What's the point of adding to your wardrobe if your current apparel is perfectly adequate? Don't feel pressured to keep up with fashion trends—they're nothing more than a marketing ploy, designed to separate you from your hard-earned money. Instead of buying each season's must-haves, invest in classic pieces that stay in style. You'll have a bigger bank account, a more spacious closet, and a lot less decluttering to do.

Narrow it down

In essence, a minimalist wardrobe is what is popularly known as a "capsule wardrobe": a small set of essential pieces that can be mixed and matched into a variety of outfits. The concept is designed to eliminate the problem of having "a closet full of clothes and nothing to wear," and involves making wise choices with regards to color, style, fabric, and accessories. Remember the Pareto principle? Well, a capsule wardrobe consists of the 20 percent of clothes you wear 80 percent of the time. By thus narrowing down your attire, you'll save money, free up closet space, and always look well put together.

Once upon a time, the clothes in my closet ran the gamut of colors—I had warm hues, cool hues, pastels, primaries, jewel tones, and earth tones. What's more, I had a variety of accessories to match this rainbow of apparel. Not only was my closet stuffed; getting dressed required serious thought, to ensure that nothing clashed. Then I discovered the secret to a minimalist wardrobe: choosing a base color.

The idea is to select a neutral color—such as black, brown, gray, navy, cream, or khaki—and limit foundation pieces (like pants and skirts) to that shade. I chose black as my base color—mainly because it's flattering on me, travels well, and hides stains—and purged all my navies, browns, and tans in the process. Not only did this strategy slash the size of my wardrobe, it helped me vastly reduce my accessories. I was thrilled to find I no longer needed footwear and handbags in multiple colors! A black purse, or pair of shoes, goes with everything in my closet—which means I can get by (and still look smart) with far fewer of them.

Don't worry—this strategy doesn't mean you have to live your life in monochrome. After you choose your base color, you get to choose accent colors. Select a handful of shades that flatter you, and work well with your neutral (I chose burgundy, plum, aqua, and teal). Stick to these colors when selecting shirts, sweaters, and other pieces to supplement your basics. For variety, you can also add a secondary neutral that complements your base: I have skirts and pants in gray, as well as black. You might choose khaki in addition to brown, or cream in addition to navy. The key is that all your colors can be mixed and matched. Ideally, you should be able to get dressed in the dark, or with your eyes closed, and still look fabulous!

After you've purged the extraneous colors from your closet, focus on versatility. Any candidate for your capsule must be multi-talented; you should be able to wear it in a wide range of weather conditions, and on a wide variety of occasions. Think of it like packing for travel: when you're dressing from a suitcase, you must be able to form a maximum number of outfits from a minimum number of items—and make sure those outfits are appropriate for any climate or activity you might encounter. Use the same principles when building your capsule wardrobe. Opt for pieces that can be layered, rather than ones that are bulky: a cardigan and shell, for example, can be worn far more often than a heavy sweater. Choose simple silhouettes over fussy ones: a v-neck shirt coordinates with more pieces than a ruffled one. Select items that go with everything, instead of next to nothing: basic black pumps are infinitely more versatile than lime green stilettos.

Furthermore, favor apparel that can be dressed up, as well as dressed down. Skip the sequins and sweatshirts, and any other items that'll be "too dressy" or "too casual" most of the time. Instead, choose the sweater that goes from the office to dinner, and also looks great with jeans on the weekend; the dress that can be glamorized with a strand of pearls, or relaxed with a pair of sandals; the shirt that works with a suit and tie, or can also be worn on its own. The more duty each item can do, the fewer items you'll need.

You may be thinking, "That's all well and good; but where can I add some pizzazz?" Ah, that's easy: with accessories! Do like the ever-fashionable French, and use chic accents—like a sharp tie, funky belt, or bold bracelet—to liven up simple, classic clothes. I've noticed something interesting: if I add an eye-catching scarf to an old ensemble, someone will invariably comment on my "new outfit." Such is the power of accessories—they freshen up a tired look in no time flat, and better yet, require very little storage space.

In summary, your minimalist wardrobe should emphasize quality over quantity. Narrow down your attire to your most classic, versatile, and well-made pieces, plus a few stylish accessories. You'll look like a million bucks—with a fraction of your current clothes!

Everyday maintenance

We've freed up space in our closets, and learned to look gorgeous with less. Let's congratulate ourselves on a job well done! Now we just have to make sure that things don't get out of hand again. With a little everyday maintenance, we can keep our minimalist wardrobes at their new, streamlined levels.

First of all, commit to keeping your closet tidy. As soon as you remove an article of clothing, hang it, fold it, or otherwise stash it in its proper place. By storing things in their appropriate modules, you'll always have a good grasp of exactly what you own—and eliminate the chance that five new sweaters will sneak their way in without notice. Moreover, if you follow the One In-One Out rule—by swapping old items for new ones— you'll never have to worry about your wardrobe expanding. In fact, your closet will only grow *more spacious* as you continue to declutter.

Second, take good care of your clothes; when you don't have a lot of them, you can't afford to have a crucial item sidelined by a mud splatter or a frayed hem. Use common sense to avoid potential damage: don't wear your suede shoes in the rain, or your white pants to your kid's soccer game. A little preventative maintenance also goes a long way: fix little tears before they become big ones, and treat stains before they turn stubborn. When you give your clothes a little TLC, you won't need backups waiting in the wings.

Third, stay out of the stores. Don't shop for fun, for entertainment, or out of sheer boredom; that's when you get into trouble! You've worked hard to eliminate the excess from your wardrobe; but one shopping spree can put you back in the same boat. You know how it goes: you're wandering through a department store, and a cute dress catches your eye. Forty-five minutes later, you're walking out the door with it—plus matching shoes, handbag, wrap, earrings, and a few other pieces you picked up along the way. Better to avoid temptation: don't set foot in a store (or surf a retailer's website) until you absolutely *need* something. In fact, make an inventory of your clothing, and take it with you when you go shopping; if you have twenty-three shirts on your list, you'll be much less likely to buy a twenty-fourth.

Finally, declutter with the change of seasons. Fall and spring are wonderful times to reevaluate your wardrobe. When you're hauling out your coats or sweaters in preparation for winter, take some time to go through them. Our tastes change, our bodies change, and so does fashion. That jacket you loved last year might look worn, outdated, or unappealing to you now; or those skinny jeans may have become a bit *too* skinny since you last wore them. Perhaps your cashmere sweater acquired a moth hole, or that "it" item you bought is now hopelessly "out." Purge anything you don't think you'll wear, and start the new season with some extra closet space!

24

Home office

Now we'll get down to some serious work: decluttering our offices. We'll dig out our desks from the mountains of paperwork, and devise systems to prevent future pileups. It may sound daunting, but we'll take it one step at a time—and I promise, it's a lot more fun than paying bills or doing taxes. Furthermore, the rewards will be well worth the effort: your new, clean, magnificent space will make you a million times more productive and efficient!

Start over

Imagine that you're sitting at your desk, hard at work on an important project. You're humming along and making good progress, when you suddenly find need for a specific document. "Uh-oh," you think, eyeing the piles of papers scattered on your desk. You clench your teeth and dive in, praying it'll somehow materialize without too much effort. No such luck. You page through the stacks with increasing desperation—in the meantime uncovering a bill that needs to be paid, a form that needs to be mailed, and a receipt that needs to be filed. You take care of these matters, then resume your search; when you're about to call the document "lost," you spot it in another pile, across the room on the printer. By that time, however, your concentration is broken and your time is short; the project will have to wait, unfinished, for another day.

When your space is clear, your mind is clear—you can work without distraction, and be more productive. A sloppy desk, on the other hand, is a veritable roadblock to progress; it makes finding things, doing things, and keeping tabs on things more difficult. In fact, if your space is too chaotic, you may not get any work done at all!

So how do we Start Over? Here, more than anywhere, we'll benefit from breaking the task into smaller pieces; otherwise, it could be simply overwhelming. Rather than move our desks, bookcases, and filing cabinets into the hall, we'll attack the *contents* of these items first. If we can reduce them so much as to eliminate a piece of furniture, fantastic! However, papers and office supplies are small and numerous; one drawer, or one file folder, may be all you're able to tackle at once. Don't be tempted to rush through it, in a bid to see instant results; take the time to be thorough, and your efforts will have much greater impact.

Totally empty out the drawer, file, or shelf on which you're working. Instead of picking out an item or two to purge, channel your inner dump truck and completely upset its contents. Once everything's laid out across your desk, table, or floor, you can give each item due consideration—and decide whether or not it's truly worth keeping. The process itself can be cathartic, giving you the upper hand over the clutter that torments you. If you've ever fantasized about playing an all-powerful deity, here's your chance: the fate of hundreds of staples, paperclips, pens, papers, and rubber bands lies in your hands. Work your divine magic, and create a minimalist paradise!

In the process, think carefully about how, and where, you store your paperwork and supplies. Just because your stapler has always been in the far left corner of your second drawer, doesn't mean it has to return there. Starting Over is a wonderful opportunity to mix things up, and try a new configuration—a chance to design your work area for maximum ease and efficiency. Your decluttering should free up a lot of extra space, so you'll have plenty of new places to put things.

Trash, Treasure, or Transfer

First, start with the easy stuff: get rid of all the junk mail, catalogs, and magazines that have accumulated. The vast majority of this stuff has little importance in the grand scheme of things; that is, the world won't end if you toss that plumbing flyer—even if your pipes spring a leak next week. You can find similar information in the phone book, on the Internet, or through the recommendation of a neighbor; there's no need to hoard a pile of solicitations. Ditto for the credit card applications, sales circulars, catalogs, brochures, leaflets, and pamphlets. If it's not important enough to act on *now*, show it the recycling bin; if you change your mind down the road, another mailer will surely arrive in the meantime. Don't labor over decision making here, just go on and purge like nobody's business. It's highly unlikely you'll live to regret tossing a piece of junk mail!

While you're at it, throw out (or recycle) all those items you come across that are clearly Trash: dried-up pens, rusty paperclips, stretched-out rubber bands, spent erasers, outdated calendars, broken pencils, torn file folders, old sticky notes, used envelopes, empty ink cartridges, and all those bits and bobs that are positively unidentifiable. I don't know how damaged and decrepit office supplies manage to hang around so long, but I suspect they've found a way to slip below our radar. Gather them up, and put them out of their misery!

That was a good warm-up, wasn't it? Didn't it feel great to clear out all that stuff? Now that we're psyched up and in the groove, we're ready to take on some bigger challenges. You may not realize it, but some of your "good" office supplies, practical as they seem at first glance, also deserve to be in the Trash pile. Before you cry "Heresy!" let me explain. Office supplies build up over time—often, over a *long* time—and we seldom clear them out. During that period, technology, tastes, and needs change, leaving some of those items decidedly less useful.

I'm embarrassed to admit it, but during my last major purge, I uncovered a package of photo corners (my pictures are all digitized), a box of floppy disks, VHS labels, and—believe it or not—typewriter correction tape! Clearly, these items no longer had any rightful place in my office. I'm sure I'm not the only one who's discovered outmoded supplies in a modern workspace; dig deep, and you may unearth a few antiquities of your own. These items may still be functional, but they're largely obsolete; and if they're of no use to you, or anyone else, you know where they belong. (Of course, choose the Transfer pile over Trash if you think you can find a taker.)

While we're on the topic of Trash, here's something else to add to the list: broken computer and electronic equipment. In most cases, we've already replaced these items with bright, shiny new ones. So then why does our six-year-old monitor, which no longer shows the slightest flicker at the press of the power button, still reside in the far corner of the office? Do we really expect to bring it back to life if our new one suddenly fails? Given that most of us don't have the technological prowess to fix it ourselves, or the resources to locate the needed replacement parts, we'd have to schlep it to a repair shop (if we could find one); and the cost to repair it may very well be comparable to buying a new one. If you're still housing a printer, computer, or other piece of equipment that has long ago given up the ghost, say your final farewell; give it a proper burial, and reclaim that valuable space.

Further candidates for your Trash pile are paperwork and supplies related to past projects and interests. If you're no longer involved with them, set the stuff free. I know from experience that it's tempting to retain such items as proof of your hard work. That's exactly how I felt about my graduate school notebooks; they represented the blood, sweat, and tears of an arduous course of study. However, the physics, calculus, and chemistry contained therein were irrelevant to my new career. The day the recycling truck hauled them away, I felt a hundred pounds lighter—and ready to embrace my future, instead of hold on to my past.

As you're evaluating your stuff, make generous use of your Transfer pile. Even though *you* no longer need fifty fluorescent file folders or a lifetime supply of No. 2 pencils, someone else might; and that someone else may be a school, hospital, or nonprofit, whose money is better spent providing services than buying office supplies. Computers, monitors, fax machines, and other equipment can be particularly valuable to such organizations. Make some phone calls, and offer up your excess; the time and effort spent to find them a new home is well worth the good karma. Save your donation receipts, and take a tax write-off if possible.

Unless your office is small, or your workload light, you'll probably find plenty of items for your Treasure pile. This is where the soul-searching, item counting, and decision making come in. Ideally, we want to strike that perfect balance where we have "just enough" to do our work, with nothing extra to hinder our productivity. Candidates for this coveted category include the following: supplies and equipment you use regularly, current issues of magazines and catalogs, paperwork you need to address, paperwork from the recent past, paperwork that needs to be held for a certain number of years, and paperwork that must be stored indefinitely. We'll address these items in detail as we work through the steps that follow.

Reason for each item

As you contemplate your reason for keeping each item, bear the following in mind: just because it's an "office supply" doesn't give it a free pass. Not every kind of office supply belongs in *your* office. Each item must prove that it's pulling its weight, or risk getting a pink slip. If your home office is like most, space and storage are at a premium. Therefore, you'll have to be brutally honest about what you use and need; otherwise, you may feel like you're working in a supply closet!

Now that you've purged the battered, the broken, and the obsolete, take a careful look at your leftover items. Ask hard questions to determine what makes the cut; you're not running a shelter for wayward supplies, after all. Do you really need five different colors of highlighters, or six different sizes of envelopes? When's the last time you used the voice recorder? How many different ways do you need to tell the date and time (i.e., if you own a watch, computer, and cell phone, are a desk clock and calendar necessary)? Does the paperweight do its job, or just hang around looking pretty? They may seem like trivial items, barely worth a second thought; but together they add up to significant desk space.

We must be similarly rigorous with our paperwork, or it can quickly get out of control. Give each piece of paper a grilling, particularly if it's not a legal or financial document. Consider whether you need the paper itself, or simply the information—if the latter, scan it or type the pertinent details into a digital file. Furthermore, think long and hard before you print *anything*—why generate more paper to deal with down the road? Leave emails in your virtual inbox, and bookmark webpages for future reference. If you're worried you won't be able to access the information at a later date, print it to a PDF file—that way, you'll have a copy on your hard drive, and can view it anytime. (To do this, you'll need software such as CutePDF, PrimoPDF, or Pdf995.) This strategy is ideal for online receipts and payment confirmations; it provides the proof you need, without all the clutter. Just be sure to back up your files regularly, to prevent any data loss.

Catalogs are also prime candidates for decluttering. First, consider whether you need to keep (or receive) them at all. Most retailers display their entire product lines on their websites; and it's often easier to find an item in an online catalog than a paper one. If you need the physical copy, retain only the latest issue, as older ones may have discontinued items and outdated pricing. If you're keeping a catalog for one item, tear out the relevant page and recycle the rest. Better yet: scan the page, or bookmark the item on the retailer's website.

Finally, question each piece of office equipment. If you only photocopy or fax something once or twice a year, would you be better off seeking these services elsewhere? Is it really worth devoting desk space to a seldom-used machine? Specialty printers (such as color and photo printers) also deserve a hard look. Are you using them enough to justify their presence, and that of their accessories (like special paper, ink, and cables)?

Does the binding machine, laminator, or digitizing tablet have a layer of dust on it? Anything that's used once in a blue moon shouldn't be taking up valuable desk space. Consider selling it, donating it, or at least putting it into storage until needed.

Everything in its place

Having a place for everything, and putting everything in its place, is the single best way to keep a tidy desk. Instead of letting all those pens, paperclips, and rubber bands run wild in your workspace, corral them into designated spots and *make sure they stay there*. Assign specific places for file folders, incoming mail, outgoing mail, catalogs, magazines, receipts, and every category of office supply and paperwork you can imagine. If it helps, label containers, drawers, shelves, or even areas of your desk, to remind you of its appropriate contents. Be positively militant about it. Check on the troops regularly, and if you find any have gone AWOL, round them up (and whip them into shape) immediately.

Paperwork, too, needs to have a place—and that place shouldn't be in a pile on your desk! Devise a filing system, and stick to it; that means every letter, bill, statement, receipt, article, or random piece of paper should have someplace to go when it enters the room. Think of it like checking into a hotel. Water bill: inbox. Bank statement: top drawer, second folder. Article on raised bed gardening: middle shelf, third binder from the left. Don't make them hang around your desk until you figure out how to accommodate them; it'll get way too crowded. Take the time to develop a system that works for you, and implement it as soon as possible. Nothing's set in stone; you can always tweak it as you go along. Above all, don't feel you have to provide shelter for every stray piece of paper that happens along; sometimes the right place for something is in the recycling bin.

With these points in mind, arrange your stuff into your Inner Circle, Outer Circle, and Deep Storage. In the office, your Inner Circle should consist of all the supplies you use on a regular basis, and the paperwork with which you're currently dealing. That means that your pens, pencils, paperclips, envelopes, stamps, notepads, checkbook, and incoming and outgoing mail (among other things) should be within arm's reach. Practically speaking, if you're sitting at your desk, you should be able to grab anything out of your Inner Circle without getting up from your chair. Therefore, the furnishings of your Inner Circle will include your desk, as well as any nearby filing cabinets or bookshelves. Reserve these spaces for the things you use most often; most importantly, don't let them become overrun with less serviceable items.

In your Outer Circle belongs paperwork with which you've recently dealt, and files you may need to reference in the future. Many of us keep bills, receipts, and statements for a certain period of time before purging them. If you use such a system, store them in your Outer Circle. You'll be able to consult them if necessary, and periodically thin them out. This is also the place for catalogs, journals, research articles, and other reference materials you don't use regularly; store them in slightly harder-to-reach areas, like high and low shelves, or file cabinets across the room. Furthermore, your Outer Circle should contain backup supplies like printer paper, ink cartridges, and extra file folders. Stash them so that they're out of the way of daily activity, but easily accessible when needed.

Even if we make little use of Deep Storage elsewhere in our homes, we'll likely need some for the office. Unfortunately, most of life's major events—like graduations, marriages, births, and house purchases—come with paperwork that must be retained indefinitely. Moreover, the government requires all of us taxpayers to keep our returns (and their supporting material) for a certain amount of time. With regard to legal documents, real estate records, and important financial statements, we have little choice but to follow the "rules" (and you know I love to break them, so I don't say this lightly).

No matter how minimalist you aspire to be, don't be tempted to "digitize and declutter" these essential documents; in most situations that require them, only the originals will do (and they can be a bear to replace if you've lost them). By all means, make digital *copies*, but accept the fact that you'll have to retain at least *some* paper documents. Since you're unlikely to reference them regularly (if ever), feel free to stow them out of sight, and out of the way. Your less sensitive Deep Storage files may be kept in a closet, attic, garage, or basement (if dry). Those of a more irreplaceable nature (birth certificates, marriage certificates, and other identification papers) should be stored in a fireproof box or safety deposit box. If you live in a disaster-prone area, consider keeping essential paperwork in a "go bag," that you can grab on the run while evacuating.

All surfaces clear

Focus the bulk of your energy on the most important surface in the room: your desk or worktable. As you're probably well aware, you can't get anything done when it's covered with stuff. Treat it as flex space, and try to clean it off when you wrap up each day's work—as if someone else might come in and use your desk tomorrow. (Of course, it'll only be you; but wouldn't it be wonderful to sit down at a clean space?) Keep office supplies in drawers or containers instead of scattered across the desk; invest in a standing or wall-mounted rack to hold incoming paper and mail; and use a bulletin board for reminders, cards, notes, and random scraps of paper, rather than let them invade your workspace.

An amazing (and distressing) thing happens in office spaces: everything that provides the least bit of horizontal space often turns into a surface! I've seen stacks of papers, and miscellaneous supplies, perched on top of shelves, filing cabinets, window ledges, printers, scanners, chairs, lamps, boxes, and planters. Please, resist the urge to "paper" your surroundings; it's chaotic, it's unorganized, and it makes it almost impossible to find stuff. Clear surfaces are not only pleasing to the eye, they're beneficial to the mind. You'll be able to think more clearly, and work more productively, without all the visual distraction.

Furthermore, it shouldn't have to be said, but I'll say it all the same: the floor is not a filing system. But you know what happens: once all those other surfaces are filled to the brim, the overflow typically lands on that big, flat surface underfoot. Office floors are fertile ground; they'll sprout stacks upon stacks of books, magazines, and paperwork that grow at alarming speeds. Avoid planting those initial seeds, or you may end up with a forest. I usually advocate some tough-love decluttering over buying additional storage; but if you've truly run out of space, and can't purge enough old stuff to make room for the new, acquire another filing cabinet. It's better than wading through piles of papers just to get to your desk!

Usually, we need only concern ourselves with horizontal surfaces. In this room, however, a common office item threatens our vertical surfaces as well: the sticky note. These little yellow squares, with their unique ability to cling to any available object, are the bane of a minimalist office. Beware: an innocent handful at the base of your monitor can multiply quickly, until you're peering at your screen through a ruffly yellow frame. Vexed by these critters, I finally started a digital document, in which I entered every scrap of information they contained; thereafter, instead of jotting down physical notes, I'd type them straight into said document. If you prefer, you can download software that manages such virtual notes for you; or you can keep such reminders, and random information, stored on your smartphone or PDA. Find a solution that works for you, and keeps your surfaces clear.

Modules

As you sort through your stuff, gather like items into modules. In the world of office supplies, segregation is a good thing; paperclips shouldn't be partying with the rubber bands, stamps shouldn't be socializing with the staples, and files shouldn't be fraternizing with magazines and catalogs. Consolidating similar items not only helps you locate them faster, it illuminates how many you actually have. When you've corralled thirty pencils into one place, you'll realize the absurdity of having so many—and with any luck, be inspired to let the bulk of them go. For each category of supplies, cull the contents and give them their own special container—even if it's just a ziplock bag, or slot in a drawer organizer.

Alternatively, consider organizing your supplies by activity. Such a strategy can boost productivity, and ensure you always have the appropriate supplies on hand to complete regular tasks. Examples include a bill-paying module, in which you keep your checkbook, envelopes, stamps, and a pen; a tax return module, in which you gather all the relevant receipts and documentation throughout the year; or project modules, in which you store materials and paperwork needed for specific business, research, or writing endeavors.

Apply the modular concept to paperwork as well, to consolidate similar information in one place. We all do a simple version of this when we file by subject matter. Take it one step further, though; instead of alphabetizing your files (or randomly throwing them in the drawer), organize them into distinct sections: investments, utilities, insurance, recipes, et cetera. If you save magazine articles, store each one in a sheet protector, and arrange them into binders by topic. That way, when you're ready to read about planting tomatoes, you can pull down the gardening binder and have at it. You can also consolidate various tidbits of information into single documents or fact sheets (like a list of emergency numbers, birthdays, or holiday gift ideas). This strategy eliminates excess paperwork, and provides pertinent information at a glance.

If you lack a dedicated workspace, your whole office may be a module. We're not all blessed with an extra bedroom or dining room that can be transformed into a home office. Some of us may be relegated to a desk in the corner of the living room, or a retrofitted closet; others may carry their entire "office" in a tote bag or plastic tub, using any available surface as temporary flex space. How wonderful would it be, actually, to reduce our office supplies, files, and equipment to a portable container! Then, when the sun is shining and birds are chirping, we can set up shop on our front porch, back yard, or local park. Ah, the minimalist dream!

Limits

When you're decluttering your workspace, you'll come to love the concept of limits. They'll help you gain the upper hand over the stuff on your desk, in your drawers, and in your files.

As you consolidated your office supplies into modules, you likely found you had far more pens, paperclips, staples, rubber bands, and other miscellaneous items than you'll ever realistically use. It's not necessarily your fault; many of these items are sold only in bulk quantities. Others, like pens, follow you home from the office, jump into your bag while you're out and about, and multiply under cover of night. Set limits for each category, and in the future, keep a minimalist mindset when shopping for supplies. Pass on the super-size packages, unless you plan to use the entire amount. Alternatively, split such purchases with a friend, family member, or colleague, or find other creative ways to distribute them: give them as gifts, use them as party favors, or simply be a good person and donate the excess.

Limits also help keep our paperwork under control. We know what happens when we file, and file, and file some more: we end up with bulging folders, the contents of which spill over into additional ones; and before we know it, we're out shopping for another filing cabinet. Filing should be a two-way street: stuff should come *out*, as well as go in. To this end, limit your paperwork on specific subjects to what will fit into one file folder—and when that folder gets too fat, purge its contents (by that time, some of the papers will surely be outdated).

Be particularly strict with nonessential papers—you know, the ones you hold on to because you "might need" the information someday. I used to tear out interesting articles, pictures, and ideas from magazines, and stash them in three-ring binders; after all, I reasoned, it was more minimalist than saving the whole issue. Eventually, however, I accumulated an entire shelf's worth of binders (and rarely referenced or re-read the material.) Thereafter, I limited myself to just one binder, devoted to the information I found most valuable; and when it became full, I'd sacrifice some of the old articles in favor of new ones. (When I bought a scanner, I eliminated that!)

We can declutter until the day is long, but one of the keys to minimalist living is controlling the *inflow*. In most cases, this power lies entirely in our hands; we can refrain from shopping, refuse freebies, and opt out of gift exchanges, effectively shutting the door on stuff. The problem: in that door lies a mail slot. And through that slot will pour all kinds of useless, unwanted, and uninvited clutter, almost every single day. We must focus our efforts, then, on limiting the incoming contents. While it's tempting to remove our mailboxes or board up our slots, such extremes aren't necessary; we'll explore some kinder, gentler ways to stop the postal deluge.

You can eliminate the bulk of your junk mail by putting a freeze on your credit report, or registering with OptOutPrescreen.com (a joint venture of the major credit reporting agencies). Once you do, companies will no longer be able to run credit checks on your name, and send you pre-approved offers. You can also contact the Direct Marketing Association (www.the-dma.org) to opt out of direct mail from their member companies; they'll add your name to their "Do Not Mail" database. Additionally, it pays to review those Privacy Policies that come with your bank and credit card statements; call the provided number, and tell them you *don't* want to receive marketing materials from them or their partner companies.

Henceforth, guard your name and address like a closely held secret. Refrain from giving this information to retailers: don't sign up for in-store rewards programs and discount cards, and decline to provide it at the checkout register. Don't participate in surveys, sweepstakes, and giveaways—more often than not, they're sneaky ways for marketers to snag your contact details. Don't send in product registration and warranty cards either, or your name and address will end up on a plethora of mailing lists;

your receipt is usually sufficient proof of purchase to obtain warranty service.

Furthermore, keep your name and address out of the local phone book; that'll also prevent it from being published online, where marketers across the country can easily obtain it. When you move, don't fill out the U.S. Postal Service change of address forms, or your junk mail will surely follow you to your new home. Instead, personally contact people and companies to provide them with your new address. Rather than subscribe to newspapers and magazines, read them online; the latter are particularly notorious for selling your information—ensuring you'll receive not only your monthly issues, but a barrage of advertisements, solicitations, and catalogs.

Speaking of catalogs: do what you can to avoid them. I learned the hard way that you can never request a catalog from just *one* company; most belong to marketing networks that share customers' contact details. Once you're in their database, you'll be getting ten different catalogs in a few months, and thirty by the end of the year. If you find yourself in this unfortunate situation (as I have), take steps to put a stop to it immediately. I use the brute force method: calling the customer service number on every catalog I receive, and asking them to remove my name from their mailing list. If you prefer, you can sign up with Catalog Choice (www.catalogchoice.org); they'll contact the merchants, and express your mailing preferences, on your behalf.

The strategies outlined above will eliminate most of your unsolicited mail. If you'd like, you can also limit incoming paperwork from companies you do business with, and opt to receive electronic communications instead. For example, sign up for online billing. Your desk will stay much neater when your gas, electric, water, sewer, telephone, cable, insurance, and cell phone bills arrive by email instead of post. You can even choose to have the amount you owe automatically debited from your bank account. Similarly, register to receive bank and credit card statements online; you'll get an email notification when they're available, and can print them to a PDF file. By doing so, you'll avoid the advertisements and offers that come stuffed in the envelopes, and reduce the paperwork you have to file.

Whew! I know it's a lot of work, but when it comes to minimizing mail and paperwork, the best defense is a good offense. Your efforts will be duly rewarded when you gaze into your lovely, empty mailbox, and sit down at your beautiful, paper-free desk.

If one comes in, one goes out

Let's face it: we've all been guilty of hanging on to old office and computer equipment. We go out and buy the latest and greatest technology, imagining the leaps and bounds by which our productivity will increase; and ask ourselves why on earth we kept that old computer, printer, or fax machine for so long. We excitedly set up our shiny new one; and after we've switched it on, made sure it's working, and congratulated ourselves on its purchase, we notice the old one sitting there, forgotten and forlorn. Before we can pick it up and haul it out to the curb, a wave of guilt and sentimentality washes over us; we can't possibly get rid of it if it's still *working*, can we? It served us well for so many years; and besides, it'd be good to have a backup if the new one should fail...

Stop right there! Your office is not a retirement home for old and outdated machines. Be realistic: if your laser printer broke down, would you really dust off the dot-matrix? After using a thirty-inch LCD monitor, could you go back to a fifteen-inch CRT? If your laptop bit the dust, would you whip out your old computer without missing a beat? Fat chance—you're far more likely to use your warranty coverage, or buy a replacement, than bring one of those has-beens back into service. From now on, whenever you upgrade such an item, donate the old one—better to let someone else *use* it, than let it waste away on the sidelines.

Apply the One In-One Out rule to the little stuff as well; the fact that something is small doesn't justify having multiples of it. How many staplers, rulers, tape dispensers, pencil sharpeners, and pairs of scissors do you have? If the answer is more than one, it's too many! Things like staplers don't need understudies; in the rare case they fail, they can be replaced cheaply and easily. Don't devote valuable space to storing backups. Ditch the duplicates, and when you bring home a better, newer, or shinier version of something you already have, send the old one on its way. (If the new one is simply an advertising gimmick—like a pen or ruler with a corporate logo—don't bring it home at all.)

The One In-One Out rule will also keep your paperwork in check. When you file a new bill or statement, throw the oldest on record away (assuming you don't need it for tax, financial, or legal purposes). In other words, if you keep a year's worth of utility bills, toss last June's when you receive this June's. When you file away that new article on real estate investing, get rid of an old, outdated one. In fact, for every piece of paper you put into a folder, challenge yourself to remove another. This method keeps your files fresh, and reduces the need to purge them later on. Do the same for magazines, newspapers, and catalogs; as soon as the new issue arrives, put the old one in the recycling bin.

Narrow it down

To have a truly minimalist office, narrow down your supplies to the bare essentials. If you mail only ten envelopes a year, for instance, you don't need five hundred on hand. If you rarely require a rubber band, eliminate the stash in your desk drawer. If you do most of your work electronically, consider culling your pens.

In this day and age, there's little need to stock up—let the big box stationers store your office supplies for you. Almost anything you require can be readily obtained at your local store or on the Internet; online orders from major retailers are commonly delivered free of charge the following day. It's like having a giant, on-demand, off-site supply closet! Find your own comfort level; if you feel you can't function without a five-year supply of paper, printer cartridges, or sticky notes, so be it. But if your space is tight, your storage sparse, or you simply enjoy sitting at a clear, empty desk, know that you probably *can* get by with less. At the very least, it's a fun experiment—and the earth won't stop spinning if you run short on paperclips.

With a little creativity, you can also narrow down your office equipment. Instead of having a fax machine, sign up for an online fax service and send documents straight from your computer. Consider dropping your landline in favor of your cell phone, and using voice mail instead of an answering machine. Make your laptop your primary computer, and ditch the separate desktop. Choose multi-functional devices—such as a printer that also scans and photocopies—instead of owning (and finding space for) three separate machines. Have a blast figuring out how to get the job done with the least amount of equipment!

Finally, call up all your minimalist might and turn it loose on your paperwork. We've already talked about ways to limit our incoming mail: like having our names removed from marketers' lists, and signing up for online statements and billing. However, we also want to narrow down the paper we already *have*. For this purpose, I highly recommend investing in a scanner (or a printer with a scanning function). Yes, it's one more piece of office equipment; but it'll likely take up less space than the stacks of paper it eliminates. You'll wonder how you ever lived without this wondrous device! I digitize articles, greeting cards, letters, bills, statements, instructions, photos, pamphlets, and more—anything for which I need the information, but not the original copy. (Of course, be diligent about purging computer files, so you don't end up with digital clutter.)

Before you go too crazy with the scanner, though, understand that you'll always need to keep *some* paper copies around. Specific time frames for retaining documents are highly dependent on your personal situation, tax and legal requirements, and common practice in your area. The following guidelines are provided only to give you a general sense of what you might be expected to keep; consult your financial advisor, or the Internet, for more specific and up-to-date details.

Typically, the papers you'll need to store forever include tax returns, real estate records, annual investment account statements, and loan documentation. It's also wise to keep your final utility bills when you move, in case you need proof of residence. Retain receipts for big-ticket items (like cars and appliances) for as long as you own them (or longer, if a tax-deductible expense); you may need them to make an insurance claim, or receive warranty service. I think I speak for all minimalists when I say that no one *wants* to hang on to this stuff; but make your peace with it, and put it into Deep Storage—it could make your life a lot easier in the long run.

As far as other financial documents go, opinions differ widely on how long you should hold them. I've seen it recommended to keep bank statements for as long as seven years, and credit card statements for as long as three. Utility bills can generally be tossed after a year, unless you need them to support your tax returns (then keep them for seven). You can also purge pay stubs annually, after you've reconciled them with your W-2 forms. ATM slips, deposit slips, and debit and credit card receipts (for minor purchases) can usually be thrown away after you've checked them for accuracy against your monthly statement. Again, these are very broad guidelines; consider your particular situation, and comfort level, when deciding what to purge.

Everyday maintenance

Our offices are dynamic spaces; there's stuff coming in, stuff going out, and stuff moving around on a daily basis. Therefore, we can't simply do a large-scale declutter and call it a day. Keeping them streamlined requires constant vigilance; the speed at which office supplies can spread out, and paperwork pile up, is astounding!

To maintain your minimalist office, set up a system for incoming paperwork so it's dealt with immediately. Be a good gatekeeper: keep a recycling bin by the front door, and stop catalogs, circulars, takeout menus, and other junk mail from even entering the house. For the mail that makes it into your office: open each piece and *act* on it at once, instead of stacking it up on your desk. Shred credit card solicitations, balance transfer checks, and other nonessential paper with personal information; scan, or file away, any documents you need to keep; and sort bills that require payment, letters that require action, or information that requires review, into the appropriate inbox or slot on your desk. In an ideal system, each piece of paper would be handled just a single time.

When you finish your work for the day, return all supplies to their designated places, and files to their appropriate folders. If it's more efficient to keep them together, set up a "working" module for that particular project—preferably in some kind of container, rather than spread out across your desk. Then, you can pick up right where you left off, without having to gather up the necessary materials; and you won't have to push them aside to use your desk in the meantime. Also, be on the lookout for refugee items from elsewhere in the house; return your child's homework, your spouse's novel, or your dog's chew toy to its respective owner, before it has a chance to settle in. You have enough to worry about with your own stuff!

Everyday maintenance will keep your desk clear, and your stuff under control. However, you'll still need to purge your files periodically. Try as you might to follow the One In-One Out rule, chances are you'll still end up with a little more "in" than "out." Scan your file folders on a monthly or quarterly basis, and toss (that is, shred or recycle) what's no longer relevant—the majority of paperwork is time-sensitive and quickly outdated. Furthermore, do a full-scale purge on an annual basis, and clear out the old to make way for the new. I like to schedule this for early January, and have a fresh start for the new year!

25

Kitchen and dining room

If asked to name the most functional room in the house, many of us would choose the kitchen. After all, it's the place where we store, prepare, serve, and consume the food that sustains us. It also serves as a popular gathering place for the family. Given its significant role in our lives, no wonder the kitchen contains a lot of stuff! Too much stuff, however, can actually diminish the room's functionality, and make it unpleasant to work and hang out in. So let's see how we can pare things down, and make this space as streamlined as possible.

Start over

Have you ever wandered through a kitchen showroom (or browsed through the pages of your favorite decorator magazine) and fantasized about trading in your kitchen for the one on display? Did you eye its gleaming surfaces with envy, thinking how wonderful it would be to cook in such a sleek and functional environment? Have you ever thought that life would be perfect if only you had more cabinet storage?

Much of the time, what attracts us to showroom kitchens isn't the high-end appliances, specialty countertops, or fancy cabinetry—it's the space! Display kitchens are invariably clean, spare, and free of clutter, and include little more than a handful of appliances and tableware. That's what makes them so lovely and inviting. The good news: you don't have to spend a fortune on renovations to achieve this look. You can give your kitchen a dramatic makeover simply by decluttering.

Remember how we talked about moving day, and how wonderful it felt to unpack your things into a fresh, uncluttered space? Think back to those beautiful empty shelves and cabinets, and how nice it was to line up your plates, glasses, utensils, and gadgets in perfect order. Unfortunately, between then and now, things have likely become a little more crowded and a little less organized. (I suspect our tableware is throwing wild, late-night parties in our kitchen cupboards!) Not to worry; we're going to recreate that first day by Starting Over, one cabinet at a time.

To this end, empty every drawer, cabinet, cupboard, and shelf in turn. As always, don't be tempted to leave something in place because you "know" you will put it back there. That's cheating! Remove every piece, until the space in question is entirely bare—that means all your plates, coffee cups, glassware, forks, spoons, knives, pots, pans, gadgets, appliances, food, foil, takeout containers, and even the contents of your "junk" drawer. Remember, the idea is not to choose the things we'll get rid of, but to choose the things we'll keep. Once everything's out, you're going to examine them thoroughly, and return only your best, most useful, and most essential items to their places. Pretend you're outfitting a brand-new dream kitchen, like the ones featured in magazines; why should yours be any less fabulous?

Should you have any lingering doubts about completely clearing the contents, this method yields a special bonus: the fantastic opportunity to *clean* those cabinets. How long has it been since they've had a good scrubbing? In the course of cooking, kitchens get greasy and dirty; and while we're pretty good at keeping the surfaces sparkling, we tend to forget about the *insides* of our cabinets. Grime, dust, and spills build up over time and lead to unhygienic conditions. So while you're eliminating the clutter, eliminate the dirt as well (how efficient we minimalists are!). Scrub them spotless, and you'll truly have a "fresh" start!

Trash, Treasure, or Transfer

As you're cleaning out your cabinets, cupboards, and countertops, you'll probably come across plenty of items for your Trash pile. If you haven't purged your pantry lately, much of it may be food; check the expiration dates of every item you touch, and ditch anything that's spoiled, expired, or otherwise past its prime. Spices, sauces, and condiments also have limited shelf lives, so don't let your decluttering pass them by. If that bottle of soy sauce is older than your toddler, toss it and treat yourself to a new one when needed. Do the same for other perishables, particularly if you can't remember how long you've had them, or the last time you used them.

Other Trash may also be lurking in your kitchen—in the form of chipped plates, cracked glasses, and bent or mangled silverware (like the fork that got caught in the garbage disposal). Give your food the respect it deserves, and serve it on (and with) undamaged tableware. Don't save these battered pieces as backups for your better stuff; they're difficult to fix, depressing to look at, and dangerous to use. Send them to that Great Kitchen Table in the sky! Discard broken gadgets and appliances, too; if you haven't already made the effort to repair them, you evidently can live without them.

In your Transfer pile belong all those items that are useful to someone other than *you*. For some reason, we tend to accumulate much more kitchenware than we need or use on a daily basis. Some of it enters our lives as wedding and housewarming gifts, others as impulse purchases. (I'm willing to bet that most of us have at least one "miraculous," "time-saving" culinary gadget we saw on a late-night infomercial—and haven't used since the day we bought it.) Some items may have seemed practical when we purchased them, but turned out to be too complicated or time-consuming for our lifestyles; so give that pasta machine or ice cream maker to someone who'll appreciate it. Be honest with yourself as you're sorting through your stuff; if you avoid using your food processor because it's a pain to clean, take this opportunity to set it free.

Don't forget that food can go into your Transfer pile as well. Our tastes and dietary needs change over time, and the shelf life of some foods can outlast our desire for them. We may grow tired of tomato soup before we finish our stash, or decide we'd rather eat fresh fruit than the canned stuff on our shelves. Don't feel bad; regard it as a wonderful chance to do a good deed! Donate any unwanted canned or packaged items to a local food bank or soup kitchen. The castoffs from your pantry can keep someone else from going hungry.

You may have difficulty purging some kitchen items out of concern that you'll need them someday (and you're pretty sure it'll be the day after you get rid of them). If so, create a Temporarily Undecided box. Put in it those things you don't use regularly, but think you *might use* sometime soon—like the bread machine, muffin tins, and fancy cake decorating supplies. Mark the box with a date, and donate whatever you don't retrieve after a specific period of time (say six months, or a year). It's a great way to deal with those "on-the-fence" items; they're available if necessary, but won't take up precious space in your cabinets and drawers. Better yet, you'll see what life is like without them—and you may decide you don't miss them at all.

Your Treasure pile should contain only those things you rely on, cherish, or otherwise use on a regular basis. These candidates are competing for a coveted spot in your cupboards, and will have to prove that they're indispensable. As we go through the following steps, we'll examine them closely, and decide exactly what's worthy of a place in our kitchens.

Reason for each item

The kitchen is a great place to have a conversation with your stuff. Some items have been lurking in the shadows for so long, you may not know them anymore. Here's your chance to get reacquainted, and make sure your relationship is still mutually beneficial.

What are you and what do you do? We shouldn't have to ask, but let's admit it—sometimes we don't have a clue. These days, there's a kitchen gadget for every conceivable task; and just because that pineapple corer or pastry wheel seemed indispensable when we bought it, doesn't mean we'll be able to identify it a few years later. In this case, a little mystery is *not* a good thing. If you don't know what something does, it's obviously not essential in your kitchen. Send it on to another home—it could make a fun gift for a culinary friend, who might actually know what to do with it.

How often do I use you? Ah, the million dollar question! Items that evoke the response "every day" or "once a week" can start making their way back into your cabinets. Just because you only use the turkey baster once a year, however, doesn't mean you have to get rid of it; such knowledge can simply help you decide where to store it. If you use something less than once a year, some deliberation is in order: is that item really worth the space it's taking up? Nine times out of ten it's highly unlikely you'll miss it.

Do you make my life easier (or more difficult)? Sure, I can cook rice and boil water on the stovetop, but my rice cooker and tea kettle make my life easier. Therefore, they earn a spot in my kitchen. On the other hand, I let go of my cappuccino machine because I hated cleaning it, and found it much more pleasant to go out for a cup instead. If something's difficult to set up, use, or clean up (and the rewards are not worth the effort), consider giving it the heave-ho—and find an alternative way to meet that particular need.

Do you have a twin? Kitchen items are like office supplies, in that they seem to reproduce of their own accord. Unless you're extremely dexterous, you can't use more than one potato peeler or can opener at a time. Furthermore, should one fail, you can easily acquire another. Ditch the doubles, and free up the space for something more useful.

Are you too good to use? I bet your stuff didn't see this one coming! Wedding china and inherited silverware can become pretty smug, figuring they can hang around for decades doing virtually nothing. Oftentimes, they're right: they get squirreled away in dining hutches, and rarely see the light of day. We're too sentimental to get rid of them, and too scared to use them (lest we break a piece and have to hunt for a replacement). In the case of silver pieces, we may simply dread polishing them. Here's a radical thought: instead of the full service, keep only one or two place settings—use them as decoration, or for romantic candlelight dinners with your spouse.

Everything in its place

The kitchen serves a number of different functions, from food preparation to dining to paying bills; therefore, dividing it into activity zones can help us keep things organized and efficient. Determine the areas in which you perform certain tasks—like prepping, cooking, serving, dining, washing up, and waste disposal—and store related tools and equipment in their designated zones. For example, keep the knives where you chop, the pots near the stove, and the dishwashing liquid under the sink. Assign specific spots to miscellaneous tasks like bill-paying, to prevent pens, checkbooks, and calculators from piling up on the counter or finding their way into your spice drawer.

Within your zones, reserve a particular spot for every last item; it's the best way to maintain order in such a crowded space. The plates should always be stacked just so, and the cups and glasses should fall into place like a chorus line. Forks, knives, spoons, pots, pans, and appliances should all have specific positions to which to return. Imagine drawing imaginary lines around each item, like a designated parking spot. If it helps, stick little adhesive labels ("pasta pot," "sauce pan," "cereal bowls") to remind you (and family members) exactly where everything goes. Otherwise, you can end up with a disorganized jumble—the perfect environment for clutter to hide.

At the same time, assign items to your Inner Circle, Outer Circle, and Deep Storage. Your Inner Circle should contain the plates, pots, pans, utensils, drinkware, gadgets, appliances, and food you use on a regular basis. They should be within arm's reach, in the zone in which they're typically needed; you shouldn't have to get on a stepladder to retrieve your coffee mug, or cross the room to get your paring knife. Dedicate your most easily accessible storage spots to these items, and keep them free of other, seldom-used stuff. That way, you won't have to root through a drawer full of miscellany to find your measuring spoons. Such organization makes the process of preparing and serving a meal much more pleasant!

Store those items you use less than once a week, but more than once a year, in your Outer Circle. Everyone's contents will be different, but will generally include things like cake pans, cookie sheets, muffin tins, waffle irons, blenders, salad spinners, ice cream makers, bread machines, crock pots, and champagne glasses. Reserve your higher cabinets, lower drawers, and deeper corners for these less frequently used pieces; you may have to bend, stretch, or reach a little in order to retrieve them. They shouldn't be *too* difficult to access, but they don't need to be at your fingertips.

Finally, put the kitchen equipment and dining supplies you use once a year (or less) into Deep Storage. Turkey roasters, punch bowls, gravy boats, soufflé dishes, dessert stands, serving platters, and specialty linens—basically, items you use only for holidays or entertaining—are likely candidates for this category. Store these in the highest, lowest, and farthest reaches of your kitchen or dining room. If you don't have the storage space, you can even stash them in the garage, basement, or attic; just be sure to properly wrap or contain them to keep out dirt, moisture, and roving critters. However, just because you *can* put things into Deep Storage doesn't mean you *have* to. If you don't need such items for entertaining (or could borrow them if necessary), don't bother keeping them at all. I don't own a single item on the above list, and have never felt less of a hostess because of it!

All surfaces clear

Our kitchen countertops are extremely important surfaces, as they're used for food preparation three times daily (or more, if we count those mid-afternoon munchies and late-night snacks). When they're covered with stuff—be it kitchen gadgets, dirty dishes, knickknacks, mail, or recipe books—it's nearly impossible to fix a nice meal. And if there's no room to wash, chop, slice, dice, pare, and peel, you'll be more likely to throw some frozen fare in the microwave or stop for takeout. Don't let clutter cheat you out of a healthy, home-cooked dinner!

Cooking is difficult when you're constantly moving items out of the way, or you're confined to a tiny section of the countertop. Therefore, your kitchen surfaces should hold only those items you use daily (if that). Consider wall-mounted racks for spices, knives, and other implements, and hanging baskets for fruits and vegetables, to keep them off the counters. Appliances that mount under upper cabinets—like microwaves, toaster ovens, and coffee makers—can also free up valuable space. For an attractive and functional kitchen, skip the cutesy tchotchkes and cookie jars, and opt for sleek and understated instead. I promise you this: simply getting all that clutter off the countertops will energize you, and inspire you to work some culinary magic.

The kitchen has long been considered the heart of the home, a place for families to gather and share quality time; but because it's such a happening hot spot, its counters are magnets for clutter. Make sure everyone who plops down a toy, book, newspaper, or piece of mail takes it with them when they leave the room. (Or warn them they may find it in your next casserole!) Be vigilant of the floor as well, and keep it free of book bags, playthings, and pet supplies; when you're carrying heavy pots and hot liquids, things underfoot can be a recipe for disaster. Do a clean sweep of the area, and return all stray items to their rightful places.

Likewise, keep kitchen and dining tables clear and at the ready for your next meal. In most households, such surfaces are used for a variety of activities, as well they should be. (Versatility is a good thing!) However, don't let homework assignments, craft projects, or tax returns swallow these tables whole, rendering them useless for their intended purpose. I've seen dining tables turned into ad hoc storage units, piled high with papers, books, magazines, toys, craft supplies, and other miscellaneous stuff. This surface certainly makes for great flex space; but when it's not being used, the dining table should hold nothing more than the next meal's accoutrements. If you *never* use the dining room for dining, consider ditching the table entirely and converting the room to serve another purpose (like a home office).

Finally, don't consider a meal "over" until every surface has been cleared. After you've finished cooking, put away all equipment and ingredients, and wipe down the countertop. Clear the table, and wash pots, pans, and dirty dishes (or at least load them into the dishwasher) immediately after each meal. Every night before you go to bed, scan your kitchen surfaces and tuck away any wayward items. It's a treat to start the next day with a clear countertop and empty sink!

Modules

You probably have a head start on this step, as the modules concept comes naturally in the kitchen. If you're already storing your cutlery, spices, or cake decorating supplies together, you're well on your way to a streamlined space.

Consolidating like with like is particularly valuable in the kitchen, where duplicate supplies and excess ingredients are common. It helps you pare down to the essentials, and prevents you from buying unnecessary extras—because you can see at a glance what you already have. If you keep all of your baking ingredients in one drawer, you'll be less likely to buy a second bottle of vanilla because you can't find the first. If you know you have six coffee cups, you'll think twice about purchasing a souvenir mug on your next trip. If you can see just how many forks, spoons, and knives you have, you may decline grandma's flatware and let your sister have it instead.

Modules reveal how certain items have accumulated (often unnoticed) over time. They make us ask questions like, "Why do we have eighteen drinking glasses for our family of four?" "Will we ever really use twenty pairs of chopsticks?" and "Why do I need two meat thermometers, three corkscrews, or four jars of cinnamon?" Culling duplicates is a fabulous decluttering opportunity. It's quick and easy, because we don't have to labor over decisions or worry about doing "without" something (we'll still have *one*, after all). It also creates breathing room in our cabinets and drawers, making it infinitely easier to put our hands on something when we need it. When we're cooking, the ability to quickly locate a certain ingredient or implement can spell the difference between "delicious" and "disaster!"

Gather your food into modules as well: store cereals, soups, and canned goods in designated sections on your shelves; keep cheese, vegetables, and condiments in their own areas of the refrigerator; and arrange cans and bottles of beverages by type. Organizing your provisions in such a way prevents overbuying and waste, as you can quickly scan your inventory before going to the store. You may even discover you have more of something than you'll ever likely consume; donate the excess to a food bank, rather than let it go to waste. On the flip side, you'll also see where you need to stock up, and can avoid running out unexpectedly.

Like it or not, most of our kitchens also contain the proverbial "junk" drawer—the place we put all those ketchup packets, takeout menus, batteries, birthday candles, twist ties, tea lights, sewing needles, scissors, plastic utensils, and other odd items that are too small, few, or uncategorizable to fit anywhere else. Does such a mish-mash of stuff have any business being in a minimalist kitchen? Sure, but under the following conditions: examine every last item, keep only those you'll actually use, and gather them into a single "utility" module (same drawer, new and improved name!). Contain related items in ziplock bags or slots of a drawer organizer. If everything is readily accessible, easily identifiable, and truly useful, there's no need to label it "junk."

Limits

Limiting our culinary items keeps them under control—and keeps our kitchens looking like those sleek, serene spaces we swoon over in magazines.

Let's start with tableware, since most of us have far more of it than we actually need. Strongly consider limiting your plates, cups, bowls, glasses, and utensils to match the size of your family; if your household contains only four people, why clutter your cabinets with sixteen place settings? Extra tableware only gives us an excuse to put off the dishwashing—making the job more difficult and unpleasant when we finally get around to it.

Ah, but what about guests, you say! By all means, take your entertaining habits into consideration when culling your supplies. Figure out the maximum number of people you regularly entertain, and save enough tableware to accommodate the group. The key word here is *regularly*—not every three years or so when you host a holiday dinner. If you throw a big extravaganza, you can always borrow pieces from family and friends; most will have extras they're willing to lend. If you feel you *must* keep all your place settings, at least limit the ones in your cabinets to your everyday needs—and put the rest into Deep Storage until they're required.

We'd also do well to limit our appliances and gadgets. Just because a tool exists for every culinary task, doesn't mean *we* have to own it. Keep the ones you use most often, and clear your space of the rest. Do the same for all those plastic takeout containers. They pile up quickly, as we hate to dispose of such potentially useful items; however, they often end up in a jumbled mess, cluttering up our cupboards. Determine the number you need, choose the sturdiest and most versatile pieces, and recycle or donate the excess.

Certainly limit the décor in your kitchen. A single bowl of fresh fruit or flowers is much more elegant than a counter full of knickknacks. Instead of decorative pieces, use your culinary ingredients to spruce up the room: pasta and beans look gorgeous in glass jars, spices are pleasing to the eye as well as the palette, and sprigs of lavender or other herbs give your kitchen a lovely, natural look. Appliances can also be decorative, as well as functional: a toaster, blender, or coffee maker in a fun color or sleek shape may be all the adornment your kitchen needs. Most importantly, limit the number of items per surface, so you can cook a meal without shoving stuff aside.

Furthermore, if space is at a premium, limit the amount of food you store. Keep enough on hand to accommodate an emergency; but question whether you really need a year's supply of beans, rice, coffee, or canned goods. Make an effort to regularly "eat through your pantry" and replenish it with fresh provisions, so that food won't spoil or go to waste. Keep good tabs on your inventory, and make shopping lists before going to the grocery store, to avoid buying (and storing) excessive amounts.

Finally, consider using limits to purge the clutter in your diet. An overabundance of food, or certain ingredients—like salt, fat, sugar, and preservatives—can lead to obesity and health problems. Limiting your fare to simple, healthy foods (like fresh fruits and vegetables) avoids the negative effects of over-processed ones. When you're making a dietary change, limits are a great alternative to going cold turkey. If you want to eat less meat, restrict it to once or twice a week; if you'd like to drink less alcohol, have one glass of wine instead of two; if you need to cut back on pastries, indulge only weekly (or monthly) as a special treat. In this way, you can pursue a healthier lifestyle without feeling completely deprived. The rewards are double: when you limit the snacks and sweets in your cabinets, you'll streamline your figure as well as your kitchen!

If one comes in, one goes out

From now on, every time you bring a new item into the kitchen, purge a similar one. As a result, you'll never have more cups, plates, forks, spoons, or garlic presses than you do at this moment.

All too often, we neglect to get rid of old tableware when we acquire a new set. The problem: in most cases, the old pieces are perfectly functional—we simply replace them because our tastes change, or we want a fresh look. So the old set gets shoved into the recesses of our cabinets, "just in case" we need some extras. Alternatively, we may inherit the newcomers or receive them as gifts—and even if we don't particularly like them, feel obligated to provide them with a home. Whatever the scenario, our cupboards become packed with an odd assortment of plates, glasses, utensils, and serving ware. No more! Henceforth, we'll no longer keep every dish or cup that comes our way. We'll pare down to our latest, greatest, or most beautiful specimens, and remove the old to make way for the new.

Kitchen equipment poses a similar problem. It's hard to put an old piece on the curb—particularly if we've replaced it before its time is up. Therefore, the darkest corners of our cupboards become hideouts for old toasters, coffee makers, crock pots, and grills. Such appliances, however, are bulky and awkward to store, and ditching them can free up significant space. Instead of housing these retirees, give them to someone who needs them—a college student or young couple may be thrilled to receive such useful items. Charity shops, nonprofits, and homeless shelters will also appreciate the donation.

Apply the One In-One Out rule to foodstuffs as well—particularly those that are used slowly, over long periods of time, like spices, seasonings, sauces, and condiments. Such items tend to linger in our drawers, and refrigerator shelves, well past their prime; we buy them for a particular meal, squirrel them away, and completely forget that we have them. Then the next time the need arises, we pick up a new one at the supermarket. If you end up with a second bottle of soy sauce, chili powder, or maple syrup, don't keep the first in reserve; replace it with the fresh stuff instead. Your shelves will be less crowded, and your food much tastier.

Lastly, let's talk about recipes and cookbooks—many more seem to enter the house than leave it. They accumulate steadily over time, and rarely do we *replace* an old one—we simply add to our collection. Recipes in particular tend to pile up, pouring into our lives from all directions: magazines, family, friends, neighbors, and the Internet. Before we know it, we have more recipes than days in the year to cook! Rather than archive them all, keep your selection fresh; when you find a better cookbook for a certain cuisine, or better recipe for a certain dish, let go of the old one. Think of your collection as dynamic, rather than static; let it evolve to suit your tastes, and diet, as they change over time.

Narrow it down

I wish I could provide a master list of the contents of a minimalist kitchen. Unfortunately, such an endeavor would be futile—mainly because we all have different ideas of what is "necessary." It would be unfair to say you can't be a minimalist if you have a bundt pan or a deep fryer. That said, I think most of us can get by with fewer kitchen "essentials" than are generally published in cookbooks and magazines.

My husband and I have found we can prepare all our meals with just four pieces of cookware: a large skillet, a saucepan, a pasta pot, and a baking pan. Our small appliances are limited to a microwave, tea kettle, rice cooker, and French press (in place of a coffee maker). In terms of other implements, we own a chef's knife, bread knife, paring knife, colander, steamer, cutting board, measuring cup, spatula, serving spoon, whisk, can opener, corkscrew, cheese grater, stainless steel mixing bowl, and a water filtration pitcher. Some of you may find our list inadequate, while others may find it excessive. For us, however, it's perfectly *enough*.

It's up to you, then, to determine your *own* "enough"—and narrow down your culinary apparatus accordingly. One particularly effective method is to choose multi-functional items over single-use ones. Unless you use them often, things like cherry pitters, melon ballers, bagel slicers, pizzelle irons, lobster shears, strawberry hullers, and crepe makers don't usually justify the space they command in your kitchen cabinets. Instead, favor simple implements that can perform a variety of functions. Similarly, it's not always necessary to have a full range of skillets and saucepans; one or two in popular sizes are generally sufficient.

Likewise, refrain from accumulating tableware in specialty sizes and shapes (like egg cups and sushi plates), and favor versatile, all-purpose dishes. Instead of storing both "good" china and "everyday" china, choose just one set and use it for all occasions. Pare down glassware as well. If you're not running a restaurant, you don't need a different vessel for every liquid—like wine glasses, champagne glasses, whiskey glasses, beer glasses, martini glasses, water glasses, and juice glasses. I have one set of glasses that suffice for all beverages (other than coffee and tea); and to be honest, I prefer drinking wine and champagne from these simple tumblers than spindly glasses or flutes.

Furthermore, consider purging the fancy specialty equipment. Going out for a treat can be more pleasurable than setting up, operating, and cleaning a complex device. Instead of dragging out a cappuccino maker, spend a lovely afternoon in the coffee shop; instead of fussing with an ice cream maker, take the family to the ice cream parlor; and instead of hoarding bakeware, head to the patisserie when your sweet tooth strikes. Likewise, if you don't cook complicated things, you don't need professional appliances with all the bells and whistles. Enjoy the challenge of preparing meals with basic implements; it's a mindful, meditative, and fulfilling way to cook.

In streamlining your kitchen, keep in mind that in some cultures, an extraordinary variety of cooking is done with the simplest of pots and utensils. It's our creativity in the kitchen—not the cookware in our cabinets—that make for delicious, satisfying meals. Good food doesn't come from fancy plates and fussy serving ware; it comes from the hands and the heart, and—as any Buddhist monk will tell you—can just as well be enjoyed in one simple bowl.

Everyday maintenance

The kitchen is such a hub of activity, it requires not only everyday maintenance—but *all-day* maintenance!

Things can spiral out of control here *within hours* if we don't stay on top of them. Dirty plates, pots, and pans pile up in the sink; food, gadgets, and packaging pile up on the counter; bills, homework, and newspapers pile up on the table; toys, backpacks, and grocery bags pile up on the floor; and leftovers pile up in the refrigerator. Generally, the more members in your household, the more stuff that ends up in the kitchen. Eventually, the clutter can become so overwhelming you couldn't possibly prepare (or eat) a meal there.

To prevent this, simply wipe the slate clean after every meal. When you're cooking, put away gadgets, equipment, and ingredients as soon as you're finished with them. After you've eaten, clear the table and counters of any remaining food or implements. Wash all the dishes, or load them into the dishwasher, immediately after use. Better to spend a few minutes cleaning up after each meal, than face the task when preparing the next; a stack of dirty dishes can quickly dampen your desire to cook. In fact, try to live by the following rule: never leave the kitchen with dishes in the sink. (At the very least, never go to bed with dishes in the sink.) It's wonderful to have a fresh start every day, but even better to have one every meal!

Furthermore, be particularly vigilant in the kitchen for OPC (other people's clutter). If you have a family, your kitchen table, counters, or breakfast bar is probably in almost constant use. All manner of books, toys, games, mail, and paperwork will find their way there, and won't always leave of their own accord (i.e., with the person who brought them in). Make sure all members of the household understand that the kitchen surfaces are flex space—and should be cleared completely after use. If that doesn't do the trick, boomerang stray items back to their owners as soon as possible. Remember, clutter begets clutter; your teenager is more likely to abandon a magazine, or bag of chips, on a messy table than a clear one.

Finally, the kitchen is a fantastic place for a One-A-Day Declutter. In this room, *something* can always go, whether it's yesterday's newspaper or last week's leftovers. Make it a habit to scan your refrigerator, freezer, and pantry shelves regularly for expired or outdated items (or stuff you have no desire to eat), and dispose of them promptly. Commit to purging at least one item every day, whether it's spoiled food, an extra coffee mug, an orphaned utensil, a mismatched plate, or a seldom-used gadget. Your junk drawer alone could probably keep you going for a year. Just think—your cupboards will actually grow more spacious with each passing day!

26

Bathroom

Ready for something easy? Let's take the minimalist strategies we've learned, and beautify our bathrooms. This room is typically the smallest in the house, with the least amount of storage—and compared to the living room, office, and kitchen, streamlining it is a breeze! With just a little effort, and a few simple habits, you can create a space that soothes your soul while you brush your teeth.

Start over

In the other rooms we've decluttered, we've often had to break the job into smaller bits. In contrast, the diminutive size of our bathrooms makes for a much more manageable task—something we can likely undertake all at once. It has just a fraction of the floor, counter, and cabinet space of our other rooms, and serves significantly fewer functions. Streamlining it, however, is not just a walk in the park. Its lack of space means we have to be particularly mindful of how we organize and use it. We're not out to determine how much stuff we can pack into it, but rather how *little* we really need in it. Our goal is to create a serene, spa-like ambience, rather than a cramped and claustrophobic one.

First, close your eyes and picture your ideal minimalist bathroom. Visualize the spare, clean countertop with nary a hairspray bottle or mascara tube in sight. Look around at the lovely, empty floor—no towels piled up in the corner, or extra supplies crammed under the sink. Take a peek at the gleaming surfaces, and carefully chosen cleansing products, in the tub. Open the drawers and medicine cabinet, and admire the orderly lineup of toiletries and grooming supplies. Not a single thing looks out of place, nor are the items fighting for space. Let your gaze rest on the votive candle, or single orchid, adorning the countertop. Ah…you could spend all day in this calm, relaxing space.

Okay, back to reality. Better yet—let's make it a reality! Start Over, just as in your other rooms, by emptying out the contents of the drawers, shelves, and cabinets. Clear everything off the countertops. Don't forget about the tub or shower stall; take the soap, shampoo, shaving cream, razors, and caddies out of there, too. Carry it all from the bathroom, and lay it out elsewhere (like on your bedroom floor, or dining room table) for examination. Decluttering is far more effective when you remove items from their usual spots, and evaluate them out of context. As you determine exactly which things you need, you'll put them back, one by one.

Starting Over is also a great opportunity to reevaluate your routine. Perhaps you're tired of using a daily toner or a weekly mud mask, or want to let your beard grow out instead of shaving. Don't be afraid to shake things up a bit! Sometimes we develop certain habits—like applying a fancy eye cream before bed—and keep doing it for its own sake, rather than any noticeable benefit. Give yourself permission to rethink what you do, why you do it, and if you want to continue. Make a fresh start—do what *you* feel is best, rather than what some beauty magazine or cosmetic ad recommends.

Trash, Treasure, or Transfer

When sorting your things into Trash, Treasure, and Transfer piles, go through the motions of your daily routine. Pretend that you're brushing your teeth, and put your toothbrush, toothpaste, and floss in the Treasure pile. Pretend you're washing your face, and add your cleanser and washcloth. Simulate shaving, putting on makeup, fixing your hair, and any other grooming activities you perform, and send the requisite supplies—razor, lipstick, mascara, comb, brush, hairspray—to join your other Treasures. This exercise reveals *exactly* which products you use every day; and therefore, what belongs in your bathroom. It also reveals which items you *don't* use, and prompts you to question why you're keeping them.

Some items belong in your Trash pile simply because of their age. Cosmetics you don't wear regularly, for example, may be past their prime before they're used up. While makeup is rarely marked with an expiration date (it's not required by law), it does have a limited shelf life. Liquids and creams—especially those worn on or around the eyes—have a lifespan of three to six months, while powdered foundation, concealer, blush, and lipstick generally last for a year. The reason for their degradation: moisture breeds bacteria. Let them hang around too long, and skin irritation and infections can result when you use them.

Be similarly diligent about tossing old medication. Most drugs—both prescription and over-the-counter—have expiration dates on their labels or packaging. (At least your job is a little easier here; you won't have to figure out how long you've had them.) Consult your doctor or pharmacist with concerns about specific medicines, such as their safety and efficacy after expiration. When it comes time to discard them, do so responsibly. Don't throw leftover medications in the trash (where they can be retrieved and consumed by people or animals), or flush them down the toilet (where they can contaminate the water supply). Instead, return them to the pharmacy for proper disposal.

Put extra towels, small electronics (like razors, straighteners or curling irons), and unopened toiletries you no longer want in your Transfer pile. Consider donating them to a local women's or homeless shelter. New, brand name cosmetics can bring in some cash on eBay, while other (unused) beauty products— including samples you've received from department store counters—make great, economical gifts. Pass along partially used potions to interested friends and family; for instance, give your unwanted perfume to the colleague who admires it, or your unloved hand cream to the friend who raves about it. You'll lighten your load, and brighten their day!

Reason for each item

The best reason to keep something in your bathroom is *because you use it*. Conversely, the best reason to declutter something from your bathroom is *because you don't use it*. As you sort through your items, set aside anything you haven't touched in the last six months. Unless you have a very good (i.e., medical) reason for keeping it, toss it and free up the cabinet space. If it's a perishable item, it may be reaching the end of its lifespan anyway.

An exception to this rule is emergency supplies. In this category, those "might need its" and "just in cases" are more than welcome! Keep a well-stocked first aid kit that includes bandages, gauze pads, adhesive tape, antibiotic cream, rubbing alcohol, thermometer, fever reducers, pain relievers, antihistamines, antidiarrheals, antacids, and more. It doesn't matter if you haven't used such things in six months or six years—keep them on hand, because you never know when you'll need them. (Of course, periodically check expiration dates and replace outdated medicines.)

The next best reason to retain an item is *because it works for you*. You know what I'm talking about: the shampoo that tames your frizzies, the cream that erases your wrinkles, or the eyeshadow that makes your baby blues pop. On the other hand, the next best reason to declutter an item is *because it doesn't work for you*—like that expensive moisturizer that irritated your skin. If you tried something and didn't like it, don't feel obligated to squirrel it away for eternity. Just because you paid "good money" for it, doesn't mean you have to keep it—or force yourself to use it. Cut your losses, admit your mistake, and pass it along to someone else before it goes to waste.

While we're on the topic, you can save a lot of cabinet space (and money) by not buying hope in a bottle. Marketers spend millions each year trying to convince us that their products will give us smoother skin, thicker hair, longer lashes, fuller lips, or a closer shave. Such claims are largely unsubstantiated—but that doesn't keep us from falling for them. We see an advertisement in a magazine, touting a miracle cream that'll make us look twenty years younger. We rush to the store, pick it up, and can't wait to try it out. We dutifully apply it each morning and night, studying the mirror for our expected transformation. Days, weeks, months go by, and…nothing. Disappointed, we shove the cream into the back of a drawer, and try to forget about how much we paid for it. Then we see another ad, hope springs anew—and before we know it, our cabinets are cluttered with useless lotions and potions. Better to stick to the tried-and-true, than accumulate bottles of broken promises.

Finally, let's consider another not-so-good reason for admittance to your bathroom cabinets: *because it was free*. In this category falls those samples you get in the mail, the freebies you pick up at the cosmetics counter, and those miniature bottles of soap and shampoo you bring home from every hotel. I know these tiny toiletries are super-cute; but if you don't use them, they're nothing but super-cute clutter. Don't bring them home to your bathroom unless you truly intend to use them. If you have a stash of them to declutter, gather them into a "beauty basket" and give them as a gift.

Everything in its place

Space in the bathroom can be tight, and storage can be scarce. Therefore, every item should have an assigned spot and stay in it—like troops lined up for battle, rather than the aftermath of a house party.

Allocate your stuff to your Inner Circle, Outer Circle, and Deep Storage. Your Inner Circle should hold the majority of things in your bathroom: in short, the stuff you use every day. Typical items might be your toothbrush, toothpaste, floss, facial wash, moisturizer, sunscreen, makeup, brush, comb, razor, shaving cream, Q-tips, cotton balls, washcloth, and any towels you're currently using. Naturally, they should be within easy reach, to make for an efficient grooming routine. Your Outer Circle should contain the items you don't use quite as often: like curling irons, nose hair trimmers, first aid kits, hair clippers, and extra towels and toiletries.

Deep Storage doesn't really apply to bathroom items, as their shelf lives are generally less than a year. The only scenario I can imagine is if you make a bulk buy of a particular item—like a case of bath soap, or a year's supply of toilet paper—and don't have room to store it in your bathroom cabinets. In that case, you could put these items into Deep Storage elsewhere in the house, and retrieve them as needed. Don't make them too hard to reach, however, as you'll require them in due course.

To keep everything in its proper place, assign a drawer or shelf to each member of the household who shares the bathroom. It'll prevent your family's toiletries from becoming a jumbled, disorganized mess. The real beauty of this strategy, however, is that it gives everyone a defined space for their stuff—and nothing more. If your teenager's hair products or spouse's shampoos overflow their designated shelves, they'll have to store the excess elsewhere. That way, one person's accoutrements won't clutter up the entire space. Keep supplies that are shared by everyone—like aspirin, bandages, and Q-tips—on a separate "community" shelf.

In order to achieve a spare, minimalist look, make sure you have adequate storage to keep everything out of sight—even if it means adding another cabinet, shelf, or drawer unit. Of course, before you do, declutter, declutter, and declutter some more. But if you've pared down to the essentials, and *still* don't have enough places to put them, consider investing in a storage solution. Tall cabinets and over-the-toilet shelves can provide plentiful space, with a minimal footprint. Tucking everything away (instead of scattering it across the counters) makes your bathroom significantly more serene.

All surfaces clear

Ideally, your bathroom surfaces should be completely free of all items when not in use. I know it's tempting, and practical, to keep your toothbrush or deodorant out on the counter—you use them every day, after all—but clutter likes to socialize.

Leave them out and before long, a hairbrush will sidle up to them; a razor will start hanging around; then, a lipstick, lotion, and bottle of perfume might join the fun. Multiply this by several family members, and your counters will get very crowded, very fast. In the end, it's easier to keep everything tucked away than decide what's "allowed" to stay out.

Clear surfaces are not only more attractive, they're also more hygienic. Bathrooms are warm, moist, enclosed environments. Dirt, mildew, and germs thrive in such conditions, and will attach themselves to any available object; the less hosts we provide for them, the better. Furthermore, a lack of clutter on your countertops makes them exceedingly easier to clean. You're much more likely to give them a daily wipe-down when you don't have to worry about moving, or knocking over, an assortment of toiletries in the process.

For the same reasons, absolutely nothing should be on your bathroom floor—no towels, laundry, or extra supplies. Corral dirty clothes in a hamper, and keep your surplus provisions in cabinets, baskets, or stackable bins (or in another part of the house). Use hooks and rods to hang up towels and bathrobes. By letting them air dry (instead of piling them on the floor), you can increase the time between laundering them—minimizing your chores, and your utility bills. Tub ledges should be clear as well; install a shelf or shower caddy, instead of lining up your soap, shampoo, and shaving cream around the perimeter. It prevents the buildup of dirt and mildew, and makes the area a dream to clean. And certainly don't perch anything on top of your toilet tank; one wrong move (or vigorous flush) and you know where that object is going!

Finally, because the bathroom is such a small, functional space, avoid any temptation to fill it with knickknacks. Save for a candle, or small bowl of flowers, keep decorative items to an absolute minimum. They'll get wet, they'll get dirty, and they'll get in the way of your beauty routine. You shouldn't have to worry about breaking something when you're blow-drying your hair. As for reading material, bring it in with you—the bathroom is not a library!

Modules

As you're sorting through your sundries, consolidate like items: for example, gather together the cold medicines, pain relievers, makeup, moisturizers, hair care, skin care, and nail care products. In each grouping, take a long, hard look at what you have. Chances are, you'll discover quite a few duplicates in the process. Weed out those extra combs, tweezers, emery boards, and nail clippers—you'd be hard-pressed to use more than one at a time. You might also discover you've gone overboard in a certain category; perhaps you've accumulated eighteen colors of nail polish, or six different scented lotions. When you see them all together, it may seem a bit excessive! Question how many you really need, and pare them down to your favorites. Of course, if you have a second bottle of shampoo in store for when your current one runs out, that's fine; as long as you plan to use it, you don't have to lose it.

Once you've culled your bathroom supplies, use containers to corral all the loose items. Keep your foundation, blush, eyeshadow, mascara, lipstick and other cosmetics in a makeup case; and round up hair accessories like clips, barrettes, bobby pins, and rubber bands into a module of their own (a ziplock bag will suffice). Do the same with medicines, beauty creams, nail items, and other grooming implements. When they're rolling around in a drawer, it's hard to keep them from multiplying; plus, the unorganized jumble provides a great hiding place for other clutter. When they're stowed in separate containers, it's easier to find them, and keep them under control. You can even get fancy, and make your modules do decorative duty as well: cotton balls, Q-tips, and bath salts look gorgeous in glass apothecary jars, and give your bathroom a chic, spa-like feel.

Family members can think of their designated shelves or drawers as their own modules. However, if storage space is scarce, consider this alternative: keep only common items in the bathroom, and have everyone store personal supplies in their own bathroom caddies. Each member then carries their caddy (containing their own cleanser, shampoo, hairbrush, moisturizer, and other essentials) into the bathroom when they use it, and takes it with them when they leave. This concept, borrowed from college dorms, cuts down on clutter and turns the room into flex space. It's a wonderful solution for bathrooms with little to no storage, or those being shared by families.

Limits

I love limits in the bathroom, and I think you will, too. They not only save you space, they save you time—and we can certainly all use more of both!

When we stumble into our bathrooms each morning, we're usually on autopilot; and hardly equipped to make decisions over which facial cleanser, shampoo, or body lotion to use. We just want to get in and out with a minimum of fuss, so we can get on with our day. The same goes for the evening: when we're ready to fall into bed, we don't want to waste time pondering which eye cream to apply—that would cut into our precious beauty sleep. When we have multiples, however, we force ourselves to do just that; and when we have to rummage through eyeshadows or lipsticks to find a particular shade, we have less time to do other (more pressing or pleasurable) things.

The magic number in the bathroom, then, is *one*. To create a truly minimalist medicine cabinet, try to limit your toiletries to one of each: one shampoo, one conditioner, one cleanser, one toner, one moisturizer, one perfume, one aftershave, one body lotion, one toothpaste, one lipstick, one eyeshadow, one mascara, one blush, one nail polish, and so on. One of each means less clutter in your cabinets, and less to think about in the morning. One of each means less impact on the environment, both in terms of manufacturing and disposal. One of each means embracing the concept of *enough*.

To this end, use something up before you buy a new one. I know that's easier said than done; we're bombarded with hundreds of ads each day, making us all sorts of promises—and sometimes when we hear about that "perfect" night cream or that "must-have" mascara, we can't get to the beauty aisle fast enough! Other times, an intriguing product catches our eye while we're shopping, or the salesperson at the cosmetics counter tempts us with an "add-on" purchase while selling us our favorite lipstick. Patience, young grasshopper, patience. If it's all it's cracked up to be, it'll certainly be worth waiting for. Resist these impulse purchases, particularly if you have a similar product at home. Make a mental note of it, and purchase it when you run out of your current one.

Now let's talk towels. Scan your bathroom, linen closet, or wherever you store them, and take an inventory. How many do you have? How many people are in your household? If there's a big difference between those two numbers, you have some decluttering to do. Decide just how many towels each member of the household needs. If you're an extreme minimalist, your magic number may be one; however, I think most people will feel more comfortable with two. With a second towel, you have a backup while laundering the other, and an extra for guests to use. Furthermore, limit your towels to one versatile size; bath towels can serve most needs, allowing you to dispense with the hand towels, face towels, fingertip towels, and other single function towels. The fewer you have to store, keep track of, and launder, the better!

If one comes in, one goes out

Oftentimes, we're too excited to try out a new beauty product to wait until we finish the old one. We buy it, bring it home, and give it a whirl. Of course, the label tells us we'll have to use it for a few weeks (or months) before we see any results, so we incorporate it into our daily routine. Our old, half-finished cleanser, lotion, or cream is relegated to the back of our cabinet and quickly forgotten. Rinse, lather, and repeat, and we soon have a growing pile of rejects languishing in our bathrooms.

Avoid this problem by disposing of an old toiletry whenever you purchase a new one. Don't feel obligated to hold on to its remnants, thinking you might go back and finish it someday; if you're happy with the new one, there's little chance that'll happen. In all likelihood, it'll probably go bad before you get to use it. Similarly, once you've started new ones, don't let those almost-empty toothpaste tubes and conditioner bottles hang around; it's unlikely you'll develop the superhuman strength needed to squeeze out the last remaining molecules. Keep tabs on your cosmetics as well. If you bring home a new lipstick from the fall palette, or a new eyeshadow from the spring collection, say "adiós" to last season's shades. A fresh selection is more fun than a cache of stale supplies!

Apply the same principle to small electronics, like electric toothbrushes, razors, hairdryers, straighteners, and curling irons.

If you've acquired a "new and improved" version, send the "old and outdated" one on its way. Don't be tempted to hold on to it as a spare. Remember, we trade a little bit of space for every item we own—and all those little spaces add up to big ones. These items can be awkward to store, and their failure isn't catastrophic enough to devote valuable space to understudies.

Finally, use the One In-One Out rule on your towels. These things can multiply like nobody's business! Why? Because when we buy new ones, we rarely ever throw the old ones away. They're just so practical, we can't bring ourselves to do it. Our fresh ones get the place of honor on the towel rack, the former get stowed away as backups, and our linen closets grow more stuffed with each passing year. Instead of perpetually accumulating them, declutter your oldest when you bring in the new; it'll give you much more breathing room. If you can't bear to let them go, at least reassign them to another part of the house; they may continue to serve you well cleaning up spills or wiping down tools.

Narrow it down

To create a minimalist bathroom, we must do more than simply organize the contents—we must narrow them down. We want to be able to meet our needs with the least amount of products.

Therefore, it behooves us to reduce our needs—or, in other words, pare down our beauty and grooming routines. Specialty products can make our *toilette* complicated and time-consuming; suddenly we find ourselves involved in a five-step cleansing program, using three different anti-aging creams, or applying mud masks multiple times a week. We're curling our hair, straightening it, moussing it, gelling it, teasing it, scrunching it, or spraying it into place. We're concealing our flaws, highlighting our cheekbones, and lengthening our lashes. Whew! Getting ready in the morning can be a job unto itself!

Take a close look at your routine, and consider where you can cut back. I'm confident you'll look just as gorgeous doing *half* what you do now. If you scaled down your skin care to a splash of soap and water, you could ditch the fancy cleansers and toners. If you decided to age gracefully, you could jettison the wrinkle creams. If you got a simple, wash-and-wear haircut, you could toss a plethora of hair products—and maybe even the hairdryer. Beauty doesn't come from a bottle—it comes from within. Instead of stockpiling miracle goop, opt for natural beauty boosters like exercise, a healthy diet, plenty of water, and a good night's sleep.

When revamping your routine, think low maintenance. That doesn't mean you have to show up for work looking like you just rolled out of bed; simply, use the fewest products possible to create a well-groomed appearance. When it comes to makeup, keep it minimal: stick with neutral colors, and play up your best feature instead of painting all of them. Embrace the hair you were born with: if it's curly don't try to make it straight, if it's straight don't try to make it curly, and if you're of a certain age, consider letting it go gray. A natural face and a simple hairdo can be much more attractive than full makeup and an elaborate coiffure.

To narrow things down further, choose multi-use products. Double duty favorites include shampoo and conditioner combos, tinted lip balms, hair and body washes, and moisturizers with a sunscreen. Some common household items are also beauty workhorses. Baking soda, for example, can be used for exfoliating, tooth brushing, hand cleansing, foot soaking, and hair care. Olive oil can be used as a facial moisturizer, makeup remover, hair conditioner, cuticle treatment, and lip balm. Petroleum jelly softens hands, feet, elbows, and knees, and can substitute for mascara. These three products alone can eliminate a cabinet full of lotions and potions!

Everyday maintenance

Everyday maintenance in the bathroom is a piece of cake! In fact, it's a great place to hone your minimalist powers, and gain the skills and confidence to take on the rest of the house.

You'll make your job much easier if you're a good gatekeeper. Don't come back from the store with an armful of beauty products you bought on impulse; don't accept the freebies from the salesperson in the cosmetics aisle; don't request samples through the mail or on the Internet; and don't bring home soaps, shampoos, and body lotions from hotels. If they're not part of your regular routine, these items will do little more than clutter up your drawers. Wait until you have *need* of a particular product before you acquire a new one. We all like to give ourselves a treat once in awhile—but spacious cabinets and empty countertops can be just as luxurious as expensive bath salts.

Even as you're guarding the gate, some wayward items will find their way in—especially if you share the bathroom with other household members. Each time you exit the room, take with you anything that doesn't belong there: like your toddler's sippy cup, your teenager's sneakers, your spouse's copy of *Popular Mechanics*, or the book you were reading in the tub. Make sure no one is using the floor as an impromptu laundry basket or temporary storage spot; if so, orchestrate a prompt pickup or return of the stray possessions. This simple habit will keep the clutter from getting out of hand, and set a great example for other members of the family.

Lastly, clear your surfaces before turning in for the night. Put all toiletries, tools, and tidbits back in their designated spots, and hang all towels on their rods or hooks. Give your countertops a quick wipe-down, to remove dirt and mildew and prevent it from forming. Make this a regular routine before falling into bed, and you'll awake to a beautiful minimalist bathroom each morning!

27

Storage spaces

Now that we've streamlined our living space, let's take a look at our storage space—like the attic, basement, and garage. Oftentimes, this is where the clutter from the rest of the house ends up when we don't know what to do with it. However, just because it's out of sight, doesn't mean it's out of mind.

Start over

Storage space seems like the answer to our problems; how orderly our lives would be if we had a full basement, big attic, or two-car garage to stash all our stuff! Unfortunately, however, this "solution" often backfires: stuff expands to fill the available space, and before we know it, we have more stuff than ever to deal with.

My husband and I once lived quite comfortably in a studio apartment, with no storage space other than a utility closet. Then we moved into a three-bedroom house, with an attic, basement, and garage. Guess what happened? Our possessions increased exponentially! During our apartment years, whenever we tired of a piece of furniture, or sports and hobby equipment, we had to get rid of it—we simply had no place to store it. Once we moved into our house, however, these things wound up in the basement—"just in case" we needed them someday. Well, these "just in cases" piled up and piled up, creating an entirely new clutter problem. Frankly, I think it's easier to live minimally when you *don't* have any storage space!

To avoid clutter buildup, keep your storage space as streamlined as your living space. Just because you have a big garage, doesn't mean you have to fill every square inch of it. Better to store your car in there (and protect your investment), than a bunch of things you don't use. What's more, these areas can serve as additional flex space: they're ideal places to pursue messy hobbies, and can even be converted into family rooms or bedrooms. Don't let useless junk prevent you from using them to their potential.

With storage spaces, you can Start Over in one of two ways: a little at a time, or the whole enchilada. If you're feeling ambitious, do it BIG! Schedule an entire weekend for your decluttering, and empty the contents of the basement, attic, or garage (whatever you've chosen to work on) into your yard or driveway. It's easy to overlook things when they're lurking in dark corners; bring it all out into the light, and expose the clutter for what it is. Sometimes, simply moving an item out of the house helps you overcome the urge to keep it; suddenly it seems ridiculous to hang on to your old baseball cleats, or the broken bicycle you haven't ridden in years.

For best results, get the whole family involved, and make a party of it! Play music, serve refreshments, and create a fun atmosphere, so it feels more like a game than a chore. A little healthy competition helps: task each member of the household with purging their own things, and declare the person with the least amount of remaining stuff the decluttering champion. For added incentive, make plans for how you'll use the "new" space; your teenager will embrace the project with much more enthusiasm if it results in a home theater, or place for his band to practice.

Alternatively, if a major purge seems overwhelming, tackle it box by box. Such a large endeavor can be less intimidating when done a little at a time. To make progress, set a regular schedule: for example, sort through one box each day or each week. Move it out of the storage area, and into another part of the house to examine its contents; when you remove things from their usual context, you're less likely to put them back. Proceeding slowly allows you to consider each item carefully, and gives you the time to digitize photos, documents, or other memorabilia before disposing of them.

And by all means, if you have a storage unit external to your property, get rid of it! It's like renting a second house for your excess stuff—*stuff you don't even like enough to live with*. Ponder the following questions: Can you list the contents of your storage unit from memory? If not, do you really *need* things you don't even know you have? When did you last use these items? Is it worth paying good money to store things you rarely (if ever) use? How important can they be, if you don't even want to keep them in your house? You may discover that in this situation, the best way to Start Over is to turn in the keys.

Trash, Treasure, or Transfer

As you divide your stuff into Trash, Treasure, and Transfer piles, keep it simple and stick to the following rule: if you haven't used an item in over a year, out it goes. This time period is sufficient to cover holiday decorations, like Easter baskets and Christmas ornaments; seasonal supplies like pool toys and snow shovels; and sports equipment that's only used part of the year, like baseball bats and ice hockey skates. Accordingly, if you didn't go skiing, use your camping gear, or put up those Halloween decorations last year (or in several years), it's time to ask *why* you're still storing these items.

You'll probably find plenty of stuff for your Trash pile here, as these spaces are often repositories for broken items. Consider how likely you are to fix that old television or lawnmower if you've already replaced it with a new one (I'll give you a hint: not very!). Likewise, question if that chair with the broken seat, or table with the broken leg, will ever enter your dining room again. If you were *really* going to fix these items, you would have done so by now; so why put extra pressure on yourself? Break free of the task by letting them go—it'll take a load off your mind, and give you time to pursue other (more pleasurable) activities. That goes double if you're dedicating precious space to a broken-down jalopy. A car is meant to get you from point A to point B; if the one in your garage is not doing the job (and is unlikely to in the near future), I think you know what to do with it.

Your Transfer pile will fill up quickly too, as storage spaces are catch-alls for abandoned projects and once-loved hobbies. We often feel guilty for giving up on activities, particularly after we've spent good money on supplies or training. We then placate (or torture?) ourselves by storing the equipment in our basement or garage, vowing we'll "get back into it" someday. Bear in mind that you're a free individual—you have no obligation to continue these pursuits. Donate the old table you never finished re-finishing, give your neighbor the fishing pole you haven't touched in years, or sell the knitting machine you never learned to use. Give yourself permission to move on—it's so liberating! When these items no longer weigh on you, you'll have the energy and enthusiasm to pursue new passions.

Furthermore, don't "furnish" these areas with rejects from your living space. Sometimes when we redecorate, we end up with furniture that no longer "fits"—but instead of setting it free, we stow it away in our garage or basement. If nobody's sitting on it, dining on it, working on it, or sleeping on it, what's the use of keeping it? Baby items in particular are often squirreled away indefinitely; but the only reason to keep those cribs, high chairs, and playpens is if you truly expect to have another child. Don't store that fifteen-year-old bassinet because it reminds you of your teenager's more charming years; it doesn't have the power to turn back time. Give these items to someone who needs them; let them help out a struggling young family, rather than gather dust in your basement.

Finally, as you gather up your Treasures, keep this in mind: as wonderful as storage spaces are, they're generally not as clean or climate-controlled as the rest of the house. Stuff stored here attracts dust, dirt, moisture, bugs, and other critters. Therefore, if you stash things in these areas for long periods of time, don't be surprised if some damage occurs. There's a good chance that if and when you need a certain item, it may no longer be in tip-top shape—and you'll have to buy a new one anyway. (So much for saving it all those years!) Many wedding gowns—meant to be "passed down" to the next generation—meet a slow demise this way. Evaluate your Treasures carefully, and make sure they can survive in this "rough" environment. If not, bring them into your main living space for safekeeping; or let someone else use them *now*, rather than let them deteriorate.

Reason for each item

In order to keep out the clutter, we must apply the same criteria to our attics, basements, and garages as we do to our living space: reserve them for things we use *now*—not things we've used in the past, or might use in the future.

Good reasons abound for storing stuff in these spaces. They're ideal for things that are used only part of the year, or are too heavy, bulky, dirty, or otherwise inconvenient to keep in the house. Examples include seasonal equipment (like your grill) and holiday decorations (like your Christmas tree); sports equipment (like bikes, balls, and helmets); lawn and garden equipment for the upkeep of your yard; tools and supplies for home maintenance and repair; tools and supplies for auto maintenance and repair; cleaning items (like brooms, bleach, and wet/dry vacuums); documents that must be retained indefinitely (like real estate records and tax returns); and hobby items that are too messy or unwieldy to store, or use, in your main living space.

These spaces should *not* be the refuge of last resort for items you don't want to use, see, or think about—but can't bring yourself to dispose of. Make your stuff apply for its position here, and evaluate its "resume": look for qualifications like "I'm used at least six times a year," "I'm necessary for trimming the hedges," or "Cleaning the gutters would be a real bear without me." Conversely, turn away candidates with nothing more to offer than, "I remind you of your high school years" or "You inherited me." If a certain item has been long unemployed, give it its walking papers—you're not obliged to shelter a garage full of slackers.

Like the first aid kit in the bathroom, emergency items get a special pass here. "Might need its" are always welcome if they might end up saving your life! Make sure you have enough water, canned goods, and other supplies to weather a natural disaster or other disruptive event. Consult preparedness books and websites for detailed lists of items you should have on hand, and tailor your inventory to your personal needs and geographic location. As a minimalist, you may be reluctant to stock up on items for unforeseen circumstances; however, if the time comes when you need them, you'll be very glad you did. Perishable supplies can, and should, be rotated throughout the year; so at least you'll get some use from them as you consume and replace them.

A popular—but not *good*—reason for storing something here is that it commemorates your past. Turn a critical eye on those yearbooks, swimming trophies, letter sweaters, graduation gowns, and other memorabilia; unless you truly plan to don your football or cheerleading uniform again (and more power to you if you still fit in it!), free yourself from these artifacts. Refrain from hoarding dusty boxes of stuff to prove who you once were, or what you once did. If a certain item is really that special, display it proudly in the house; it's not proving anything to anyone stashed away in the basement. Remember, your stuff is not a record of your life—*you* are. Give similar thought to any heirlooms hidden here: if they're not special enough to keep in the house, question whether they're special enough to keep at all.

Everything in its place

In these storage areas—as in other parts of the house—it's critical that everything have (and stay in) a designated spot. Haphazard piles of miscellaneous things can swallow up these spaces in no time flat. Resist the temptation to throw something in a corner, or jam it on the nearest shelf; if you do, you'll end up with a huge, disorganized mess that'll only attract more clutter.

Plan out the space carefully, and assign items to appropriate zones. For example, keep your lawnmower, rake, pruning shears, potting soil, and seeds in a lawn and garden zone; store your boxes of Halloween, Christmas, and Easter decorations in a holiday zone; gather your tennis rackets, roller blades, snowboard, and soccer balls into a sports zone; consolidate your windshield wiper fluid, wrenches, motor oil, and jack stands in an auto repair zone; and stash your screwdrivers, hand saw, power drill, touch-up paint, and pest control products in a home maintenance zone. Dividing your storage space into specific sections helps you find what you need when you need it, and keeps useless clutter from sneaking its way in.

You might assume that everything in these spaces would be categorized as Deep Storage, but that's not the case. Our basements and garages contain items we use on a regular basis; therefore, we need to organize the space so that the most frequently used items are within easy reach. In your Inner Circle, store everything you access often—like cleaning supplies, lawn equipment, and tools for home and car repair—on the most accessible shelves, racks, and hooks. Think of your Inner Circle as "active" space; it serves a functional role, housing all the necessary supplies and equipment (and perhaps even the work area) to perform regular tasks.

Your Outer Circle, on the other hand, is primarily storage space. It should consist of higher and lower shelves, and farther reaches of your attic, basement, or garage. In this section store your holiday decorations, perishable emergency supplies, and out-of-season maintenance and sports equipment (like your snow blower and skis in summer, or your sprinklers and camping gear in winter). Generally speaking, your Outer Circle should house items that are used only once a year, or part of the year. You may find it convenient to move seasonal equipment back and forth between your Inner and Outer Circles as needed.

Finally, Deep Storage is for items you have little intention of laying eyes on again, but are obligated to keep for some reason or other. This category shouldn't contain much; in fact, non-perishable emergency supplies, and financial or legal documents, are about the only things that come to mind. Most importantly, don't use Deep Storage to hide things you don't want to deal with: like your grandmother's tea service, or the comic books you collected many moons ago. It may be tempting to sock them away for a few decades, in hopes they'll bring a fortune on eBay; but the chances that they'll grow that valuable (and stay in mint condition) are rather slim. And if you don't feel like dealing with them now, will you really want to deal with them later?

All surfaces clear

In your attic, basement, or garage, keep anything that serves as functional space—like workbenches or tables—completely clear. The tasks performed in such areas are sometimes dangerous; therefore, maintaining clutter-free surfaces is an essential safety precaution. In other words, you don't want tennis balls rolling around when you're working with a power saw or handling hazardous chemicals. Furthermore, when you set out to tackle a project, having to clear the area of junk first is discouraging. The mess may prompt you to go back inside, plop on the couch, and call out a handyman instead. To keep your worktop clear, install a pegboard panel above it; all your tools, screws, nails, bolts, and other bits and bobs will then be off the surface, yet within reach.

Likewise, do everything you can to keep the floor clear. These spaces can be awkward and dark, providing a ripe tripping hazard if anything is underfoot. When you're negotiating the terrain with a ten-foot ladder, or fifty-pound bag of rock salt, it's a bad time to discover that your child's wagon is out of place. Make liberal use of vertical storage space—such as shelving, and wall-mounted hooks and holders—to store things off the floor. Hang garden tools like rakes and shovels, sporting equipment like skis and skates, and mesh bags of smaller items like soccer balls, helmets, and other accessories. Install overhead racks to stow bicycles and large items out of the way. Ideally, you should be able to walk through the space without stepping over, skirting around, or bumping into any objects. For a tidy look, opt for a uniform, wall-mounted shelving system, rather than an ad hoc assemblage of stand-alone racks.

In addition to creating a neater, safer environment, vertical storage has other benefits as well. First, it makes items easier to access. You won't have to wade through boxes to find your scuba equipment, or dig through piles to unearth your weed whacker. Second, it protects them from damage. Items stored on the floor are susceptible to moisture, insects, and other critters—and in danger of people, or cars, running into them. Third, it keeps the clutter in check. Stuff on the floor tends to gradually spread out, creeping through the space like a lava flow. If the floor is off-limits as storage space, you'll accumulate a lot less junk!

Modules

Because these storage areas house a wide variety of items—from coolers to kayaks, and rakes to roller blades—modules are the single best way to keep them organized. They help us maintain order in what can be a crowded and chaotic space.

First, consolidate like items, from the largest down to the smallest: in addition to grouping your shovels and rakes, sort your nuts, bolts, and screws by type and size. (For the natural born organizer, it's the stuff of dreams!) Divide your supplies into the most specialized categories possible. Rather than label a handful of boxes "home repair," separate the contents into plumbing, electrical, woodworking, painting, and exterior care modules. Likewise, sort decorations according to occasion or season—that way, you won't have to root through your Christmas balls in order to fetch your birthday streamers. Organize sports equipment by activity or participant, and store winter gear (like boots, hats, and gloves) in a separate module from summer gear (like flip flops and beach towels).

In the process of consolidating, you may be surprised to discover how many hammers and screwdrivers you have. We often buy extra tools and hardware when we have trouble finding the ones we own—resulting in even more clutter in our workspace. Other times, we acquire specialized implements for certain projects, and never use them again. Take this opportunity to streamline your supplies to the essentials: cull the duplicates, save the necessities, and purge the rest.

Next, find appropriate containers for small to medium-sized items; left on their own, they're apt to wander off and get themselves in trouble. I like transparent bins and boxes, as they enable you to see the contents at a glance. Clearly label or color code opaque containers—like green for garden tools, or red for emergency supplies—so you don't have to comb through a dozen boxes to locate what you need. Better yet, take it one step further: make an inventory of each container's contents, print off the list, and tape it to the front of the box. With such a system in place, you'll be able to lay your hands on anything in a matter of minutes—as well as keep out any stray items.

Arranging your stuff into modules makes it a breeze to locate things, put them away, and survey them before purchasing anything new. However, it can be easy to forget what you own once it's out of sight. Therefore, consider listing or photographing items as you pack them up (particularly those in long term storage). It's a great way to keep track of things for insurance purposes and project planning. Having an inventory at your fingertips is invaluable when filing a claim; and if you're wondering if you have a certain tool, searching your computer for it may be more pleasant than searching a cold, dark basement.

Limits

Consider limiting the contents of your attic, basement, or garage to what fits on your shelving or vertical storage. By taking the floor out of the equation, you'll remove volumes of potential clutter and free up the space for other activities (like parking your car, working on a hobby, or forming a garage band). Besides, it just *feels* good when you're not weighed down by so many things!

Limit your possessions by category as well. For example: restrict yourself to just one or two boxes of seasonal decorations, and select your favorite pieces until you've filled the allotted container(s). Thus, you'll have a lovely collection, rather than a random hodgepodge. Such limits are not only beneficial to your storage area, but also to your home—for when it comes to décor, less is more. A room looks more elegant when decorative pieces are kept to a minimum; and it's easier to retrieve and display your best items when you don't have to rummage through a boatload of boxes.

If you're not careful, tools and garden equipment can commandeer a large swath of your basement or garage. Limit them to a certain section of the room, or a certain number of containers, to prevent their expansion. Retain only the finest and most useful items, and refrain from purchasing a specialty tool for every task. Similarly, limit the amount of hardware you own; if you'll never use a thousand screws, don't buy (or store) that many. Assign a particular container to them, and when it's full, declutter the excess. Limit your lawnmowers, leaf blowers, circular saws, orbital sanders, drill presses, and other equipment, too; unless you employ a maintenance staff, one should be sufficient.

Sports equipment can also multiply quickly. Keep it under control by limiting the number of sports in which you (and your children) participate; one per season is a reasonable amount. This strategy not only cuts down on clutter, it provides an opportunity to develop expertise in particular pursuits. When we focus our efforts on fewer activities, we increase our potential to master them—an achievement which can be far more satisfying than trying every sport known to man. Such limits are particularly beneficial to children, who may feel overscheduled and overwhelmed when shuttled between baseball, karate, tennis, and ballet lessons.

Finally, strictly limit any memorabilia or sentimental items you choose to keep. For instance, dedicate just one box to high school and college stuff, and save only those items of greatest importance to you—rather than every test you took, award you won, poem you wrote, uniform you wore, or fraternal item you owned. Do the same for wedding items: keep only what will fit in a single box. Choose your most special mementos, instead of hoarding every card, favor, and decoration associated with the event. Apply similar limits to any souvenirs, heirlooms, trophies, baby keepsakes, and children's art and schoolwork you decide to store as well.

If one comes in, one goes out

Our storage spaces are like black holes: stuff goes in, but it never comes out (maybe scientists should look here for the missing matter of the universe!). Fortunately, we can stop their growth—by purging an old item each time we add a new one.

When we buy new electronic, computer, or office equipment, we often relegate the old stuff to these areas. Why we're storing them, I have no idea—I don't know anyone who has actually dug out one of these dinosaurs and put it back into service. I know if my current laptop failed, the last place I'd look for a replacement is in my basement; I'd be shopping for a new one before you could say "out of warranty." Yet we save these relics nonetheless, turning our attics and basements into museums of old technology. If you haven't already cleared out these "antiques," there's no time like the present. From now on, when you purchase a new piece of technology, don't preserve the old one for posterity—let it back into the world, where it still may be of use.

Apply the same philosophy to your home and garden tools. If you acquire a shiny new lawnmower, tree trimmer, or power drill, sell or donate the old one; why keep duplicates, when you can only use one at a time? If it helps, pretend you don't have the space for two, and *must* make a choice between them. If your old one is on its last legs, or the new one lightens your workload, the decision is easy—send the former on its way. However, if you can't bear to part with the old one, and it continues to meet your needs, return the new one to the store—because there's no reason to spend your hard-earned money on it.

Likewise, if you decide to pursue a new sport or hobby, give up an old one—along with the related equipment. It'll prevent your attic, basement, or garage from being haunted by the Ghosts of Activities Past. You certainly don't need stuff that reminds you of failed pursuits or lost interests; better to cut the cord, free your mind, and sell the supplies to recoup some money. You only have so much time in your day, and precious little of it is leisure time. By dropping an old pastime, you can devote your energy, space, and resources to a new one.

Finally, a word about furniture: in short, if your attic, basement, or garage isn't a living space, it doesn't belong there. All too often, these spaces provide refuge for old tables, chairs, beds, and sofas that have been displaced by new ones. Unless you have very specific plans for their future—like giving the couch to your college-bound daughter, or moving the table to your beach house—let them go. From now on, follow the rule: when one piece of furniture comes in, one goes out (and *not* out to the garage!).

Narrow it down

Even though it's out of sight, the stuff in our attics, basements, and garages is always there—hanging over our heads, piled beneath our feet, and pressing in on us. Just the thought of being surrounded by junk can be psychologically suffocating. Therefore, narrow down the contents of these spaces as much as possible: store only what you regularly use (or expect to in the near future). Don't fill them with "just in cases"—just in case you take up skiing again, just in case your new printer breaks, just in case you need to prove you lettered in track and field. Life is more exhilarating when you live with less!

First, lighten your load by ditching the holiday decorations. Why squirrel away store-bought décor, when nature's bounty is much more elegant? Instead of adorning your Christmas tree with manufactured baubles, string it with popcorn and cranberries; instead of decorating with artificial wreaths, make fresh ones each year with evergreens; instead of dragging out a ceramic centerpiece, spruce up your table with sprigs of holly. Beautify your home with acorns and leaves in the fall, and fresh and dried flowers in spring. Use pebbles, branches, and fruit—rather than mass-produced tchotchkes—to provide texture and color to your rooms. When you decorate with nature, you have a "fresh" look in every sense of the word—and better yet, nothing to store!

Second, pursue sports and hobbies that require little equipment. You can play soccer and tennis with far less stuff than hockey and football; and you can practice yoga, karate, and dance with next to nothing. You can walk or run in the great outdoors instead of buying a treadmill, and focus on calisthenics instead of exercise machines. In fact, sports are often more enjoyable when you don't have to fuss with accoutrements. By the time you don all those hockey pads, you could have gone for a three-mile run! Take a similar approach to hobbies: while woodworking, pottery, or metalsmithing are wonderful activities, they require numerous specialty tools and supplies. Learning a language, writing poetry, or sketching, on the other hand, may bring you similar satisfaction without all the stuff.

Third, resist the urge to buy the latest and greatest tools; many tasks can be completed with the most basic of implements. For example, you don't need fancy equipment to be a great gardener; in most cases, a shovel, hoe, fork, rake, spade, hose, and watering can will suffice. Working with simple hand tools can be much more satisfying than operating high-powered ones; it brings you closer to your work (both physically and psychologically), and gives you a greater sense of achievement. Pare down your toolbox further by choosing versatile items that can tackle a variety of jobs, over those that perform just one. A multi-purpose rotary tool with interchangeable bits (like those made by Dremel) can eliminate an entire workbench full of specialty equipment.

Finally, be a borrower. If you only go ice skating a few times each winter, rent skates instead of owning them; if you only pressure wash your siding once a year, hire the equipment from a home improvement center; if you only need a nail gun once in a blue moon, borrow one from your neighbor. Consider participating in community tool shares instead of storing your own; they give you access to a wide variety of maintenance and garden equipment. Furthermore, if you rarely use your automobile, sell it off and join a car share program—you'll decrease your costs, and increase your garage space. You can also give items you don't use regularly to a friend or relative with greater need for them—with the understanding you can borrow them when necessary. Your handyman neighbor can then use (and store) your ladder all year round, and lend it to you when you need it.

Everyday maintenance

To maintain clutter-free storage spaces, you *must* be a good gatekeeper—because once stuff gets settled in, it takes some serious effort to flush it out. Question any item headed for the attic, basement, or garage *before it gets there*; if something's leaving the living space, it can just as often leave the household altogether. Don't use these spaces to avoid facing reality or making tough decisions; if you find yourself walking up the attic steps with your aunt's music box collection, stop and think about alternative ways to deal with it. Giving it to your sister-in-law, or donating it to a charity shop, may be a better solution than squirreling it away.

Monitor these spaces on a regular basis, to make sure things don't go haywire behind your back. Such vigilance is particularly necessary in a multi-member household, where everyone may not have the same minimalist goals. If you spot a foreign object, figure out who owns it and why it's there; if it's simply out of place, determine its appropriate spot and return it there immediately. The longer you let it lounge around, the more likely it is to attract friends. Keep a close watch on the floor, and put the brakes on any "clutter creep" that might be occurring. When you (or family members) are finished using tools, sports equipment, or hobby supplies, see that everything is returned to its proper place, instead of left lying around.

Additionally, consider doing a One-A-Day Declutter—these areas provide ample opportunity to purge your household of excess stuff. Better yet, it's *easy*: since the items reside outside your main living space, you're already somewhat detached from them. You don't look at or use them on a daily basis, and you have a pretty good idea of what it's like to live without them. Think of it this way: if you were making a cross-country move, would you bother to drag them along? If they're not special (or useful) enough to wrap up, box up, and cart around, you may as well set them free. At the end of the year, you'll have 365 fewer things to store—that's wonderful incentive in itself!

At minimum, conduct a massive decluttering session once a year; schedule it for a holiday weekend for a particularly festive atmosphere. Unload the entire contents of the attic, basement, or garage into your backyard, and strive to return less than *half* to the space. Purge unused tools, unloved hobby supplies, outgrown sports equipment, and anything else that may have snuck its way in during the previous twelve months. To increase motivation, plan a yard sale for the following week, and earmark the proceeds for something fun—like a family vacation or swim club membership. Make it a tradition, and everyone will look forward to the annual "fresh start."

28

Gifts, heirlooms, and sentimental items

During the course of your decluttering, you'll run across certain objects that give you pause. They're neither useful nor beautiful, yet you can't bring yourself to get rid of them. Ironically enough, you may not even have chosen to bring them into your life. What am I talking about? Gifts, heirlooms, and sentimental items.

GIFTS

Gifts are supposed to be "good," right? We're supposed to give them with joy, receive them with joy, and cherish them for the rest of our days—or so we've been told to believe. Throughout history, gifts have symbolized a special transaction between two people; they've been used to convey respect, curry favor, express love, extend hospitality, seal friendships, ask for forgiveness, and more. The key word here, however, is *symbolize*. The gift itself is nothing more than an object representing a certain emotion or intention—which, absent that object, still remains. If the ceramic rooster you received from your best friend suddenly vaporized into thin air (would that it were so easy!), your friendship would be no less for lack of it.

Furthermore, much of the gift-giving that occurs nowadays is inspired less by noble intentions, and more by aggressive marketing. Around every major holiday, we're barraged with ads urging us to buy this, that, and the other thing for our loved ones. They promise that happiness will reign if we give our wife the right diamond necklace, our husband the right electronic gadget, our friend the right cashmere scarf, and our children the right trendy toys—and on the flip side, hint at the disappointment they'll suffer if we don't. Consequently, our gift-giving often has more to do with fulfilling obligations, satisfying expectations, and avoiding guilt than anything else.

Thanks to such marketing, nary a holiday, birthday, housewarming, wedding, or anniversary goes by without gifts exchanging hands—the evidence of which can be seen in our overstuffed drawers and closets. Multiply these occasions by the number of friends, relatives, and colleagues with which you exchange, and the stuff can build up quickly! Our challenge when we become minimalists, then, is two-pronged: to purge unwanted gifts we already have, and to avoid receiving new ones.

The upside of all these gifts flying around is that most givers will have already forgotten what they gave you—particularly if some time has passed since the occasion. Can *you* remember what you gave your boss for Christmas, or your spouse for his birthday, two years ago? If so, have you seen it since—and do you care? For most people, the *act* of giving is what's important, and they don't give a second thought to the object after it changes hands. In other words, when your sister-in-law comes to dinner, it's highly unlikely she'll be scanning your shelves for the candleholder she gave you last year. It's the thought, not the thing, that counts.

Therefore, keep only what you truly love, and set free those things you don't—that holiday sweater, Chia Pet, or piano key necktie may bring a great deal of joy to someone else. Think of it as spreading the giver's generosity into the world! From now on, when you receive gifts that are not to your taste, put them right in your donation box—it's much easier to part ways with them if you don't let them settle in. In all likelihood, several months will pass before you fill up your box and take it to your local charity; if the giver visits in the meantime, retrieve the item temporarily and set it out for display.

Dealing with unwanted gifts that come long distance is even easier: express your gratitude with a heartfelt thank you note, and a photo of the gift in use. For instance, if your aunt sent you a crystal clock, take a snapshot of it on your mantelpiece; if your cousin made you a hand knit scarf, have someone photograph you wearing it. Send the picture to the giver, and the item to charity, and everyone will be happy. In the unlikely event you're asked to produce it years later, you can always resort to "the dog broke it," "it wore out," or "it was lost in our last move." Be careful not to sound too broken up about it, though—or you may receive a replacement!

Alternatively, you could sell the gift in question, and use the proceeds to buy something new. That way, you'll still have a symbol of the giver's sentiment, in a more functional or beautiful form. Or consider re-gifting it; you'll save some money, and keep the "spirit" of the gift alive. When passing on your unwanted presents, just be sure to follow a few simple rules: make sure the item is appropriate for the recipient, and similar to what you would have bought them in a store; re-gift outside the social circle (and preferably region) of the giver; and re-gift only those items you haven't already used.

You can avoid these situations altogether, of course, by opting out of gift exchanges. I know, I know—easier said than done! It might be no problem at the office, or among casual acquaintances, but it's usually another story regarding friends and family. Changing holiday traditions can be a challenge, and must be approached with diplomacy and grace. To increase your chance of success, put a positive spin on your proposal: emphasize spending time with each other in lieu of gifts, or express a desire to conserve the planet's resources. Explain that you have all the "things" you could possibly want, and prefer to explore other (non-material) ways to celebrate the occasion. If a "zero gift" policy doesn't fly, suggest a Secret Santa or Pollyanna exchange; at least then you'll receive only one gift, instead of five, ten, or twenty.

If people insist on bestowing you with gifts, express your preference for consumables. Tell them how glorious a gift of homemade pasta, gourmet olive oil, or exotic coffee beans would be; or mention your sweet tooth, and speak longingly of baked goods and artisan chocolates. Make it known that you love fancy bath salts, hand rolled candles, or scented body lotions. Remind them of your green thumb, and request plants, flowers, or seeds for your garden. A consumable gift will satisfy the giver, and enable you to indulge in a luxury you might not splurge on yourself. The best part—after you've enjoyed it, there's nothing left to store!

Alternatively, suggest "experience" gifts—like music lessons, theater tickets, or membership to a museum or cultural institution. Point out that while "things" can break or wear out, the memories of a wonderful experience last forever. Or propose that everyone exchange gifts of service, like babysitting, snow shoveling, a car wash, or computer assistance. Give each other "coupons" for specific tasks, which can be redeemed when needed. The gift of someone's help can be far more valuable, and appreciated, than another sweater or kitchen gadget. In fact, simply committing to spend time together in a certain way—like having a picnic, taking a hike, or doing lunch—is a wonderful substitute for something from the store.

Finally, consider making charitable donations instead of exchanging gifts. The money we spend buying each other gadgets, knickknacks, and tchotchkes can do a world of good for those less fortunate. Instead of shopping, spend an afternoon choosing favorite charities with your loved ones (be sure to involve the kids!); the experience can be much more fulfilling (and fun) than fighting the crowds at the mall. Engaging in philanthropy with friends and family opens up a wonderful dialogue with them, and brings you closer together for a common cause. It'll make your occasions richer and more meaningful, and you won't have anything to return, re-gift, or declutter later on.

As if gifts from our acquaintances weren't enough, we also receive gifts from companies and retailers—otherwise known as freebies. I used to accept all those toasters, tote bags, and trial sizes without question, figuring I'd deal with them later. Then one day I opened a new bank account, and found myself carting home a George Foreman grill. I had absolutely no use or desire for one; however, the bank manager presented it with such flourish, it seemed downright rude to refuse it. No problem, I thought—I'll simply accept it, then turn around and give it away. Ha! It wasn't as easy as I thought. It took me three weeks to find a taker, as almost everyone to whom I offered it already had one.

Since then, I've become much more wary of the freebies that try to enter my life…and I'm much less likely to accept them. These little samples, trials, and tchotchkes are a particularly invasive form of clutter. At least when you purchase things, you make the decision to pay for them—a formal invitation, if you will, to bring them into your home. Freebies, on the other hand, slip into our drawers and cabinets rather stealthily, disguised as gifts. Visit any place of business, and you'll likely receive a pen, calendar, or magnet with the company's name. Attend a professional sports event, and you're sure to leave with some kind of fan memorabilia. Purchase makeup at a department store, and your bag will be stuffed with complimentary, pint-sized potions.

You can, however, shore up your defenses; it's just a matter of developing "freebie phobia." Instead of automatically extending your hand for whatever's being proffered, cultivate an instinct to reject it. At the very least, stop for a moment to consider if you need it. If the answer is "no," then politely decline. You may receive some strange looks on occasion; after all, turning down free stuff is unexpected behavior in a consumer society. However, this simple act of refusal will go a long way toward keeping out the clutter!

HEIRLOOMS

When it comes to decluttering, heirlooms are a sticky wicket. In many cases, we would have never chosen to bring such objects into our lives—let alone commit to caring for them the rest of our days. Yet suddenly we find ourselves dusting around Hummel figurines, wondering where to hang a painting of poker-playing dogs, or trying to incorporate a Victorian fainting couch into our contemporary family room. Oftentimes, we don't hold on to these objects because they're useful or beautiful; we keep them out of a sense of guilt, sentiment, and responsibility to preserve our family "heritage."

Unfortunately, heirlooms usually come into our lives because the original owner passed away. That fact itself can paralyze us when we're trying to deal with them. We feel like the objects are all we have left of the person we loved; and that in letting them go, we'll give up our final connection with them. It's an extremely emotional, and difficult, situation. Give yourself plenty of time to grieve before handling these items. An adequate waiting period will enable you to take a more logical, and less emotional, approach to them. If possible, keep them boxed up or stowed away until you're ready to make some decisions; if they've already settled into your home, it can be even more difficult to declutter them.

The most important thing to remember is that *the stuff isn't the person.* These were simply things they owned—just like the things you own. Do you feel like you're embodied in your dinner plates, or that your coffee table symbolizes your very being? Of course not! Likewise, your loved one was far more than that object on the mantelpiece, and shouldn't be equated with it. Do you really think grandma would want you dusting "her" each week? (Or worse yet, stashing "her" in a stuffy attic?) Instead of squirreling away mementos, honor the person you lost by sharing stories and photographs of them with friends and family. Your memories are infinitely more precious than any "thing" they left behind.

Our obligation then, is not necessarily to keep the items we inherit, but to find the best possible use for them. We've been entrusted to steward them to a new home; but it doesn't *have* to be ours. In fact, another relative may be thrilled to own such a piece of family history; if so, pass it along. By all means, don't let petty squabbling or notions of "inequity" compel you to retain them—that is, don't hoard twelve place settings of china just so your cousin "doesn't get them." If you don't want them, you should be more than happy to hand over the responsibility for their safekeeping.

If your heirlooms are valuable or historically significant, consider lending (or donating) them to a local museum or historical society. Such an institution might welcome the opportunity to display your grandfather's World War I uniform, or your uncle's collection of regional landscape paintings. It's a wonderful way to share your loved one's legacy with the public, and transfer the care and responsibility for such precious items into more capable (and secure) hands. Even if your pieces aren't particularly valuable, try to place them in a setting where they'll be appreciated. For example, offer up the grandfather clock or old phonograph you inherited to a nearby retirement home. Give your aunt's doll collection to a little girl who would love it, or donate her boxes of books to the local library. Try to find ways in which these objects can bring joy to others, rather than gather dust in your attic.

Alternatively, sell the items, and put the proceeds to good use. I'm sure Uncle John would be thrilled if his sports memorabilia paid for his favorite nephew's baseball camp; as would Aunt Jane be tickled to see her old crystal punch bowl finance your new kitchen cabinets. Their objective was not to burden you with musty antiques, but to do something special for you—and all the better if you can transform their generosity into something you'll truly appreciate. Another idea: donate the proceeds to their favorite cause or charity. I'm hard-pressed to think of a better way to honor someone's memory.

If an heirloom has monetary value, treasure it, gift it, donate it, or sell it; but don't hold on to it because it "*might* be worth something." We may have fantasies that the stamp collection or oil painting we inherited will fund our retirement; but most often, it's just a handy reason to squirrel it away and avoid dealing with it. Instead of making million dollar excuses for your clutter, *find out what it's worth*. The Internet is a fabulous resource for determining the value of antiques and collectibles. Spend some time searching for similar items; find out how much they cost in online shops, and what prices they've brought at auction. In the process, you'll learn whether your piece is run of the mill, or exceedingly rare. If the latter: obtain a professional appraisal, or contact an auction house like Christie's or Sotheby's for an evaluation.

Use eBay to value more common heirlooms. The site features a mind-boggling array of items, complete with auction prices—making it quick and easy to find the market value of your stuff. Remember, something is only worth what someone else is willing to pay for it. However, don't despair when you discover that grandma's "good" silverware sells for bargain basement prices; now that you *know* its value, you can decide what to do with it. No longer will you have to drag it around with each move, thinking that one day it'll put your child through college. If you keep it, it'll be for its own merits, rather than hope of a future financial windfall.

No matter what their value, you'll probably still have trouble parting with particular items—because you're too attached to their sentiments to let them go. In such cases, consider "miniaturizing" them. Just because you inherited a big collection of pottery or glassware doesn't mean you have to keep *all* of it. Preserve the sentiment by retaining just a few special pieces, and displaying them proudly. If the heirloom in question is a single item, consider saving just *part* of it: snip a few squares off that old quilt, or salvage the pulls from that antique dresser. You'll still have something to remind you of the person who left it;

only that something will be much smaller, and more manageable.

Digitizing heirlooms are another way to save the sentiment, without saving the stuff. You can scan old postcards, letters, documents, and prints directly into your computer, and store the files on your hard drive. Alternatively, take digital photographs; a picture of your aunt's treadle sewing machine will bring back the same memories as the item itself—without taking up an inch of space. Just one word of caution: while it may take a fire, flood, or other catastrophe to wipe out your physical heirlooms, the digital versions can be erased in a single system failure. Therefore, make regular backups of your files—to the Internet, or external media—to protect against data loss.

Finally, perhaps *you're* planning to pass down items to future generations. It might sound a little harsh, but keep this in mind: there's a good chance that your kids don't want them. They have their own style, their own stuff, and their own décor—and your Victorian settee, or Art Deco sideboard, isn't likely to fit in. Likewise, they probably won't have the foggiest idea what to do with your snow globe, cookie jar, or garden gnome collection. Don't burden your heirs with the task of sorting through your clutter, and agonizing over its fate. Streamline your possessions as best you can while you're still here, instead of passing on your junk to the next generation. If you have significant items you'd like to bequeath, consult your children about them *now* and gauge their interest. Certainly don't guilt them into taking things they don't really want, just to get them off your hands. That's not a good way to declutter!

SENTIMENTAL ITEMS

Unfortunately, heirlooms aren't the only sentimental items we need worry about; over the course of our lives, we accumulate plenty of our own. Events, milestones, and rites of passage all seem to come with their own "accessories"—and these commemorative items can be tough to get rid of!

We begin accumulating such objects as early as birth—or at least long before we have a say in the matter. Your parents likely kept your first spoon, rattle, or baby cup, and may have even bronzed your first pair of shoes. They probably stowed away your report cards, swimming trophies, and the pictures you drew in art class. They may have even held on to your peewee sports uniforms or your Boy (or Girl) Scout badges. (Which is all well and good, until they try to unload them on *you*.) As we get older, we pick up the torch where they left off: saving our high school yearbooks and graduation gowns, our fraternity (or sorority) memorabilia, ticket stubs from the theater, trinkets from our travels, postcards, greeting cards, letters, and more. Then we get married, have kids of our own, and start saving *their* stuff…(oh boy!).

We find it hard to declutter these items because of the memories and emotions attached to them—as if parting with them means giving up part of our lives. But we all know that's not true! Getting rid of your old football jersey won't make you any less of an athlete, and tossing the leftover favors from your wedding won't invalidate your marriage. Likewise, selling your collection of Pez dispensers won't erase the fun you had hunting for them at flea markets. We just have to understand that the events and experiences of our lives are not embodied in these objects. While things can be broken, tarnished, or taken away, the memories they represent persist—with or without them.

With that in mind, let's consider a few categories of sentimental items that can trip us up while we're decluttering.

Wedding Stuff

Your wedding is one of the most important, and memorable, events of your life. However, it can seem like you married not only your spouse, but a whole pile of stuff. You might feel like you've made a lifelong commitment to preserve a dress, train, headpiece, veil, shoes, garter, favors, invitations, flowers, ribbons, cake toppers, serving pieces, centerpieces, guest books, photo albums, frames, cards, candles, decorations, and other keepsakes that entered your life that day. Remember, though: you promised "to have and to hold" your spouse—not boxes full of bridal-themed clutter.

Use limits to deal with such items. Select a container, and reduce your wedding keepsakes to what will fit inside; or, choose a handful of special pieces for preservation. Trust me, you won't lose sleep over a few trinkets or baubles, and your marriage won't suffer a bit. The biggest challenge is the dress; and as far as decluttering goes, this one's a doozy! Most of us married women have wedding gowns stashed away—and though they're fragile, they're bulky, and they're awkward to store, we can hardly imagine discarding them. But consider this: if you're never going to wear it again, is there any point in keeping it? It's probably well-documented in photos or videos; and when you share memories of your wedding, you're far more likely to whip out the pictures than the actual dress.

Perhaps you envision passing it down to your daughter someday. It's a lovely idea, but question how likely it is that she'll actually want to wear it. (Did you wear *your* mother's dress?) Most brides-to-be love shopping for the "perfect" gown, and pore over magazines and catalogs for months in the process; frankly, the chance of them selecting a thirty-year-old one from the attic is pretty slim. The sentiment may be more appreciated, however, in different form. Consider "miniaturizing" your dress by using the fabric or lace to create another item—like a purse, ring pillow, or jewelry case—that your daughter can use as "something old" on her wedding day. In fact, such an item can also make a wonderful, and more manageable, keepsake for yourself.

Furthermore, keep in mind that storage conditions can be particularly harsh on such a fragile garment. You may faithfully stow it for decades, only to discover damage or deterioration when you finally retrieve it. Therefore, consider giving it a second life while it's still in good condition. For example: have it shortened, dyed, or otherwise altered into a top, skirt, or cocktail dress. Alternatively, spread the joy to other brides by selling it online, or in a consignment store. Or do some good with it, and donate it to a charity shop or Brides Against Breast Cancer (www.bridesagainstbreastcancer.org).

Children's Stuff

You could be decluttering like a pro, until you come across those pictures your son drew in kindergarten—your heart melts, and your resolve evaporates in an instant. You have such pride in your children, your instinct is to save every last item they've owned or created. However, if such items are taking up precious space in your home, it's not fair to you or to them. Your children will benefit more by having a spacious, uncluttered environment, than a record of every homework assignment they've completed. Still—how can you possibly part with the evidence of their genius?

Again, limits to the rescue! Instead of saving every piece of your child's schoolwork, select the most important, special, and unique. (Why let future presidential historians know he ever turned out anything mundane?) If your "baby" has already left the house, the decisions are up to you; it's highly unlikely your grown son will have any interest in the project. If he's still under your roof, though, enlist his help; by doing so, you can find out what he treasures most. At the end of each school year, have your child pick his favorite essays, projects, and drawings for his keepsake box. If you like, you can digitize the "rejects" for posterity, and pass the originals on to proud grandparents and relatives.

If you're downsizing your empty nest, and would like to declutter these items entirely, offer them to your adult children. If they take them, wonderful! They can decide for themselves what to do with them. If they refuse, then realize this: if such things are of that little significance to them, you have no obligation to keep them either. Your success as a parent is evident in the men and women they are today, not the math homework they did in the third grade. Instead of reminiscing about the past, be part of their lives in the present—and celebrate their current achievements, rather than their former ones.

Handmade Stuff

Hobbies are a wonderful outlet for our creativity; sometimes, however, our homes can get cluttered with our works of "art." When we're learning a craft, we find that practice makes perfect—and turn out all manner of drawings, paintings, scarves, socks, bowls, stained glass, origami, cards, candles, jewelry, and more while we master the techniques. The problem comes when we're unable to discard these things, simply because *we made them by hand*. We need to realize that many of our efforts (especially our early ones) are not exactly masterpieces, and hence do not require preservation. Keep only your favorites, and give away the rest. If the results were less than stellar, recycle the materials into new projects: unravel that misshapen scarf and reuse the yarn, or remove the beads from those crooked earrings and incorporate them into a new piece.

On the flip side, you may be the recipient of someone else's handmade stuff—like the socks your sister knitted, or the bowl your friend made in pottery class. Graciously accept the item, and wear (or use) it a few times in the giver's presence (send a photo if they don't live nearby). However, if it's not to your taste, don't feel obligated to keep it forever. Stash it in your donation box, and find a new home for it after some time— better for it to be loved and enjoyed than stuffed away in your closet. Don't feel too guilty, as the giver may very well have been trying to clear out *her* clutter. When you receive such a gift, express your gratitude; but don't overdo the enthusiasm, or you'll likely end up with more "art" in the future!

Collectible Stuff

Perhaps you've spent the last five years collecting vintage lunchboxes, Fiesta dinnerware, or first edition books, and have recently begun to question why. Maybe your enthusiasm for the item has waned, or the thrill of the hunt has disappeared. Whatever the reason, you've grown tired of the collection, and would love to reclaim the space it's taking up in your home. The solution: unravel it. While you *may* be able to sell the collection in its entirety, you'll likely have more success unloading it piece by piece. No, it's not easy, and not half as fun as acquiring the stuff; but if you spent several years amassing the lot, you can't expect to get rid of it overnight (unless, of course, you give it away). Take heart in the fact that you're not stuck with it for good; online auction sites like eBay enable you to recoup your investment, and move on with your life.

If you're not ready to part with the entire lot, consider downsizing it. Sometimes we get so caught up in the excitement of collecting, we're not too discriminate about our purchases; we focus on quantity rather than quality, and simply add, and add, and add some more. In the past, our collections were limited by accessibility; we'd have to drive around to antique stores and flea markets to find new items. Today, however, we can acquire scores of new pieces with the click of a mouse, and can easily go overboard in our enthusiasm. Clear the clutter by retaining only the rarest, most beautiful, or most unique pieces, and selling off the rest. Alternatively, cap your collection at a certain number, and give up old pieces when you find something "better." The end result will be a well-edited, high-quality selection that takes up much less space in your house.

Of course, you won't have to deal with collections if you don't start them in the first place. I sometimes wonder if the urge to collect is hard-wired in the human race. We start when we're young, collecting dolls, stuffed animals, action figures, or baseball cards. In our teens, we accumulate comic books, t-shirts, or pop memorabilia. As our age (and budget) increases, we move on to pottery, glassware, jewelry, and watches. I don't know whether this drive is innate, or simply encouraged by society, but I do know this: you don't have to indulge it. If you're tempted to start a new collection, first question why: are you truly passionate about the particular item, or simply seeking a new activity? If the latter, apply your energy to something more productive—like exercising, learning a new skill, or doing community service. It'll save you money and space, and can be considerably more satisfying.

Souvenirs

Visit any famous landmark or monument, and you're sure to see it nearby: the ubiquitous souvenir shop. And more likely than not, it'll be teeming with tourists. For some reason, we feel we haven't really been someplace unless we bring home a tiny replica of it—or a mug, t-shirt, key chain, or tote bag emblazoned with its image. Snatching up some proof of our visit seems perfectly natural while sightseeing; after all, everybody else is doing it. It's not until later—when we get home, unpack that miniature Mount Rushmore, and wonder where on earth to put it—that we begin to question our judgment. Too late! That item is now a symbol of our trip, and we feel stuck with it forever.

That's not true, of course. On the contrary, our travel experiences have *nothing* to do with tacky trinkets. Tossing that Hawaiian lei, or Eiffel Tower paperweight, won't erase your honeymoon or that romantic weekend in Paris. Your memories are far more valuable than mass-produced tchotchkes, so purge the tourist clutter without regret. In the future, resist the urge to commemorate your trips with material items; don't feel obligated to buy beer steins in Germany, kimonos in Japan, nesting dolls in Russia, or commemorative key chains from anywhere. If you must bring something home, make it something small: postcards or foreign coins afford ample "evidence" of your travels. Digital photos are even better: they take up no space at all, and provide wonderful documentation of your trip. That said, don't let keepsake-hunting or picture-taking distract you from fully experiencing the places you visit. Your memories make the best souvenirs!

PART FOUR

Lifestyle

Now that we've streamlined our homes, let's take our minimalist philosophy beyond our four walls! We'll declutter our schedules as we did our rooms, and learn some wonderful techniques to reclaim our time. Then we'll discuss how a "lighter" lifestyle benefits the Earth, its inhabitants, and future generations—providing us with even more incentive to reduce our consumption, and live joyfully with less.

29

Streamline your schedule

In our quest to become minimalists, we typically focus first on the stuff that clutters our homes. We want to purge the excess and reclaim our space, so that we have ample *room* to live, play, learn, and grow. However, we also need ample *time* for such pursuits, and therefore must streamline our schedules as well. In this chapter, we'll discuss ten techniques to minimize our to-do's, and maximize our efficiency—and thereby gain a little more serenity in our daily lives.

Say "no"

Unfortunately, we can't do everything, please everyone, and be everywhere at the same time. Of course, that won't stop others from asking us to do so! But we only have so many hours in each day, and so many days in each week; and unless we develop some superhuman powers to work at the speed of light, or transcend the physics of time, there comes a point when we have to say "no."

It sounds easy—but for many of us, it's one of the most difficult things to do. (If you're a born people pleaser, you know what I'm talking about!) If someone asks for help on a project, assistance with a fundraiser, volunteers for a school event, or companionship for the afternoon, your mouth just refuses to form that tiny, two-letter word—no matter how overscheduled you may already be. You may be motivated by a sense of guilt, duty, responsibility, obligation, or simply a desire to help people; but in the end, your "do-gooder" instinct may do more harm than good.

How can that be? Well, just as every object takes away space in your home, every task takes away space in your schedule—space that could be devoted to more important, productive, or fulfilling activities. Accepting additional responsibilities at work may mean later hours, and less time with your spouse. Playing on your company's softball team may mean missing your son's baseball games. Baking cookies for the PTA may mean cutting back on volunteer work. Taking on extra carpool runs may mean skipping yoga sessions or art class. Chances are, your schedule is tight as it is; and if you can't say "no," something has to give.

It may help to look at it this way: saying "no" to a less important activity means saying "yes" to a more important one. All right! We like to say "yes!" Saying "no" to new duties ensures that your current ones aren't neglected, and that the people who deserve your time most aren't cheated out of it; in essence, it's saying "yes" to your present responsibilities and your loved ones. Furthermore, it's also saying "yes" to yourself: scheduling a little "me time" is essential to your personal development, spiritual growth, and mental health. Nurturing yourself leaves you more energetic, more willing, and more capable to nurture others.

So if you'd like to say "no," how exactly do you do it? As simply as possible. When the request is made, respond with

"I'm sorry, but I just can't do it at this
need to provide detailed excuses, or long
The quicker you get it over with, and the
the better. Don't leave it open for neg
think it over; that'll only make it harder to ...
Above all, don't say "yes" to avoid feeling guilty; you'll get over
it in short order. In fact, dealing with a little guilt can be a lot
easier than squeezing another obligation into your schedule!

Eliminate the excess

When we have a lot of extra stuff around, sometimes we just
stop "seeing" it; we turn a blind eye to the clutter, and resign
ourselves to the fact that we just "don't have enough space." By
the same token, we often fail to recognize the junk in our
schedules. We sigh, throw up our hands, and complain that we
just "don't have enough time." You know what that means,
don't you? Our schedules—just like our shelves, drawers, and
closets—can benefit from a good decluttering!

Start Over by examining how you spend your day. "Dump
out" the contents of your schedule: put every activity and
commitment on paper, so you can see it all laid out in front of
you. List everything: going to work, getting your nails done,
shopping for groceries, going for coffee, doing the laundry,
reading the newspaper, cooking dinner, watching television,
browsing websites, driving your daughter to ballet class, playing
poker with your buddies, and anything else that occupies your
hours. Sometimes we move through our days on autopilot,
jumping from one activity to the next without thinking; this
exercise makes us "see" exactly where our time goes.

Now, imagine your ideal day. Which activities would you
include, and which would you omit? Of course, you'll probably
still need to go to work and cook dinner; but would you visit the

instead of the coffee shop, or do yoga instead of surfing the Internet? How closely does your ideal schedule match your real one?

With that in mind, go through your real schedule, and start scratching out the nonessentials. In other words, decide which activities you'd like to Trash. Would the world stop spinning if you didn't watch the evening news? Would your life lose meaning if you skipped the salon? Would your social life collapse if you missed the weekly poker game? I'm not suggesting that you give up activities you love; but rather that you examine each one, and determine its importance. You may find you're perfectly happy to ditch a few in exchange for some extra free time. Cross out those two hours of television each night, and you'll gain over half a day each week. That's quite a windfall!

As you consider each activity, state your Reason for doing it. Perhaps you drive your kids to school for the conversation time, or lunch with your sister to build your relationship. Perhaps you volunteer at the local library to give back to your community. Obviously, those items belong in your schedule. On the other hand, perhaps you get manicures because your friends do, watch television to keep up with water cooler chat, or read certain magazines out of habit. Here's your opportunity to do some purging! When we ask ourselves *why* we do certain activities, we may be surprised at the answers; we probably never stopped to think about it before. Such mindfulness helps us decide what to "put back" into our schedules, and what to leave out.

Prioritize

Sometimes we can feel positively overwhelmed by our to-do list. We know we have a million things on it; so we jump from task to task without rhyme or reason, tackling each new chore as it pops into our head. However, while we're trying to do one thing, we're worrying that we're not doing another—and may even start to panic that we won't get everything done. We've already said "no" to anything extra, and eliminated the excess; so what's a minimalist to do?

The problem isn't necessarily the size of the list, but the fact that we don't know where to start. That's the beauty of prioritizing—it gives us an action plan. Instead of drifting aimlessly (or running frantically) between tasks, we line them up and knock them out, one by one. When we set priorities, we take control of our time. We know what needs to be done, and in what order. We can then focus our energies on wiping out our tasks, rather than worrying about them.

The most straightforward way to set priorities is by ranking them. List everything you need to do, and order them from most urgent to least. For example, answering time-sensitive emails, or completing a project due in the next few hours, will rank much higher than working on your development plan or picking up your dry cleaning. Furthermore, highlight those tasks that *must* be done today. That'll make it crystal clear what you have to complete, and prevent something crucial from falling through the cracks. Then simply go down the list like a wrecking ball, toppling those to-do's until there's none left standing!

Of course, the brute force method may not appeal to all personalities; some people prefer to work in more organic, non-linear ways. That's fine; right-brainers can (and should) set priorities too. Instead of ranking to-do's in single file, group them according to Most Urgent, Next Urgent, and Least Urgent. Then, within each group, mark each task as a Quick & Easy (Q&E) or a Slow & Hard (S&H). How you approach them next depends on your personality, schedule, and what mood you're in when you wake up in the morning.

One strategy is to tackle the S&H's first. That way, you'll eliminate the most difficult and time-consuming tasks as soon as possible—rather than having them hang over your head all day. This method discourages procrastination by addressing the most dreaded jobs immediately, and leaving the lighter stuff for later on. It also rewards you with a tremendous sense of accomplishment, which can provide a real boost to your energy and efficiency. Best of all: your day will get easier as it goes along. The one drawback is the possibility of getting hung up on the S&H's—and thereby risking the chance that your Q&E's won't get done.

The opposite approach is to breeze through the Q&E's first, before diving into the hard stuff. This is my personal method of choice. I love to blast through all those little things on my to-do list, before I settle in to tackle the big ones. My mind is clearer when there are fewer tasks on the horizon (even if the remaining ones are daunting). Getting the minutiae out of the way improves my concentration, and warms me up for the challenge. Of course, this strategy is not without its disadvantages either; if my Q&E's aren't as quick and easy as I expect, or if something additional comes up during the day, I might have too little time left for my S&H's.

Therefore, some of you may feel more comfortable with a mixed approach. Complete an S&H, followed by a few Q&E's, followed by another S&H, and so on. It doesn't matter what plan you follow—as long as you have a plan. At the very least, proceed from your Most Urgents, to your Next Urgents, to your Least Urgents; how you order the tasks within each group is entirely up to you. Arrange them by degree of difficulty, time consumption, or simply your mood—whatever system motivates you best. By setting priorities, you can tackle your to-do list in a determined and straightforward manner; and minimize the time it takes to do so!

Consolidate

When we streamlined our rooms, we used Modules to organize our stuff; by keeping like items together, we found we could purge, store, and access them with far greater ease. We can apply a similar strategy to our schedules: by consolidating like tasks together, we can manage our time, and our to-do lists, much more efficiently.

Consider the following scenario. You visit the grocery store in the morning to buy your food for the week. After lunch, you realize you forgot about your dry cleaning, and hop back in the car to get it. Later that afternoon, you remember you have to make a bank deposit, so you're out the door again. That evening, your family decides they want to watch a movie, so you dash out to pick up a rental. By running your errands as you think of them, you not only waste gas—you waste time! Alternatively, imagine that before you stepped out of the house, you made a to-do list. After leaving the grocery store, you hit the dry cleaners, stopped off at the bank, and swung by the video store (since you know your family likes to watch movies on Saturday nights). By consolidating your errands, you completed them in a fraction of the time, and still had the rest of the day ahead of you.

We can apply the same principle to all of our tasks: whether it's preparing food, doing household chores, making phone calls, answering emails, completing work assignments, or scheduling appointments. Whenever we tackle a new activity, there's a certain amount of setup (and sometimes cleanup) involved. It may be as simple as launching an email program, or it may be somewhat more laborious—like dragging out cleaning supplies, or gathering the materials for a particular project. We may also require some mental warm-up, to put us in the right frame of mind for the particular task. That's why jumping randomly from chore to chore is so inefficient; we must continually adjust to the new job at hand, and may end up repeating some prep work.

By grouping similar activities, and tackling them at once, we minimize the time needed for setup, cleanup, and warm-up. Instead of doing a little bit of ironing each night, do it all in one session; instead of working on a project in dribs and drabs, knock it out in as few sittings as possible; instead of returning phone calls sporadically throughout the day, schedule a block of time to make them all at once. Once you get in the groove of doing a particular activity, you work more efficiently and expertly; if you stop, it can take some time to attain that point again.

This strategy is particularly effective for dealing with email. Many of us keep our email programs open all day, so we can see our messages arrive in real time. Sometimes, we'll even dash off immediate replies to get them out of the way. Although we feel like we're staying on top of things, we're letting it interrupt whatever else we're working on. If an email pops up while I'm writing this paragraph, I can't help but look at it; and even if I don't answer it right away, it's already broken my train of thought and slowed me down. It'll take a little extra time to regain my concentration, and get back up to speed. Therefore, I find it significantly more efficient to check and answer emails during defined periods: like at the beginning and end of my workday. By consolidating this task into one block, I avoid a million little interruptions during the day, and am much more productive.

As you peruse your to-do list, brainstorm creative ways to consolidate its contents. For instance, try batch cooking—a method by which you make several meals at once (for anywhere from two to thirty days) and freeze them. Set aside one weekend per month for household maintenance—and tackle all those niggly little repair jobs in one no-holds-barred session. Do all your vacuuming, mopping, and dusting in one shot instead of cleaning room by room. Limit your errand running to one or two days per week, and knock out all your necessary trips with the minimum amount of driving. It takes a little more planning, but can free up a significant amount of time.

Standardize

I once saw an interview with a prolific author who had turned out hundreds of books over the course of his career—and could write a single one in a matter of days. His secret? He had developed a computerized template for outlining his plot, and simply changed the premise, locations, characters, and other details for each new story. In essence, he had created an assembly line for books, just as Henry Ford had done for his Model T's. Although far from the creative ideal, his method brought him great success in the genre of mass-market fiction. Such is the power of standardization!

Although I don't condone such a formulaic approach to writing, I think it's perfect for the repetitive tasks we face on a daily basis. After all, there's no sense in reinventing the wheel for every item on our to-do lists. By making templates, we can complete them more quickly, more efficiently, and with a minimum amount of effort—leaving us time and energy to devote to more important activities.

A common example of such standardization is document templates. If you often need to produce paperwork with a specific format—such as an invoice, memo, or letter—save a blank version of it as a template. Then, you can dispense with all the setup each time you start a new one. Simply open the template, save it as your new file, and get right to work. This method also saves time creating webpages, making spreadsheets, and writing reports—just about any task that involves putting new data into a specific framework. It's like having the foundation already in place when you begin to build a house.

Standardization can also be useful when answering emails. If you find you're often fielding similar questions, make a database of common answers—then simply cut and paste the appropriate block of text when replying to them. The technique is convenient for a variety of communication: from requesting information, to providing updates on projects, to sending out confirmations or notifications to customers or clients. Just use the "standard language" for the task at hand, changing the details to fit the particular situation. You may even find it handy in your personal life—like when you're answering ten different emails asking about your kids, or what you did on your recent vacation.

Even household tasks can be streamlined with this strategy. Take cooking, for instance. Develop a standard repertoire of dishes you can make with your eyes closed: like a pasta dish, a chicken dish, a tofu dish, and a fish dish. Then add a twist—such as different sauces and spices—for variety. I love to make a simple meal of steamed tofu and vegetables, and vary the sauce—curry, peanut, black bean, sweet and sour, or ginger and garlic—according to my particular mood or craving. The possibilities are endless, and the process quite efficient: instead of learning an entire recipe from scratch, you simply cook your standard dish and vary the topping. You can also standardize your cleaning, laundry, and grooming routines—say, by arranging tasks in a certain order—to complete them with minimum fuss and maximum efficiency.

Delegate

Between work, family, and household responsibilities, most of us have a full plate. Even after we've eliminated the clutter from our to-do lists, we sometimes still don't have enough hours in the day to get everything done. In that case, we have to recognize that we can't do it all ourselves, and learn to delegate tasks to others.

This technique is particularly effective in (and usually associated with) the office. If you're overworked, and lucky enough to have a staff, consider delegating more of your responsibilities to them. It not only lifts a burden from your shoulders; it helps your employees develop the necessary skills to move to the next level. Of course, delegation comes with a certain responsibility on your part; rather than simply dumping your work in their laps, be prepared to mentor them as they tackle it. Explain how such projects can enhance their resumes and advance their careers, and make yourself available for advice and assistance. Most importantly, instill them with confidence, and empower them to make necessary decisions on their own; if you insist on micromanaging their progress, you may just as well do the job yourself.

Delegation can be especially beneficial if you're running your own business. As an entrepreneur, you're likely "doing it all." In addition to your day-to-day responsibilities, you may be completing your own tax returns, writing your own press releases, creating your own website, designing your own advertising, handling client inquiries, and trimming the hedges outside your office or store. Consider shifting some of these responsibilities to employees or outside contractors; it can free up significant time for you to develop and expand your business. If you're concerned about cost, realize that your time may be far more valuable than what you pay an accountant to do your taxes, or give your nephew to build your website. If you need temporary help, consider hiring a "virtual assistant"—a Web-based worker who can handle administrative, marketing, or other duties as the need arises.

Don't stop delegating at the office door; employ this technique at home as well. For example, involve children in household chores from an early age. Initially, you may spend some extra time supervising; but before you know it, they'll be handling the vacuum, and loading the dishwasher, like pros. As they get older, consider teaching them how to pay bills and reconcile your bank statement. Not only will you see your to-do list shrink; you'll instill in your kids a sense of responsibility, and help them develop valuable skills. Sending your teenage son out into the world, armed with the knowledge of how to cook, balance a checkbook, and iron his own shirts, is a major accomplishment in itself!

Of course, the main stumbling block to delegating tasks is perfectionism. When we feel that nobody else can do as good a job as we can, we insist on doing everything ourselves. In the next section, we'll discuss the solution: recognizing that not everything has to be done perfectly.

Embrace "good enough"

Have you ever spent too much time writing the perfect email, cooking the perfect dinner, preparing the perfect presentation, or finding the perfect gift? (I know I have!) The quest for perfection can throw our to-do lists in a tailspin; what we should have been able to complete in short order takes us two, three, or four times as long!

I was born a perfectionist. I got straight A's in school, kept my room neat as a pin, and gave 110 percent to every activity I undertook. I dotted every "i," crossed every "t," and never ended a sentence with a preposition. I cleaned, cooked, dressed, decorated, spoke, and wrote as flawlessly as possible. Then one day, my husband and I were redecorating our apartment (we were young, poor, and DIY newbies), and I watched in horror as he installed a piece of carpet *ever so crookedly.* He was proud of his efforts, and couldn't understand the distressed look on my face. "What's wrong?" he said. "It's good enough."

"Good enough." Those two words changed my life, and put me back in control of my time. They lowered my stress, brightened my outlook, and made me more enthusiastic to take on life's challenges. No longer did I have to labor over every detail of every project, every word of every paragraph, every ingredient of every meal. Perfect wasn't necessary; "good enough" was good enough.

And it's true. In 99 percent of the stuff we do, perfection is superfluous. It's not necessary, not expected, and likely won't be noticed or appreciated. So here we are, devoting extra time and effort to making everything just so—and nobody cares. It's actually a wonderful realization; because when we stop striving for perfection, we get our stuff done faster, and with greater ease. We fly through our to-do lists in half the time, and the world keeps on turning.

I'm certainly not suggesting that you shouldn't have pride in your work, or put forth your best effort. In fact, doing a poor or sloppy job will likely increase the amount of work you do in the end—when you have to start over, make corrections, or apologize for your incompetence. Rather, I'm saying there's a point of diminishing returns. Once you've reached "good enough"—where the work you've done is respectable—there's often little point in pushing further toward perfection. The extra time and effort isn't worth what little reward might result—and instead, may keep you from attempting and accomplishing other (perhaps greater) things.

Likewise, accept "good enough" for the work you delegate. Don't redo an employee's report because you think you can make it incrementally better; don't chide your daughter if the dishes have a few spots; and don't review minor projects with a fine-tooth comb. Give the work a once-over to make sure it's acceptable; just don't get bogged down in making it perfect. Delegation means trusting others to do the job, and letting them take responsibility for its quality.

Once you accept "good enough" from yourself and others, you'll be amazed at how much you can accomplish. By recognizing that perfection isn't always necessary, you'll increase your productivity—and free up your schedule, and mind, for things that really matter.

Reduce expectations

Expectations—we all have them. We expect to get the deal of a lifetime on our new car, we expect our children to get perfect grades, we expect to get that big promotion at work, we expect to make a 10 percent return on our investments, we expect to move into that ideal house in that ideal neighborhood with that ideal school system—and have ideal chats with our ideal neighbors in our ideal yards. Furthermore, we expect that life won't be complete until all of that happens.

Conversely, people have plenty of expectations of us. They expect us to cook delicious meals, bring home a bigger paycheck, keep the house sparkling, volunteer to coach Little

League, help with the school's bake sale, climb the corporate ladder, maintain a beautiful lawn, provide wise advice and immediate assistance, and generally be the perfect husband, wife, mother, father, brother, sister, parent, child, or friend.

No wonder we're so exhausted! We're all running ourselves ragged trying to live up to each other's expectations, as well as those we set for ourselves. What we really need to do is give ourselves a break. We need to step back, examine all these expectations, and question whether they're really worth the time and energy we're expending to fulfill them.

Let's take an example. Suppose you've recently gotten engaged, and are planning your wedding—your expectations for this day have been building since you were young. They may involve a country club venue, elegant ice sculptures, and a guest list in the hundreds. Perhaps you envision dozens of bridesmaids and ushers, color-coordinated favors, and a small orchestra playing your favorite songs. The tradeoff for these expectations: countless hours of planning and coordinating, plenty of stress over making decisions and arrangements, and tens of thousands of dollars spent (meaning more hours of work to pay the bill, or pay down the debt). Consider instead if all you expect is a simple ceremony with friends and family. Wow—you instantly save oodles of stress, thousands of hours, and some serious money. And in the end, you accomplish the same objective: marrying your sweetheart.

In another scenario, perhaps you have high expectations regarding where you live. If you envision yourself in a big house in the best school district, or a swanky condo in a fashionable neighborhood, anything less may disappoint you—leading you, perhaps, to work long hours or take a second job to make the mortgage or rent payments. However, if you want nothing more than a roof over your head, you'd be equally delighted with a modest apartment or bungalow. In the latter case, you'd not only have a warm place to sleep; you'd sleep much easier, without the stress, anxiety, and extra work.

That's the beauty of minimalist living—being satisfied with what's enough to meet our needs, rather than wasting our time, money, and energy to fulfill lofty or unrealistic expectations. This philosophy applies not only to big things (like weddings and houses), but to small ones as well. We have myriad opportunities to reduce our expectations in our everyday lives: for example, by being content with simple, healthy meals instead of insisting on gourmet; by buying solid, quality clothes rather than splurging on trendy or designer ones; by letting our kids be kids, instead of overscheduling them with activities and lessons; and by telling our spouse we'd prefer him home for dinner each night, rather than working overtime toward a promotion.

Reducing what we expect from ourselves and others takes a tremendous amount of pressure off our minds, our schedules, and our bank accounts. When we're content with "enough," life becomes infinitely easier, more pleasant, and less harried. It's very liberating!

Set limits

While decluttering our homes, we discovered that setting limits helps us reclaim, and preserve, our space. By restricting our place settings to four, our trousers to ten, or our DVDs to twenty, we purged the excess from our homes and put the brakes on further accumulation.

Setting limits also helps us reclaim, and preserve, our time. By restricting the number of activities we engage in, or the amount of time we devote to them, we purge the excess from our to-do lists and avoid overscheduling ourselves.

We only have twenty-four hours in each day. Sure, we'd love to take a cooking class, learn a new language, practice yoga, volunteer at the library, coach our daughter's soccer team, lead a Boy Scout troop, join a book club, study Tai Chi, and participate in our community theater. But when we spread ourselves too thin, we wind up feeling too harried to enjoy the activities we're pursuing. Everything starts to feel like an obligation, and suddenly we resent the two hours we "have" to spend in the pottery studio. Furthermore, we never have the time and energy to explore, or master, any particular pastime in depth—leaving us with little sense of satisfaction or accomplishment.

One solution: set limits on the *number* of activities in which you're involved. Consider pursuing a single "extracurricular" interest at a time—then you can devote your full attention to learning how to play the piano or ballroom dance. Or choose one personal and one community endeavor, balancing your "me time" with some volunteer time. At work, limit the number of meetings you attend each day, or the number of assignments you tackle at once—assuming, of course, that it's under your discretion. If you're running your own business, limit the number of clients you accept, or the number of projects you take on, in order to provide better service and allow yourself some work-life balance.

Alternatively, set limits on the *time* you spend on certain activities. For instance, restrict your hobbies to two nights per week, or your volunteer work to two weekends per month, to keep some breathing room in your schedule. Limit the hours you spend on meal preparation (like one per day), and household cleaning and maintenance (like three per week). Pay particular attention to "time sink" activities like watching television and surfing the Internet. How many times have you intended to do a "quick" Google search, and found yourself still in front of your computer three hours later? Limit such pursuits to a reasonable period (like one hour per day) to prevent them from completely draining your leisure time.

Use time limits in the office as well. Allot a certain number of days to complete a project, or a certain number of hours to finish a report. Such limits will prevent you from laboring too long on a particular task (perhaps in an effort to "perfect" it), and ensure you have adequate time to complete your other work. Limit the minutes you devote to making phone calls and answering emails each day. Also, do what you can to limit the amount of overtime you work each week. Staying late at the office won't necessarily be seen as a sign of your ambition or devotion; in contrast, it may be regarded as an inability to do your job, or manage your time effectively.

When we set limits on our stuff, we had to give up something old before adding something new—like tossing a book we already read in favor of the new bestseller. When we set limits on our schedules, we must do the same. If we decide to take on a new commitment, we must give up an old one. It keeps our to-do lists from spiraling out of control, and ensures we have adequate time for the activities most important to us.

Just "be"

A few years ago, I was involved in a group conversation about work and careers. One of the men, in his late twenties, was asked what he did. He simply smiled and said, "Not much," offering no further explanation. An awkward silence fell over our crowd of young professionals. Many of us were putting in sixty-hour weeks, and madly juggling work, family, and social commitments. His casual response was akin to heresy.

Unfortunately, busyness seems to be a prized trait in our culture—as if the more activities, events, hobbies, committees, appointments, meetings, and responsibilities we can jam into our schedules, the better people we are. Ask a friend what she's doing today, and you'll likely get an exhaustive rundown of various tasks. We're always in a rush to do something, go somewhere, or meet someone; it's almost as if we're trying to out-do each other in how many things we can "get done." In fact, an entire industry has evolved around personal productivity and time management—with books to teach us strategies, software to "optimize" our schedules, and gurus to dispense advice. The techniques may differ, but the objective is the same: to show us how to *get more done*.

Minimalist living is the opposite. We've been learning how to say "no," eliminate the excess, consolidate, standardize, and delegate not so we can get more done—but so we have *less to do*. We're not freeing up space in our schedules so we can fill it with something else; and we're not slashing the time spent on one activity, so we can squeeze in two or three more. Perish the thought! The objective is to leave some time open, empty, and free—instead of always "doing," we want some time to just "be."

Just "be"—it's a foreign concept to many of us. How often are you able to kick back with a cup of tea, and simply let your thoughts wander? How long has it been since you stared out the window and daydreamed? When was the last time you sat on your porch and listened to the birds, or soaked for an hour in a bubble bath? In our "busy is best" culture, we can hardly imagine "wasting" time on such idle pursuits. And God forbid if someone caught us, or otherwise found out—they'd think we have nothing to do!

However, when we set aside time to just "be", we're not wasting it—we're cherishing it. We're engaging in an incredibly fulfilling pursuit; one that'll relax us physically, strengthen us mentally, and nourish us spiritually. It doesn't matter whether we're meditating, taking a walk, or just lying on the bed and staring at the ceiling. What matters is that we're stopping, tuning out distractions, and embracing the silence. We're taking the opportunity to *think*: about ourselves, our families, our hopes, our dreams, and our world.

What's more, we *need* this time. When we're always "doing," it's easy to lose sight of our true selves. We come to think of ourselves as the overworked middle manager, the guy who owns an auto repair shop, or the stay-at-home parent who cooks, cleans, and drives the kids around—instead of the person who loves haiku, dreams of being a singer, or yearns to make a difference in the world. Remember the quote, "Music is the space between the notes"? When we take the time to just "be," we're appreciating that space—those moments between meeting clients and paying bills and picking up the dry cleaning. And in the process, we stop defining ourselves by what we *do*—and start to realize who we *are*.

30

The greater good

Something wonderful happens when we become minimalists: our efforts ripple out to effect positive change in the world. Every time we decide against a frivolous purchase, make do with something we already have, or borrow from a friend instead of buying, it's like giving a little gift to the planet (and the rest of its inhabitants). The air will be a little cleaner, the water a little clearer, the forests a little fuller, the landfills a little emptier. We may have embraced minimalism to save money, save time, or save space in our homes, but our actions have far greater benefits: they save the Earth from environmental harm, and save people from suffering unfair (and unsafe) working conditions. Not bad for wanting some clean closets, huh?

Our consumption has both an environmental and human toll. There's a back story to each item on retailers' shelves: the natural resources used in its production and distribution, the people involved in its manufacture, the environmental consequences of its disposal. Before buying, we must consider the entire life cycle of a product, to make sure its purchase won't do more harm than good. With this in mind, let's discuss some further minimalist habits we can cultivate—not only to lighten our personal load, but to lighten our footprint on the planet, and conserve its bounty for future generations.

Become a minsumer

Advertisers, corporations, and politicians like to define us as "consumers." By encouraging us to buy as much as possible, they succeed in lining their pockets, growing their profits, and getting re-elected. Where does that leave us? Working long hours at jobs we don't like, to pay for things we don't need. Putting in overtime to purchase items that'll be obsolete, or out of style, in a matter of months. Struggling to make credit card payments on stuff that's cluttering up our homes. Breathing polluted air, and drinking polluted water, so that retailers can fill their shelves with more gizmos, and corporate executives can take home bigger bonuses. Hmm, something about that doesn't seem quite right...

But here's some wonderful news: minimalist living sets us free! It unshackles us from the "work and spend" cycle, enabling us to create an existence that has little to do with big box stores, must-have items, or finance charges. Instead of toiling away as consumers, we can become "minsumers" instead: minimizing our consumption to what meets our needs, minimizing the impact of our consumption on the environment, and minimizing the effect of our consumption on other people's lives.

Becoming minsumers doesn't mean we can never set foot in a store again. I don't know about you, but I'm not that comfortable foraging or dumpster diving for the stuff I need— and I certainly don't expect to get anything for free. I appreciate the ease with which we can obtain basic necessities, and the fact that (unlike our ancestors) we don't have to devote our days to securing food, clothing, and shelter. However, I believe that once these needs are met, consumption can be put on the back burner. Once we're warm, safe, and fed, we shouldn't feel compelled to browse a shopping mall, or surf the Internet, to find *more* things to buy. Instead, we could devote that time and energy to other, more fulfilling pursuits—such as those of a spiritual, civic, philosophical, artistic, or cultural nature.

So what do we have to do to become minsumers? Not much, actually. We don't have to protest, boycott, or block the doors to megastores; in fact, we don't even have to lift a finger, leave the house, or spend an extra moment of our precious time. It's simply a matter of *not buying*. Whenever we ignore television commercials, breeze by impulse items without a glance, borrow books from the library, mend our clothes instead of replacing them, or resist purchasing the latest electronic gadget, we're committing our own little acts of "consumer disobedience." By simply *not buying*, we accomplish a world of good: we avoid supporting exploitative labor practices, and we reclaim the resources of our planet—delivering them from the hands of corporations into those of our children. It's one of the easiest and most effective ways to heal the Earth, and improve the lives of its inhabitants.

Reduce

We're all familiar with the phrase, "Reduce, Reuse, Recycle." Of the three "R's," Recycling is the superstar. It's a media darling, and features prominently in environmental campaigns and community programs. When we decide to go "green," it's usually the focal point of our efforts. Reducing, however, is the unsung hero of this trinity—because the less we buy in the first place, the less we need to recycle! Reducing neatly sidesteps the entire resource-, labor-, and energy-intensive process, and is therefore the cornerstone of our minsumer philosophy.

Every product we buy involves three important steps in its life cycle: production, distribution, and disposal. In the production phase, natural resources and energy are used to make the item; in some cases, harmful chemicals are released into the air and water as a byproduct of the manufacturing process. In the distribution phase, energy (typically in the form of oil for trucks, ships, and airplanes) is used to transport the item from the factory to the store; these days, that often means a trip halfway around the world! In the disposal phase, the item has potential to clog our landfills, and leach toxins into the environment as it degrades.

The items we recycle have already taken a toll on the environment—resources have been lost, and energy expended, in their production and distribution. By recycling, we're trying to do some "damage control," by avoiding the problems of its disposal, and using its material to make new goods. Reducing, on the other hand, eliminates the entire troublesome process altogether; each item we *don't buy* is one less thing to be produced, distributed, and disposed of. Better to never own the item in the first place, than have to worry about how it was made, how it got here, and how to get rid of it later on.

The best way to reduce is to buy only what we truly need. Rather than shopping mindlessly, we must *think* about every purchase—whether it's clothing, furniture, electronics, décor, or even food. We should develop a habit of asking "why" before we buy. For example: am I purchasing this because I really need it, or because I saw it in an ad, on a friend, or looking pretty in the showcase? We should stop and consider whether we could get along just as well without it. In fact, regard a line at the register as a blessing in disguise, as it gives you ample time to evaluate what's in your shopping cart. I've walked away from many a checkout counter, after pausing to reflect on potential purchases.

The techniques you can use to reduce your consumption are countless. Enjoy the challenge of meeting your needs in alternative ways, and cobble together a creative solution instead of running to the store. It can be as easy as borrowing a tool from a neighbor, or as resourceful as devising your own drip irrigation system from materials you have on hand. Additionally, favor multi-purpose items over single-use ones. A simple vinegar and water solution can eliminate the need for a plethora of commercial cleaners, and versatile clothing can be dressed up or down to suit any occasion. Finally, don't replace something that works simply because you want a new one—be proud of keeping your old car going, or getting a few more years out of your wool coat. The less resources, energy, and landfill space we each require, the better for all of us in the long run.

Reuse

The second "R," Reuse, is also central to our minsumer efforts. The longer we can keep a particular item in service, the better—especially if it prevents us from having to buy something new. Since resources have already been devoted to its production and distribution, we have a responsibility to get the most use possible from it. That's why I'm such a big fan of versatile products; the more functions an item serves, the less likely it is to end up in a landfill.

Like reducing, reusing is preferable to recycling. While recycling requires additional energy to make something new, reusing requires none. We simply adapt the product, in its original form, to meet different needs. My reuse hero is Scarlett O'Hara; if she could fashion a gorgeous dress from some old curtains, we can certainly make seedling planters from our yogurt cups, and rags from our old t-shirts. We don't even need to be *that* creative. We have plenty of opportunities to reuse things on a regular basis: like the packaging materials we receive (boxes, bubble paper, packing peanuts), and the wrapping paper, ribbons, and bows on our gifts. In fact, before you toss a glass jar, Christmas card, or takeout container in the recycling bin, consider if you can repurpose it for something else you need—like a vase, holiday postcard, or hardware organizer.

Of course, as minimalists, we don't want to clutter our drawers and cabinets with stuff we might *never* use. Therefore, if *you* don't have need for something, give it to someone who does. Reuse doesn't necessarily mean that *you* have to reuse it; the planet will be just as well off if somebody else does. To this end, sell your old stuff on Craigslist or eBay, or give it away on Freecycle or to charity shops. Ask friends, family, and colleagues if they can use your castoffs. Offer up your excess to local schools, churches, shelters, and nursing homes. Finding another home for something takes a little more effort than putting it out on the curb; however, it keeps perfectly useful items in circulation longer, and keeps someone else from having to buy new.

By the same token, consider reusing someone else's stuff for *your* needs. Suppose you've been invited to a wedding, and don't have an appropriate outfit. Before you hit the department stores, try to find something pre-owned: check out the thrift stores and charity shops in your area, and search online auctions and classifieds. Failing that, raid the closets of friends and relatives, or make use of a rental service. Do the same for tools, furniture, electronics, and almost anything you can think of; regard the secondhand market as your default source, and only buy retail as a last resort. You'll avoid putting additional pressure on our overtaxed environment, and prevent something useful from winding up in the trash.

Recycle

Our ultimate goal as minsumers is to live lightly on the Earth—using as few resources, and putting as little into landfills, as possible. Our primary strategy is to Reduce our consumption to the bare bones, and our second is to Reuse whatever we can. However, we'll still sometimes end up with items that are no longer useful; and in those cases, we should make every effort possible to Recycle them.

Fortunately, recycling has become much easier in recent years. Many communities operate curbside programs for picking up glass, paper, metal, and some plastics. Others maintain convenient drop-off stations for recyclable materials. If such resources are available to you, take advantage of them. Remember, when we purchase an item, we assume responsibility for its entire life cycle—including its proper disposal. None of us want our grandchildren to inherit a world of landfills; keep them in mind when you're tempted to toss that soda can or newspaper in the trash. We want to minimize not only the junk in our homes, but also the junk in our environment.

In fact, don't limit your recycling efforts to the usual suspects; investigate the prospects for other items as well. Some office supply and electronic stores offer "take-back" services for computers, monitors, peripherals, printers, fax machines, cell phones, and personal electronics. Other companies offer mail-in programs, with prepaid boxes or shipping labels, for returning used products; when I replaced my laptop, I was thrilled to be able to send my old one back to the manufacturer. Look around, and you'll find programs for recycling eyeglasses, shoes, furniture, batteries, printer cartridges, clothing, carpets, mattresses, light bulbs, and more. In fact, before you put *anything* in the trash, take some time to research recycling options; call your community offices, or search for "recycle" plus the item in your favorite search engine. You may be surprised at the possibilities!

You can even do some recycling in your own backyard. Instead of bagging up your leaves, twigs, grass clippings, pine needles, and other yard waste for the garbage collector, start a compost pile. Add kitchen scraps like vegetable matter, coffee grounds, tea bags, and eggshells to the heap; when everything decomposes, you'll have a wonderful, organic substance with which to enrich your garden soil. Consult a gardening book or website for a complete list of "eligible" waste, and to learn how to layer and stir the materials. Composting is doubly good for the environment: it keeps trash out of the landfill, and eliminates the need to buy packaged, commercial fertilizer.

Although recycling occurs at the end of a product's life cycle, keep it in mind from the very beginning. When you're shopping, favor products that can be recycled over those that can't; they'll usually be marked with the universal recycling symbol (a triangle formed by three arrows). Different plastics are identified by the number inside the symbol; make sure the particular type is recyclable in your community. If not, consider a more eco-friendly alternative. Likewise, avoid acquiring hazardous and toxic materials (like paints, cleaners, oils, and pesticides). Improper disposal of such items is harmful to the environment, and a threat to human health; you'll need to drop them off at special collection sites to get rid of them. Take the easy way out, and seek safer, non-toxic products to meet your household needs.

Consider the lifespan

As minsumers, we aim to purchase as little as possible; therefore, we want the stuff we buy to last a long time. We must consider the lifespan of an item in our decision to acquire it. Why waste all those precious resources—for production, distribution, and disposal—on a product we have for just a few months?

For this reason, favor items that are well made and durable. That sounds like a no-brainer; but how many times have you let price, rather than quality, influence what you buy? When you're shopping, it's easy to compare prices, but it can be difficult to determine quality. How do you know if that chair will collapse next month, or if that watch will stop ticking next week? You have to put on your detective hat, and look for clues: like where the product was made, the materials out of which it's constructed, and the reputation of the manufacturer. Although price isn't always a gauge of quality, low cost isn't typically associated with longevity; and while replacing the item may not break the bank, we must consider the environmental costs of doing so.

Accordingly, refrain from purchasing trendy items—like the handbag that's "hot" one moment, and "out" ten minutes later; the décor that'll look dated next season; or the electronic gadget that'll be obsolete in a few months. These items will never wear out before you tire of them (or before you're too embarrassed to own them). Even if you donate them, resources were still wasted on their manufacture and distribution; better to have never purchased them in the first place. Instead, choose pieces you truly love, or classic items that'll stay in style forever; then, you'll be able to measure their lifespan in decades, rather than days.

Finally, avoid disposable products whenever possible. We certainly don't want to deplete our natural resources on items we use for *minutes!* Unfortunately, "single-use" stuff has become increasingly popular in our society: from plates to razors, napkins to diapers, cameras to cleaning cloths. Many such items are used daily, and generate a tremendous amount of waste. You can slash your carbon footprint dramatically by favoring reusable versions: like handkerchiefs, canvas shopping bags, rechargeable batteries, proper tableware and utensils, and cloth napkins, diapers, and towels. As always, let the lifespan be your guide; if it's ridiculously short, look for a longer-lasting alternative.

Consider the materials

When evaluating a potential purchase, give due consideration to the materials from which it was made. By choosing items produced with sustainable or renewable resources, you can minimize the impact of your consumption.

As a general rule, favor products made from natural materials over man-made ones. Synthetic substances like plastics are typically made from petroleum, which is a non-renewable resource. Not only is the manufacturing process energy-intensive; it can emit harmful toxins, and expose workers to hazardous fumes and chemicals. Furthermore, some plastics contain additives that can leach into food and water, and pose a health risk. Disposal presents an additional problem. Plastics degrade very slowly, and can persist in landfills for hundreds (or even thousands) of years; burning them, on the other hand, can create toxic pollution.

Natural materials don't require the same energy inputs, and are significantly easier to dispose of and recycle. But just because we're buying something made of wood, doesn't mean we're in the clear. We must still be vigilant with regards to its origin and harvesting. Large swaths of land have been deforested to produce paper, furniture, flooring, lumber, and other products. Illegal logging and unsustainable harvesting have destroyed ecosystems, displaced indigenous tribes, and altered local climates. To avoid contributing to such tragedies, look for wood that has been certified as coming from sustainable sources, and favor rapidly renewable types (like bamboo) over endangered species (like mahogany and teak).

Alternatively, reduce your environmental impact by purchasing products made from recycled content. You'll find paper, clothing, handbags, shoes, flooring, furniture, décor, jewelry, glassware, and plenty of other items that are enjoying a second life as something new. Buying recycled goods preserves natural resources, saves energy, and prevents the original items from ending up in a landfill. Show your true minsumer spirit, and take pride in the fact that your tote bag was made from soda bottles, or your dining table from reclaimed wood.

Finally, consider the packaging. The ideal, of course, is none at all—especially considering the brevity of its lifespan. However, many of the items we buy will come with some sort of outer casing. Favor those products with the least amount of packaging, or packaging that can easily be recycled. And by all means, don't bring home your purchases in a plastic bag; make it a habit to use cloth ones instead. This action alone can save a significant amount of energy and waste!

Consider the people

Not only must we evaluate the materials from which a product was made; we must consider who made it, and under what conditions. That tchotchke on the department store shelf, or that dress on a retailer's rack, didn't materialize out of thin air.

Some person either constructed it by hand, or operated the machinery to do so; and before we buy it, we want to know if that person was treated fairly, provided with safe working conditions, and paid a livable wage.

In my "world of the future" fantasies, I imagine being able to scan the barcode of a product with my cell phone to discover its history: like what natural resources were used in its production; whether it can be recycled, or how long it will take to degrade in a landfill; where it was made, and the manufacturer's track record with respect to wages and working conditions. Imagine having such data at our fingertips! We'd understand the impact of each purchase, and could make a truly informed decision whether or not to buy it.

Decades ago, such information was easy to obtain. Factories were located in our towns and cities, and we could see with our own eyes whether smokestacks were belching out pollution, or chemicals being dumped into lakes and rivers. We could visit the factory floor, or ask our neighbor, cousin, or friend who worked there if they were treated properly and paid adequately. We could trust that unions, laws, and regulations ensured a fair wage and safe environment for the people who made our stuff. With the advent of globalization, all that changed. Most of the things we buy now are made in far-flung locales where labor is cheap, and companies volunteer little information about their supply chains or production methods. Some use foreign subcontractors for their manufacturing, and may themselves be unaware of the conditions under which their products are made.

Why should we be concerned? Because even though our Uncle Joe isn't making our jeans anymore, there's still a human being making them; and all too often, that person may be suffering in the process. In order to cut costs and increase profits, more and more corporations are outsourcing manufacturing to where wages are lowest. Unfortunately, where wages are low, regulations are usually scarce. So the person making our hip-huggers may very well be working excessive hours, in cramped, filthy, and dangerous conditions. They may suffer injuries, breathe harmful fumes, be exposed to dangerous chemicals, and endure verbal or physical abuse. They may make only pennies per hour, and have no hope of pulling themselves, or their families, out of poverty. Worse yet, they may be children—removed from their homes, denied an education, and forced to work.

How will we know? Well, that's the tricky part. Obviously, no company is going to put out a press release on how little they pay their workers, or run commercials showing the miserable conditions in their factories. Our best option is self-education. We should take it upon ourselves to learn which manufacturers employ fair labor practices, and which ones don't. Search the Internet for information from watchdog groups and human rights organizations; and pay attention to exposés on companies that have been tied to child labor, sweatshop conditions, and abuses of human rights. Research the retailers and brands you patronize, to make sure their practices are in line with your values; if they're not, take your business elsewhere. Also, inspect the origin label before you buy something; if the product was made in a region known for environmental destruction or exploited labor, pass up the purchase and move on.

In many cases, you'll suspect—but won't be sure—that a product was made under substandard conditions. For example, the price may be too low for anyone to have earned a decent wage in the process; or it may be from a Third World country known for slum-like working conditions. That may be enough to make you return it to the rack, lest you inadvertently contribute to someone else's suffering. Bravo! You'll find that such concern makes you more of a minimalist—because it's usually easier to *not buy* something, than uncover its particular background. Your desire to save the world saves space in your closet; and your desire to save space in your closet saves the world. How wonderful is that?

Buy local

We've talked a lot about production and disposal, and how we can minimize our footprints with respect to them. We're not done yet, however. We must also consider distribution—and how the transport of goods from where they're made, to where we buy them, adds to their environmental toll.

Once upon a time, the majority of our goods were produced close to our homes. We bought our vegetables from the farmer who raised them, our clothes from the tailor who sewed them, and our tools from the blacksmith who forged them. In most cases, such items traveled no more than a hundred miles (and usually quite a bit less) to reach us. Now, our stores carry produce from Chile, apparel from India, and hardware from China. Much of the stuff in our households originated halfway around the globe. The problem: the additional energy (in the form of fuel) that must be expended to transport it.

Oil is a non-renewable energy source that gets scarcer by the minute. Yet, instead of conserving it, we fill up planes, ships, and trucks with it to move consumer goods from one corner of the world to another. Unfortunately, that means more pollution in our atmosphere, and less resources in our future. Is it really worth the environmental consequences to send a mango, or a mini skirt, on a three-thousand-mile journey?

Not to us minsumers. We prefer to buy our goods locally, keep our air cleaner, and save all that energy. We'd rather purchase our chairs from a local craftsperson, than a furniture superstore; our décor from the community arts fair, instead of a global retailer; and our clothes from a manufacturer in our own country. It's certainly not as easy as popping into the megamart, and it can be challenging to find a pair of socks without an exotic pedigree. But the least we can do is *try*. In fact, the more we demand domestic goods over imported ones, the more likely we'll see a revival in local manufacturing.

Fortunately, there's one category in which buying local is a breeze: food. Many of us have access to local farmers' markets, where we can purchase fresh fruits, vegetables, honey, meats, dairy products, and more. Since the items are grown, raised, and produced locally, the energy expended in transportation is minimal. Furthermore, freshly picked produce tastes better, and is more nutritious, than food that's been sprayed with pesticides and spent a week in a shipping container. Therefore, plan your menu according to what's in season. Instead of buying tomatoes in January from some far-off land, enjoy the fruits of your local harvest throughout the year. Nothing's more delicious than corn, blueberries, and watermelon in summer; apples, squash, and pumpkin in fall; oranges, chestnuts, and turnips in winter; and spinach, snow peas, and strawberries in spring.

When we buy local, we not only save the environment; we also strengthen our communities. Instead of sending our hard-earned dollars to foreign nations, we put them right back into our own neighborhoods—where they can provide the services, build the infrastructure, and fund the programs we need. We save our farmland from developers, thereby preserving open space and agricultural traditions. We foster strong and diverse local economies, which are far less dependent on (and better able to weather disruptions in) global markets and supply chains. Best of all, we build long-lasting, personal relationships with the people who supply our stuff. It's wonderful to know that our consumption is helping a farmer maintain his livelihood, or a local merchant's child attend college—rather than paying the bonus of some distant corporate executive.

Share and share alike

I once lived in a charming, inner-ring suburb of a major city. The streets were lined with rows of bungalows, each on one-tenth of an acre with a postage-stamp backyard. On my block alone stood twenty houses, each an arm's length away from the next. I always thought it funny that on a Saturday morning, twenty lawnmowers would emerge from twenty garages, to mow the twenty postage-stamp backyards. We could just as easily have done with one or two, and passed it down the row in turn!

Sharing is a wonderful minsumer strategy. Imagine if, instead of each of us buying and storing infrequently used items, we could borrow them from a common pool. We'd only pay a fraction of the cost for acquisition, maintenance, and repair—and we wouldn't have to worry about where to put them all. We'd also give the Earth a break; instead of demanding the resources to make tens (or hundreds) of a certain item, we'd only need enough for one.

We're all familiar with this concept from our public libraries. It would be ridiculous for us all to own such vast quantities of books; we'd lose entire forests in the process! It's much more efficient, economical, and eco-friendly to establish a common collection and share them. We should look for opportunities to apply this model to other items as well. For example, consider organizing a tool share in your neighborhood; collect funds from members, and purchase a shared set of equipment to store in a central location. Participants can then "check out" the ladder, chainsaw, or weed whacker when they need it—rather than having to purchase one of their own.

Car share programs are another example—and a fabulous way to cut our carbon footprints. They're popular in urban areas, where residents have only occasional need for such transportation. The cars are distributed in convenient locations throughout the city, and members pay hourly rates (which typically include gas and insurance) to use them. Such programs not only save us money on registration, insurance, maintenance, and parking; they also reduce the congestion on our roads, and the pollution in our air. What's more, they decrease the sum total of cars that need to be manufactured, distributed, and disposed of—conserving a significant amount of resources and energy.

The possibilities for sharing are practically limitless. They can be as informal as two friends swapping clothes, so that each "doubles" her wardrobe; or as formal as a co-housing arrangement, in which residents share common facilities and appliances. The key is realizing that we don't have to *own* everything we need. Why duplicate the energy, expense, and extraction of resources to fill all our households with the same stuff? Sharing enables us to meet our needs, while bypassing the consumption cycle—making our homes more spacious, and our planet more sustainable.

Be a butterfly

When we overconsume, we're like bulls running through a china shop—leaving a destructive path of downed forests, dirty waterways, and overflowing landfills in our wake. In our quest for more goods and unfettered growth, we break the Earth's fragile ecosystems, shatter the lives of indigenous peoples, and leave future generations to clean up the mess.

As minsumers, we want to do the opposite. Instead of being bulls, we strive to be butterflies—living as lightly, gracefully, and beautifully as possible. We want to flit through life with little baggage, unencumbered by excess stuff. We want to leave the Earth and its resources whole and intact, as if we alighted just for a moment and barely touched them.

The Earth has a finite number of resources for a growing number of people; and as more countries become industrialized, the greater the pressure on the system. When we act like bulls, we grab more than our fair share. We feel entitled to support our consumptive lifestyles at any cost, and worry little about the effects on the environment. We don't give a second thought to what's left over for others, or whether we'll have enough land, food, water, and energy to go around. What's worse: in a "growth at all costs" economy, such behavior becomes the norm. Imagine hundreds, thousands, even millions of bulls stomping through the world and stripping it bare of its bounty.

When we act like butterflies, on the other hand, we're satisfied with the barest of essentials. We consume as little as possible, conscious of the fact that resources are limited. We celebrate the gifts of nature—a spring breeze, a clear stream, a fragrant flower—rather than trampling them. We're aware that we're stewards of the Earth, and have a responsibility to nourish and nurture it for future generations. We exist harmoniously with each other, and within the ecosystem.

Furthermore, we inspire others with the beauty of our actions. We don't need power or money to further our agenda; we simply need to do what we do, day in and day out, and set a wonderful example for our neighbors and our children. By embracing minimalist living, we have a unique opportunity to change the current paradigm: from one of overconsumption and profiteering, to one of conservation and sustainable growth.

We can be pioneers of social and economic change, simply by consuming less, and encouraging others to do the same. It's the easiest form of activism imaginable, yet has the power to transform our lives, our society, and our planet. And someday, perhaps we'll have nations of butterflies, rather than bulls!

Conclusion

Everyone has their own reasons for embracing a minimalist lifestyle. Perhaps you picked up this book because your drawers are stuffed, your rooms are cluttered, and your closets are bursting at the seams. Perhaps you realized that shopping at the mall, and acquiring new things, isn't making you happy. Perhaps you're concerned about the effects of your consumption on the environment, and worried that your children and grandchildren won't have the clean air and water that should be their birthright.

I hope that the advice on these pages has inspired you to declutter your home, simplify your life, and live a little more lightly on the Earth. It's a message you won't hear very often in our "more is better" society; in fact, you'll almost always hear the opposite. Everywhere we turn, we're encouraged to consume—by commercials, magazines, billboards, radio, and ads on buses, benches, buildings, bathroom stalls, and even in our schools. That's because traditional media outlets are largely controlled by people who profit when we buy more stuff.

Practicing a minimalist lifestyle can sometimes feel like you're swimming upstream. You'll encounter people who feel threatened by any deviation from the status quo; they'll say you can't possibly get by without a car, a television, or a full suite of living room furniture. They'll imply that you're not successful if you don't buy designer clothes, the latest electronic gadgets, and the biggest house you can afford. They may even go so far as to say you're unpatriotic, and a threat to the national economy, if you don't consume to your full capacity.

Don't believe it. We all know that quality of life has nothing to do with consumer goods, and "stuff" is not a measure of success. A sustainable economy has more widespread benefits than one of unbridled growth; and you can support your country far more effectively by participating in community and civic affairs, than by shopping at the mall.

And don't worry—you're not going it alone. Look beyond "big media," and you'll find plenty of kindred souls. In fact, mention offhand to your colleague or neighbor that you're "downsizing your possessions," and you'll likely be met with a knowing sigh, and a comment to the effect of "I'd like to do that, too." After the economic excesses of the last few decades, there's a growing disillusionment with consumerism, and a groundswell of interest in living simpler, more meaningful lives.

The Internet in particular is a treasure trove of information and support. In recent years, the number of blogs and websites about minimalist living, voluntary simplicity, and alternative lifestyle design has increased exponentially. Whether you're seeking advice on cleaning out your closets, wondering what it's like to unplug the TV, or dreaming about selling all your stuff and living out of a suitcase, you'll find others who have been there, done that, and are sharing their experiences. Consider participating in a discussion forum on the topic; it's a great way to connect with fellow minimalists, trade decluttering techniques, and find inspiration and motivation to continue on the path.

Once you've stepped outside the status quo, you'll feel a wonderful sense of calm and serenity. When you ignore advertisements, and minimize your consumption, there's no reason to long for items, no pressure to buy them, and no stress to pay for them. It's like taking a magic wand, and eliminating a host of worries and problems from your life. You no longer care about the "it" handbag, the latest car models, or the newest trend in kitchen cabinets—much less have any desire to work longer hours, or max out your credit cards, in order to acquire them.

With minimalist living comes freedom—freedom from debt, from clutter, and from the rat race. Each extraneous thing you eliminate from your life—be it an unused item, unnecessary purchase, or unfulfilling task—feels like a weight lifted from your shoulders. You'll have fewer errands to run, and less to shop for, pay for, clean, maintain, and insure. You'll feel footloose and fancy-free: able to move on a dime, and pursue opportunities, without fussing over all your stuff. Moreover, when you're not chasing status symbols or keeping up with the Joneses, you gain time and energy for more fulfilling pursuits: like playing with your kids, participating in your community, and pondering the meaning of life.

Such freedom, in turn, affords a fabulous opportunity for self-discovery. When we identify with brands, and express ourselves through material items, we lose our sense of who we are. We use consumer goods to project a certain image of ourselves—buying a persona, in essence, to show to the rest of the world. We start to think of ourselves as the guy who wears Gucci, the lady who loves Tiffany, the man who drives a Mercedes. Furthermore, we're so busy dealing with *stuff*— running to and fro, buying this and that—that we find little time to stop and explore what really makes us tick.

When we become minimalists, we strip away all the excess—the brands, the status symbols, the collections, the clutter—to uncover our true selves. We take the time to contemplate who we are, what we find important, and what makes us truly happy. We emerge from our cocoons of consumerism, and stretch our wings as poets, philosophers, artists, activists, mothers, fathers, spouses, friends. Most importantly, we redefine ourselves: by what we do, how we think, and who we love, rather than what we buy.

There's an old Buddhist story about a man who visited a Zen master, seeking spiritual guidance. Instead of listening, however, the visitor spoke mainly of his own ideas. After a while, the master served tea. He filled the visitor's cup, and then kept pouring as it spilled over onto the table. Surprised, the visitor exclaimed that the cup was full—and asked why he kept pouring when nothing more would fit! The master explained that like the cup, the visitor was already full of his own ideas and opinions—and that he couldn't learn anything until his cup was emptied.

The same thing happens when our lives are too full—of commitments, of clutter, and of nonessential stuff. We don't have "room" for new experiences, and miss out on chances to develop ourselves and deepen our relationships. Becoming minimalists helps us remedy this. By purging the excess from our homes, our schedules, and our minds, we empty our cups—giving us infinite capacity for life, love, hopes, dreams, and copious amounts of joy.

About the Author

Francine Jay, also known as "Miss Minimalist," writes about living with less at www.missminimalist.com. On her website she provides advice, shares her experiences, and discusses the joys of minimalist living with a growing community of kindred souls. When she's not writing, she enjoys hiking, doing yoga, and traveling the world with a tiny bag.

Also by Francine Jay
Frugillionaire:
500 Fabulous Ways to Live Richly
and Save a Fortune

Internet Resources

Amazon: www.amazon.com

Brides Against Breast Cancer:
www.bridesagainstbreastcancer.org

Catalog Choice: www.catalogchoice.org

Craigslist: www.craigslist.org

CutePDF: www.cutepdf.com

Direct Marketing Association: www.the-dma.org

Dress for Success: www.dressforsuccess.org

eBay: www.ebay.com

Freecycle: www.freecycle.org

Goodwill: www.goodwill.org

Miss Minimalist: www.missminimalist.com

OptOutPrescreen.com: www.optoutprescreen.com

Pdf995: www.pdf995.com

PrimoPDF: www.primopdf.com

Red Cross: www.redcross.org

Salvation Army: www.salvationarmy.org

Made in the USA
Middletown, DE
20 November 2015